amigos 1

Vincent Everett

Emma Díaz Fernández

Pippa Mayfield

Guía del profesor

OXFORD

UNIVERSITY PRESS

Great Clarendon Street, Oxford OX2 6DP

Oxford University Press is a department of the University of Oxford.
It furthers the University's objective of excellence in research, scholarship,
and education by publishing worldwide in

Oxford   New York

Auckland   Cape Town   Dar es Salaam   Hong Kong   Karachi
Kuala Lumpur   Madrid   Melbourne   Mexico City   Nairobi
New Delhi   Shanghai   Taipei   Toronto

With offices in

Argentina   Austria   Brazil   Chile   Czech Republic   France   Greece
Guatemala   Hungary   Italy   Japan   Poland   Portugal   Singapore
South Korea   Switzerland   Thailand   Turkey   Ukraine   Vietnam

Oxford is a registered trade mark of Oxford University Press
in the UK and in certain other countries

British Library Cataloguing in Publication Data

Data available

ISBN: 978-0-19-912624 8

10 9 8 7 6 5 4 3 2

Printed in United Kingdom by Synergie Basingstoke

Acknowledgements

Front cover photograph by Martin Sookias.
The authors would like to thank the following people:
Pippa Mayfield (editor of the Teacher's Book); Carmen Suárez Pérez (language
consultant)
The publishers would like to thank:
Colette Thomson (sound production); Keith Faulkner for music composition and
María Jesús Pascual García, Paqui Giménez Pérez and students from the
IES Gilaberto de Centelles, Nules.
Every effort has been made to contact copyright holders of material reproduced in
this book. Any omissions will be rectified in subsequent printings if notice is given
to the publisher.

Contents

Teaching notes for Amigos

Symbols used in this Teacher's Book:

🎧	listening materials
C1	copymaster materials available
W1	consolidation and extension activities available in Workbooks
AT 1.1	reference to National Curriculum attainment level

AMIGOS 1   SUMMARY OF UNIT CONTENTS

	Contexts	Grammar	Skills	Pronunciation	Culture	PoS coverage	Framework
Puente	• Language awareness • Learn about Spain • Classroom language • Students' Book instructions; how to find your way around the coursebook	• un/una • el/la/los/las • Recognition of imperatives	• Understanding instructions in Spanish • Speaking Spanish spontaneously • Classroom language • Familiarization with the coursebook	• Discriminating between Spanish and English sounds	• Spanish towns • Famous Spanish-speaking people	1a, 1b, 1c, 2a, 2b, 2g, 2h, 3a, 3b, 3c, 4a, 4d, 5a, 5d, 5e, 5g, 5h, 5i	Launch: 7W3, 7W4, 7W7, 7L4, 7L5
Unit 1	• Greetings, name, alphabet, spellings • When your birthday is and how old you are • Contents of school bag • Numbers 0–31	• tener • Difference between tú and usted • hay • un/una/unos/unas • Plurals	• How to form questions in Spanish	• Alphabet • Important features of Spanish pronunciation	• Mayan civilization • San Fermín • tú and usted	1a, 1b, 1c, 2a, 2b, 2c, 2d, 2e, 3b, 3c, 3e, 4a, 4c, 4d, 5a, 5b, 5c, 5d, 5e, 5f, 5g, 5h, 5i	Launch: 7W1, 7W5, 7W6, 7W8, 7L1, 7S2, 7S4, 7S5, 7S9, 7T1, 7T6, 7C3, 7C4, 7C5 Reinforced: 7W4
Unit 2	• Nationalities • Countries • Family members • Pets and colours	• ser • Adjectival agreement with colours • Adjectival agreement with nationalities • Possessive pronouns • Comparatives			• Fernando Alonso – Formula 1 champion	1a, 1b, 1c, 2a, 2b, 2c, 2d, 2e, 2f, 2i, 3b, 3c, 3e, 4a, 4c, 4d, 5a, 5b, 5c, 5d, 5e, 5f, 5g, 5h, 5i,	Launch: 7W2, 7S1, 7S3, 7S8, 7L2, 7T3, 7T5, 7T7 Reinforced: 7W3, 7W4, 7W5, 7W8, 7T2, 7T6, 7C3, 7C4
Unit 3	• Places in town • Directions • Weather	• ir • estar • Imperatives • de • muy and mucho	• Spelling • Using estar with directions		• Valencia • Weather in Spain	1a, 1b, 1c, 2a, 2b, 2c, 2d, 2f, 2g, 2h, 2i, 3b, 3c, 3d, 3e, 4a, 4c, 4d, 4e, 5a, 5c, 5d, 5e, 5f, 5g, 5i	Launch: 7S7, 7L3, 7L6, 7T2 Reinforced: 7W5, 7S1, 7S2, 7S3, 7S4, 7S9, 7T2, 7T5, 7T6, 7T7, 7C1, 7C3, 7C5
Unit 4	• Saying where you live • Talking about rooms in the house • Types of house • Daily routine • Telling the time	• Prepositions • Reflexive verbs • ser and estar	• Avoiding repetition of hay • Small, useful words	• Avoiding traps with words that look as if they are pronounced the same as English words	• Latin American and Spanish housing	1a, 1b, 1c, 2a, 2b, 2c, 2d, 2f, 2g, 2h, 3b, 3c, 3e, 4a, 4c, 4d, 4e, 5a, 5c, 5d, 5e, 5f, 5g, 5i	Launch: 7S6, 7T4, 7C2 Reinforced: 7W1, 7W2, 7W4, 7W6, 7S3, 7S4, 7S7, 7S9, 7L1, 7L3, 7L6, 7T1, 7C3
Unit 5	• Free-time activities • Household chores • Going out • Days of the week	• Infinitives • Opinions • -ar verbs • The immediate future	• Forming compound sentences	• How accented letters affect where a word is stressed	• Spanish sports • Free time in Spain and Argentina	1a, 1b, 1c, 2a, 2b, 2c, 2d, 2f, 2h, 2i, 3b, 3c, 3e, 4a, 4c, 5a, 5b, 5d, 5e, 5f, 5g, 5h, 5i	Reinforced: 7W1, 7W5, 7W7, 7S5, 7S6, 7L2, 7L5, 7C2, 7C3, 7T3, 7T4
Unit 6	• School subjects • Opinions • Times • Transport • Numbers 10–100	• me gusta(n) • Radical-changing verbs	• Building on your understanding of verb + infinitive		• Differences between Spanish and English schools • Schools in Spain and Latin America	1a, 1b, 1c, 2a, 2b, 2c, 2d, 2f, 2i, 3b, 3c, 3e, 4a, 4c, 4d, 5a, 5c, 5d, 5e, 5f, 5g, 5i	Reinforced: 7W2, 7S8, 7C3

YEAR 7 LONG TERM PLAN							
	Puente	Unit 1	Unit 2	Unit 3	Unit 4	Unit 5	Unit 6
W1: everyday words		L			R	R	
W2: high-frequency words			L		R		R
W3: classroom words	L		R				
W4: gender and plural	L	R	R		R		
W5: verbs present (+ past)		L	R	R		R	
W6: letters and sounds		L			R		
W7: learning about words	L					R	
W8: finding meanings		L	R				
S1: typical word order			L	R			
S2: sentence gist		L		R			
S3: substitute words			L	R	R		
S4: simple questions		L		R	R		
S5: simple negatives		L				R	
S6: compound sentences					L	R	
S7: time phrases and past and future events				L	R		
S8: punctuation and orthographic features			L				R
S9: simple sentences for routine communication		L		R	R		
T1: simple texts		L			R		
T2: read aloud simple texts		L	R	R			
T3: appraise texts			L			R	
T4: use basic resources					L	R	
T5: assemble short texts			L	R			
T6: respond to prompts		L	R	R			
T7: check written work			L	R			
L1: engage with sound patterns		L			R		
L2: improve capacity to follow speech			L			R	
L3: gist and some detail				L	R		
L4: respond to face-to-face instructions	L						
L5: spontaneous talk	L					R	
L6: improve quality/fluency				L	R		
C1: geographical facts	L			R			
C2: aspects of everyday culture					L	R	
C3: authentic materials		L	R	R	R	R	R
C4: simple stories, songs or jokes		L	R				
C5: social/linguistic conventions		L		R			

L = where a Framework objective is **launched**

R = where a Framework objective is **reinforced**

Introduction

Course aims and objectives

¡Bienvenidos a Amigos 1 !

Amigos is a three-part broad-ability course for 11–14 year olds with a single volume Students' Book in Parts 1–3 that provides differentiation in particular via the Uno/Dos pages at the end of the Students' Book, and the parallel workbooks. The course:
- meets the requirements of the MFL Framework
- is easy to use
- is fully differentiated to teach the whole ability range

Rationale

The aims of **Amigos** are to provide:

- **a clear structure**
  - There are six units per Part, which makes it easy to teach one unit per half-term.
  - There are five main spreads in each unit, which makes it easy to teach one core spread per week.
  - Regular assessment is provided via the end-of-unit checklists, revision and formal assessment.

- **clear progression**
  - Clear teaching and learning objectives are provided to show students exactly what they will learn.
  - There is careful and systematic presentation and practice of key grammar, skills and pronunciation points

- **clear differentiation**
  - The core material that all students must cover is clearly identified.
  - There are plenary activities on each spread.
  - There are Uno and Dos differentiated activities at the end of each unit, as well as Lectura uno and dos, that students can work through on their own.
  - Parallel workbooks at Uno and Dos levels accompany each part of the course.

- **clear presentation**
  - The bright and attractive location photos provide a vivid cultural backdrop that will motivate students.
  - The Students' Book activities are colour-coded by skill so that students can find their way easily around a spread.
  - All the language that students will need to use is highlighted in the Frases clave.

- **clear and comprehensive support**
  - For students, there is an end-of-unit vocabulary and checklist together with a clear grammar section and Spanish–English, English–Spanish glossary.
  - For teachers, full support is provided with Scheme of Work and lesson planning via the Teacher's Book and **Coursemaster** CD-Rom.

The components of Amigos 1

Students' Book

The Students' Book has 160 pages and is divided into six units, plus an introductory unit (Puente). Each unit is divided into four core spreads plus a reading/culture spread which is ideal for independent study.

At the end of the Students' Book there is differentiated end-of-unit practice with one page of activities for more able learners and one page for lower attainers per unit. Following this is the Lectura section which provides differentiated reading activities: two pages per unit. Then there is the grammar reference section with activities and lastly, the Spanish–English and English–Spanish glossary.

Workbooks (Uno and Dos)

There are two Workbooks: one for reinforcement (Uno) and one for extension (Dos).

The Workbooks provide one page of reading and writing activities per Students' Book double-page spread. This is followed by a page focusing on the grammar of the unit, a Reto page which offers further extension, the unit vocabulary page and unit checklist.

The Workbooks are designed to be written in, and so are ideal for homework and coverwork.

Copymasters

The Copymaster contains 126 pages of photocopiable worksheets. These provide opportunities for further practice and extension of the language of the unit.

Each unit contains the following worksheets:
- Unit vocabulary list (Vocabulario)
- Unit checklist (Ya sé…)
- Starter activities (¡A sus marcas!)
- Plenary activities (Reto)
- Differentiated listening, speaking, reading and writing activities
- Grammar (Gramática)
- Learning strategies (Técnica)
- Cultural information (Cultura)
- Pronunciation (Se pronuncia así)
- Higher and lower tests (Controles) in listening, speaking, reading and writing

At the end of the Unit 6 copymasters, there are also differentiated end-of-year tests in listening, speaking, reading and writing and this is followed by attainment target setting and student progress pages. There is a CD-Rom of all the Copymasters in an editable format to accompany the Copymasters.

Teacher's Book

The Teacher's Book contains all the summary information and framework guidance that you will need to plan your lessons. Each unit contains the following:

- A unit overview grid
- A Medium term plan showing Framework objectives coverage
- A Planner section for each core teaching spread to help with lesson planning
- Answers to all of the Students' Book activities
- Notes on all of the Students' Book activities
- Information about the Copymasters, including answers
- Information about the Workbooks, including answers
- Transcripts for all of the recorded material

ICT

Presentation, practice and assessment is provided by an interactive CD-Rom, Amigos Integral, which also contains a video element.

CDs

The CDs provide the audio material to accompany the Students' Book, Copymasters and assessment material. The recordings contain a range of short dialogues, longer conversations, songs, interviews and surveys.

Digitised (mp3) versions of all recordings are available on request, but require proof of CD purchase.

CD contents:
CD 1 Puente, Units 1–3
CD 2 Units 4–6
CD 3 Copymasters, including assessment for Units 1–6 and end-of-year assessment

Coursemaster

This CD-Rom is to accompany all Parts of **Amigos**. It provides teachers with editable schemes of work on both PC and Apple Macintosh platforms as well as a Students' Record of Progress and Class Records of Progress.

Flashcards

There are 160 colour flashcards to accompany Parts 1 and 2 of **Amigos**.

Amigos and the Modern Languages Framework

Amigos has been carefully planned to ensure that all Framework objectives are covered in familiar contexts.

- ### Long Term Plan (LTP)

See page 5 of this book. These provide an overview of objectives to be covered, typically, in Year 7. Each objective is to be specifically launched (L) and reinforced (R) at least once within that year.

Year 7 objectives are covered in **Amigos 1** Units 1–6
Year 8 objectives are covered in **Amigos 2** Units 1–6
Year 9 objectives are covered in **Amigos 3** Units 1–6

- ### Medium Term Plans (MTPs)

These relate to individual units within the course and aim to cover six weeks' work. The MTPs provide a clear picture of the context for learning and give an outline of how the Framework objectives, identified in the LTP, might be taught.

- ### Short Term Plans (STPs)

These are planning guides designed to focus on whole-class teaching strategies, specific resources and activities to meet objectives within each unit. They typically cover a week's work, and facilitate the easy generation of individual lesson plans.

To help you plan and write all your departmental documentation, the Long, Medium and Short Term Plans are all provided on the **Amigos Coursemaster CD-Rom** in an editable format. In addition, an annotated example of a lesson plan and an editable lesson plan template are also provided on CD-Rom.
This Teacher's Book includes copies of the relevant Medium Term Plans at the start of each unit, as well as Planners for each core spread that mirror the Short Term Plan format.

The **Amigos** teacher's notes reflect the focus of the MFL Framework on key areas of teaching and learning. These include:

Starters
Setting lesson objectives
Modelling
Questioning
Practice
Plenaries

Assessment for Learning

Assessment for Learning (AfL) helps students to know and understand the standard they are aiming for, and also to understand what they need to do in order to achieve their objectives. It involves not only sharing learning goals with students, but also involving them in both peer- and self-assessment. AfL stresses the importance of ensuring that the information gathered about students' progress is used, by both teachers and learners, to identify the next steps for learning. This might involve giving students opportunities to talk about what they have learned and what they have found difficult.

The *Reto* plenary activities, the *Ya sé…* checklist and end-of-unit Adelante tasks at three levels of difficulty provide opportunities for students to evaluate their own learning in a meaningful way.

Formal assessment

Regular assessment of student progress is an integral part of the learning process. Amigos offers an approach to assessment in line with the National Curriculum and the Scottish 5–14 National Guidelines.

Amigos provides summative assessment material on *Control* copymasters for every unit. This is designed to coincide with the *Repaso* pages in the Students' Book after every unit. There are four *Controles* per assessment section to assess individual skill areas: *Escuchar, Hablar, Leer,* and *Escribir.* There is also a differentiated end-of-unit assessment in all four skills. Answers, a mark scheme and assessment criteria are provided for all assessment material. Each assessment copymaster has a total of 25 marks so that each test can be graded as a percentage. The assessment materials are graded *Uno* (lower level) and *Dos* (higher level) so you can easily select the appropriate activities for your students.

End-of-unit assessment is also provided in **Amigos Integral.**

Thinking skills

One of the key aims of **Amigos** is that students should be able to learn in a meaningful way, to think flexibly and give reasons for their answers. Even in the early stages of language learning this can be encouraged, by allowing students time to reflect on what they have just learnt and applying this knowledge to other contexts. It is important to allow students time to reflect, analyse, problem-solve and make predictions based on previous knowledge if they are to move towards becoming more independent language learners. If students take a more active role in their language learning, they make quicker progress and the thinking skills learned can be applied to other curriculum areas.

Amigos helps students to develop their thinking skills by offering them challenging tasks on a regular basis so that they have to think through a problem which may have more than one correct answer.

The *Zoom gramática, Técnica, Se pronuncia así* and *Cultura* sections usually contain open-ended questions that encourage students to draw on their existing knowledge to work out a new problem. It is often best to work on these sections as a whole class with students so that you can discuss the problem or question together and listen and respond to each other's proposed solutions. By doing this, students will learn more about the thinking process involved.

The *Reto* plenary activities provide an opportunity to check learning against the spread objectives and to check students' reasoning for their answers.

The *Ya sé…* checklist activities on the Copymasters, in the Workbooks and in the Students' Book also help students to reflect on their own learning.

ICT

Amigos Integral provides a series of short authentic video clips of interviews with Spanish teenagers. There are quick, easy-to-complete activities to assess understanding of grammar, vocabulary, pronunciation and listening. The results are saved to provide a full assessment profile for each of your students. There is a Students' **Integral** for independent study in class or at home and a Teacher's version for network use.

Differentiation

There will be a broad range of students within any beginners' class. There are particular features of **Amigos** which will make it easier to differentiate work:

For each unit there is an *Uno* and a *Dos* page at the back of the Students' Book. The *Uno* pages are intended for students who require more support, and who may need to take some of the points of the main unit at a slower pace. The *Dos* pages are intended for more able students and could be used in several ways. More able students could do the activities on this page when they have completed other activities quickly. Both pages could be used for homework or independent work in class including coverwork.

The *Ya sé…* checklist provides activities at three levels of difficulty to test students' knowledge, so students can choose the one they feel most comfortable with. Differentiation by outcome will play a major part of the assessment of these activities..

The *Lectura* reading section contains two pages of differentiated reading (*Uno* and *Dos*) per unit.

The Copymasters provide differentiated activities on the *Escuchar, Hablar,* and *Leer y Escribir* worksheets.

The *Uno* and *Dos* Workbooks provide differentiated support material for each unit. The *Uno* Workbook provides consolidation and reinforcement activities for lower attainers whilst the *Dos* Workbook provides extension activities for more able students. Both Workbooks can be used in class or for homework.

Teaching with Amigos

Summary of main characters

In **Amigos** students are introduced to a group of friends who live in Valencia. The characters are introduced in the *Puente* unit and as students progress throughout the book, they learn more about each of the characters.

The four main characters are: Carlos Pérez Brito, Fátima Ahad, Raquel Martínez, Jorge López García and Adam Johnson (who has recently moved with his family from England to live in Valencia).

Features of an Amigos unit

Unit opening page

Each unit opens with an overview of the learning objectives to be covered and is accompanied by starter activities to introduce students to the context and language of the unit. The setting for each unit is Valencia and the surrounding area and the five main characters who live there.

Presentation and practice activities

New vocabulary is best introduced using the **Amigos** flashcards.

New language is presented in the Students' Book in a variety of ways through the photos featuring the five characters, other photos and illustrations. The conversations between the main characters are provided on CD and should be used for repetition by the students, as this will ensure the best possible pronunciation and intonation. Students will enjoy learning these short exchanges and 'performing' them to the rest of the class. More able students can adapt the conversations by substituting phrases with other items of key language.

Underpinning the course structure are the Modern Language objectives. Each objective is carefully launched and reinforced via the Students' Book units, specifically through the *Zoom gramática*, *Técnica*, *Se pronuncia así* and *Cultura* sections, and each spread has been written with the MFL Framework teaching and learning methodology in mind. For details of where the Year 7 objectives are launched and reinforced, see page 5 of this book.

Students should be encouraged to learn by heart, on a regular basis, both items of vocabulary and also short conversations. This will promote good language-learning habits and ensure that students are able to transfer the language that they have learned to new contexts. The key language of the unit is then developed through a wide variety of mixed-skill practice, with activities to ensure language development from supported/guided to more open-ended. **Amigos** intends each activity to have a purpose for learners, to ensure that they find the activities interesting as well as useful in terms of their linguistic development. The Copymasters and *Uno/Dos* Workbooks provide further consolidation and practice activities for each unit. Reinforcement and extension activities are provided on the *Uno/Dos* and *Lectura Uno/Dos* pages at the end of the Students' Book. Further grammar practice activities are also provided at the end of the Students' Book in the grammar reference section.

Core spreads

There are four core spreads per unit through which the key language and skills are presented and practised.
Each double-page spread includes:
- Specific objectives given in English in student-friendly language to provide students with a clear understanding of what they are going to learn and to motivate them by the speed of their progress.
- A starter activity (*¡A sus marcas!*) at the beginning of each spread.
- Activities in all four skills to practise the key language of the spread. The rubrics for these activities are bilingual where an instruction is first introduced, then in Spanish only. There are colour-coded words for each skill *Escuchar*, *Hablar*, *Leer* and *Escribir*.
- *Frases clave* in Spanish. The key language of the spread is summarized in these boxes to provide support and reference for students. Students will find these sections useful for revision and they may wish to copy this key language into their vocabulary books, although a summary of the key language for each unit is also provided on the *Vocabulario* page of each unit, on copymaster and in the *Uno/Dos* Workbooks.
- Plenary activities (*Reto*). These activities are ideal for informal class or group assessment.

Zoom gramática

Grammar is included as a central part of each unit, as students need to understand how the language works from an early stage if they are to manipulate and use it successfully in other contexts. Students are exposed to examples that occur naturally in context in the units and are then encouraged to reflect on these and work out the rules. There are practice activities on the Students' Book page itself, on copymaster and in the *Uno/Dos* Workbooks, and in the grammar reference section at the back of the Students' Book.

Técnica

This feature promotes language-learning skills in a systematic way throughout **Amigos**. The learning skills are then developed further with additional practice activities on the Students' Book page and on copymaster pages for each unit. The development of language-learning skills is considered to be an integral part of the language-learning process and should be given sufficient time during whole-class work. Students who are given opportunities to practise these skills from the start will develop into effective independent language learners.

Se pronuncia así

This regular feature encourages learners to focus on improving their pronunciation and intonation, enabling them to develop good habits in spoken Spanish. There is a great deal of emphasis on sound–spelling links in the early units. Sounds which are traditionally more difficult for English speakers are featured. This section should be made as much fun as possible in class, with whole-class repetition, followed by group- and individual work. Students who find pronunciation difficult should be given opportunities to practise these sections further on a regular basis, perhaps by recording them for independent use. Further practice of the pronunciation points is given on the *Se pronuncia así* copymasters in each unit.

Cultura

This feature points out items of cultural interest that are relevant to the unit, with a practice activity on the Students' Book page, on copymaster and in the *Uno/Dos* Workbooks.

Songs

Songs and raps are a feature of **Amigos** and are intended to provide enjoyment as well as to develop language skills. Where possible, encourage students to sing along with the recording, as this will provide additional pronunciation and intonation practice. Some students will enjoy writing additional verses, and more musical students should be encouraged to compose other songs to practise the language of the unit further.

Repaso

This is a revision page and covers the language and structures that have been learnt in the unit.

Vocabulario

This is the full list of the key language for each unit and is also provided on copymaster and in the *Uno/Dos* Workbooks.

Ya sé...

This bilingual checklist summarizes the learning objectives covered within each unit and contains plenary activities at three different levels of difficulty for students to check their own progress. Use this checklist actively with the students to help them review what they have learned in each unit and to reflect on areas for further revision and practice.

Bilingual checklists for each unit are also available on copymaster and in the *Uno/Dos* Workbooks.

| Puente Overview grid | | | | | | National Curriculum | |
Pages/Contexts/Cultural focus	Objectives	Grammar	Skills and Pronunciation	Key language	Framework	PoS	AT level
4–5 **¡Hablamos español!** Where Spanish is spoken in the world Famous Spanish-speaking people Gender	Learn where Spanish is spoken in the world Learn about gender in Spanish Recognize some famous Spanish-speaking people	*un/una*	–	*un/una*	(L) 7W4	1a, 1b, 1c, 3b, 3c, 4a, 4d, 5a, 5g	1.1, 2.1, 3.1–2
6–7 **España** Some main Spanish towns Introduction to the main characters	Students learn where some of the main towns in Spain are Introduction to the five main characters of the Students' Book	–	–	–	(L) 7C1	1a, 1c, 3b, 3c, 4a, 5a, 5d, 5h, 5i	3.2
8–9 **Las instrucciones** Classroom instructions	Learning about classroom instructions How to speak spontaneously in Spanish Definite article	*el/la/los/las*	–	*el/la/los/las* *Escuchad, Sentaos, ¿Cómo se dice? ¿Qué página?, Mirad la pizarra, Callaos, Leed, Escribid los deberes.*	(L) 7W3, 7W7, 7L4, 7L5	1a, 1b, 1c, 2a, 2b, 2g, 2h, 3a, 3b, 3c, 5d, 5e, 5h, 5i	1.1–2, 3.1–2, 4.1–2
10 **¡Bienvenido a Amigos 1!** How to find your way around the coursebook	Develop the ability to find your way around the coursebook	–	How to find your way around the coursebook	–	–	–	–

AMIGOS 1 PUENTE MEDIUM TERM PLAN

About this unit: This initial unit introduces students to aspects of the Spanish language and the Spanish-speaking world, including an opportunity to get used to Spanish 'sounds'. It is intended to whet the students' appetite and to draw on their own experience and knowledge. It also provides preliminary guidance in how to use the coursebook: how to use the key language to express what they want to say, how to keep a record of vocabulary, how to understand and use classroom language and how to find their way around the coursebook.

Framework objectives (launch)	Teaching and learning	Week-by-week overview (assuming 3 weeks' work or approx. 5–6 hours)
		Week 1
7W3: classroom words	Understanding written target language instructions in the **Amigos 1** Students' Book	Gain an awareness of foreign languages; say what language(s) you speak; discriminate between English and Spanish sounds; adapt a simple sentence to communicate personal information
7W4: gender and plural	All Spanish words have a gender; importance of learning gender as well as word itself	
7W7: learning about words	Memorising techniques to remember instructions	**Week 2**
7L4: respond to face-to-face instructions	Understanding instructions in Spanish	Gain cultural awareness: Spanish language, places and people; record vocabulary effectively; recognize gender:
7L5: spontaneous talk	Importance of speaking in the target language in class; recap on what learnt so far	*el/la*, *un/una*; recognize cognates and near-cognates
7C1: geographical facts	Students learn some of the main towns in Spain	**Week 3**
	Teaching and learning (additional)	Accumulate and apply a stock of words for language learning and classroom talk; understand instructions and follow speech of different kinds in different contexts; respond to instructions, questions, etc.; contribute to spontaneous talk in the target language; recognize verbs in the imperative; develop the ability to follow instructions in the coursebook; find your way around the coursebook
	Spain and neighbouring countries	

Puente

Unit objectives

Contexts: Where Spanish is spoken in the world; gender in Spanish
Grammar: indefinite and definite articles
Language learning: common classroom language expressions; the importance of using Spanish in the classroom; getting to know the coursebook
Cultural focus: famous Spanish people; some main cities in Spain

Planner

● ● ● ● ● ● ● ● ● ● ● ● ● ● ● ● ● ● ● ●

¡Hablamos español! páginas 4–5

Objectives

▶ Learn where Spanish is spoken in the world

▶ Recognize Spanish words used internationally

▶ Learn about gender and indefinite articles in Spanish

Resources

Students' Book, pages 4–5

Key language

un/una

Programme of Study reference

1a, 1b, 1c, 3b, 3c, 4a, 4d, 5a, 5g

Framework reference

(L) 7W4

● ● ● ● ● ● ● ● ● ● ● ● ● ● ● ● ● ● ● ●

| AT 1.1 | **1 ¿Dónde se habla español?**

Students look at the map and list at least one country on each of three different continents where Spanish is spoken.

Answers: North America: parts of the USA (California, Texas); South America: Spanish is spoken in all the countries labelled on the map; Europe: Spain

| AT2.1 | **2 ¡A contrarreloj!** Con tu compañero/a, mira el mapa. Cierra el libro. ¿Cuántos países puedes recordar en un minuto?

Students work in pairs. They test each other to see how many Spanish-speaking countries they can each remember in one minute.

| AT 3.1/2 | **3 ¿Conoces estas palabras? ¿Conoces otras? Escríbelas** con tu compañero/a.

Students work in pairs. They decide if they know the meaning of the Spanish words given, and write down any others they can think of.

| AT3.2 | **4 Personajes del mundo hispano. ¿Qué quieren decir estas palabras?**

Students look at the sentences about famous Spanish-speaking people and see if they can understand what the highlighted words mean.

Answers: cantante = singer; príncipe = prince; futbolista = football player; tenista = tennis player; director = film director; guitarrista = guitarist; actriz = actress; actor = actor

Zoom gramática

This section introduces the idea of gender and indefinite articles.

Planner

• •

España   páginas 6–7

Objectives

▶ Learn about the regions of Spain

▶ Learn common terms for talking about yourself

Resources

Students' Book, pages 6–7

Programme of Study reference

1a, 1c, 3b, 3c, 4a, 5a, 5d, 5h, 5i

Framework reference

(L) 7C1

• •

AT 3.2   **1 Mira el mapa y lee las descripciones de las fotos. Empareja las descripciones (1–5) con las ciudades (a–e) en el mapa.**

Students look at the map and read the descriptions. They try to match the descriptions with the places shown on the map.

Answers: 1 a; 2 e; 3 c; 4 d; 5 b

AT3.2   **2 Lee las presentaciones. ¿Qué significan…?**

Students read the information about the different people who will feature in the book, and decide what the Spanish words mean.

Answers: nombre = first name; apellido = surname; nacionalidad = nationality; edad = age; años = years

Planner

●●●●●●●●●●●●●●●●●●●●●●●●●●

Las instrucciones

páginas 8–9

Objectives

▶ Learn classroom phrases in order to use Spanish spontaneously in the classroom

▶ Learn definite articles

Resources

Students' Book, pages 8–9
CD 1, track 2

Key language

el/la/los/las
Escuchad, Sentaos, ¿Cómo se dice…? ¿Qué página? Mirad la pizarra, Callaos, Lee, Escribid los deberes.

Programme of Study reference

1a, 1b, 1c, 2a, 2b, 2g, 2h, 3a, 3b, 3c, 5d, 5e, 5h, 5i

Framework reference

(L) 7W3, 7W7, 7L4, 7L5

●●●●●●●●●●●●●●●●●●●●●●●●●●

| AT 1.1/2 | **1 Escucha y lee. Escribe el número de la frase adecuada.** Students listen and match each instruction they hear to the appropriate picture. |

| AT3.2 | ***Answers:** 1 b; 2 d; 3 f; 4 c; 5 a; 6 e* |

 CD 1, track 2   página 8, actividad 1

1 – Buenos días. Sentaos. Abrid el libro.
  – ¿Qué página?
  – La página tres.
2 – Mirad la pizarra y escuchad las respuestas.
  – ¡Más despacio, por favor!
3 – ¡Hasta mañana, chicos!
  – ¡Hasta mañana, profesor!
4 – Lee, Marga.
  – ¡No entiendo!
5 – Sssshhh… ¡Callaos! ¡El profesor!
6 – Escribid los deberes.
  – ¿Cómo se dice en español 'exercise book'?
  – El cuaderno.

| AT 3.1/2 | **2 Empareja los dibujos con las frases.** Students match the pictures with the most appropriate sentence according to the context. |

***Answers:** a 7; b 8; c 5; d 2; e 4; f 1; g 6; h 3*

Zoom gramática

This section continues with the introduction of gender, this time focussing on the definite article.

***Answers:** el: profesor, libro, cuaderno; la: página; los: deberes; las: respuestas*

Técnica

This section gives some ideas for using Spanish in the classroom and ways of learning and remembering the phrases. Point out to students that unless they go on holiday to a Spanish-speaking country, their Spanish lesson is the only opportunity they have to practise the language, so it's important to use the language as much as they can in class.

Copymasters

Hoja 1

This can be used after page 4 of the Students' Book.

| AT3.1 | **1 ¿Dónde se habla español? Rellena los espacios.** Students complete the country names. |

***Answers:** Méjico; Guatemala; Nicaragua; Belice; El Salvador; Cuba; La República Dominicana; Puerto Rico; Honduras; Costa Rica; Panamá; Venezuela; Colombia; Ecuador; Perú; Chile; Bolivia; Paraguay; Uruguay; Argentina*

Hoja 2

This can be used after page 7 of the Students' Book.

| AT3.1 | **1 Mira el DNI de Francisco. ¿Qué significa la información de su carné?** Students read the information on the identity card. |

***Answers:** Nombre = name; Apellidos = surnames*

AT3.1

AT4.1

2 Lee la información al final de la página y rellena los carnes 1 y 2.

Students read the information and complete the next two identity cards.

Answers: 2 Nombre: Ana, Apellidos: González Pérez;
3 Nombre: Antonio, Apellidos: Díaz Rodríguez

AT
4.1/2

3 ¿Y tú? ¿Cómo sería tu carné español?

Students complete identity card 4 with their own name and surname(s).

Unit 1	Overview grid					National Curriculum	
Pages/Contexts/ Cultural focus	Objectives	Grammar	Skills and Pronunciation	Key language	Framework	PoS	AT Level
12–13 **1.1 Mis amigos** Greetings; age; name; alphabet and spelling	Greetings in Spanish Say how you are and ask how somebody else is The alphabet Spelling your name in Spanish	*tú* and *usted*	–	¡Hola! ¿Cómo te llamas? Me llamo…. Encantado/encantada. ¿Cómo se escribe tu nombre? Buenos días, Buenas tardes, Buenas noches, ¿Qué tal? ¿Y tú? Fenomenal, Regular, Fatal, Adiós, Hasta luego	(L) 7W1, 7W6, 7S9, 7T1, 7T2, 7T6, 7C5	1a, 1b, 2a, 2b, 2c, 2d, 2e, 3c, 4c, 5a, 5b, 5c	1.1–2, 2.1–3, 3.1–2, 4.1
14–15 **1.2 ¿Cuántos años tienes?** Age; numbers 1–16	Count from 1–16 Say how old you are Ask other people how old they are	*tener*, when used for age	Pronunciation of *c*	uno, dos, tres, cuatro, cinco, seis, siete, ocho, nueve, diez, once, doce, trece, catorce, quince, dieciséis ¿Cuántos años tienes? Tengo…. años. Yo también. ¿Cuántos años tiene Marga? Tiene… años.	(L) 7W5, 7S2, 7S4, 7L1, 7C4	1a, 1b, 1c, 2a, 2b, 2c, 2d, 3b, 3c, 3e, 4a, 4c, 4d, 5a, 5c, 5d, 5e, 5g, 5i	1.1–2, 2.1–2, 3.1–2, 4.1–2
16–17 **1.3 ¿Cuándo es tu cumpleaños?** Months; numbers 15–31; birthdays	Months of the year in Spanish Count from 15–31 Say when your birthday is Ask other people when their birthday is	Months in Spanish not taking a capital letter How to form questions in Spanish	–	¿Cuándo es tu cumpleaños? Mi cumpleaños es el… primero, dos, tres de enero, febrero, marzo, abril, mayo, junio, julio, agosto, septiembre, octubre, noviembre, diciembre	(L) 7S4	1b, 1c, 2a, 2b, 2c, 2d, 3b, 3c, 3e, 4a, 4c, 4d, 5a, 5d, 5e, 5h, 5i	1.1–2, 2.1, | 3.1–2, 4.1–2
18–19 **1.4 ¿Qué hay en tu mochila?** School bag; plurals	What you have in your school bag Plurals in Spanish	*un/una/unos/unas* Negatives	–	una goma, una regla, una pluma, una agenda, una carpeta, un estuche, unos patines, una revista, un equipo de gimnasia, un i-pod, unas canicas, un diccionario, un cuaderno, un libro, un bolígrafo, un sacapuntas, un lápiz, un móvil, una botella de agua, una bolsa de caramelos, un monopatín, ¿Hay? Hay…, No hay…, Hay un/una/unos/unas…, ¿Qué hay en tu mochila? ¿Tienes…? Sí, tengo…, No, no tengo…	(L) 7W8, 7S5 (R) 7W4	1b, 1c, 2a, 2c, 2d, 2e, 3a, 3b, 3c, 3e, 4a, 4c, 4d, 5a, 5c, 5d, 5e, 5f, 5g, 5i	1.1, 2.2, 3.1–2, 4.1–2
20–21 **1.5 Entre amigos** Mayan civilization	Use the language and structures learnt in the unit in a different context	–	–	–	7C3	2a, 3b, 3c, 3e, 4a, 4c, 4d, 5d, 5e, 5f, 5g, 5h, 5i	1.1, 3.1–3, 4.1

AMIGOS 1 UNIT 1 MEDIUM TERM PLAN

About this unit: In this unit students learn and use a range of new language through the context of self and classroom items. They carry out simple conversations and use basic strategies for understanding short written and spoken texts. Students are introduced to gender and the plural form of nouns. Students learn how to ask questions and learn some important features of Spanish pronunciation. Students also learn some simple facts about the ancient Mayan civilization.

Framework objectives (launch)	Teaching and learning
7W1: everyday words	*Tengo…, ¿Y tú? ¿Qué tal? ¿Cuándo es tu cumpleaños? ¿Cómo te llamas?*
7W5: verbs present (+ past)	*tener (tengo/tienes/tiene)*; its use as 'to have' and its use with age
7W6: letters and sounds	Spanish alphabet; spelling words; vowel and consonant sounds
7W8: finding meanings	Use knowledge of cognates and false friends to work out the school bag items
7S2: sentence gist	Learning about the difference between Spanish and English when talking about age
7S4: simple questions	*¿Cuántos años tienes? ¿Cuándo? ¿Cómo? ¿Qué tal?*
7S5: simple negatives	How to form basic negatives using *no* before the verb
7S9: using simple sentences	Basic personal information: students introduce themselves following model conversation on p. 12.
7T1: reading using cues	Read conversation on p. 12 using photos as clues to understanding
7T2: reading aloud	Read conversation on p. 12 or p. 13
7T6: texts as prompts for writing	In pairs make up a conversation based on the model conversation on p. 12
7L1: engage with sound patterns	Students learn pronunciation of new sounds and words containing those sounds
7C3: authentic material	Students learn about the Mayan civilization and its numbering system
7C4: stories and songs	Numbers song on p. 14
7C5: social conventions	*tú* and *usted* in greetings
Framework objectives (reinforce)	
7W4: gender and plural	*un/una/unos/unas*
	Teaching and learning (additional)
	The festival of San Fermín

Week-by-week overview (assuming 6 weeks' work or approx. 10–12.5 hours)

Week 1
Introduction to unit objectives. Learn how to say hello, goodbye, how are you?; introduce yourself; understand the Spanish alphabet

Week 2
Learn how to count from 1–16; how to say how old you are and how to ask other people how old they are

Week 3
How to say the months of the year in Spanish; count from 15–31; say when your birthday is and ask other people when their birthday is

Week 4
Students say what they have in their school bag and learn how to form plurals in Spanish

Week 5
Students apply the language and structures learnt in this unit to reading and answering questions on longer texts which focus on an aspect of Spanish or Latin American culture

Week 6
Recycle language of the unit via *Uno, Dos* and *Lectura* pages; students check their progress via the *Ya sé…* self-assessment checklist in the Students' Book and on Hoja 6.

¡Yo!

Unit objectives

Contexts: numbers 0–31, the alphabet, birthdays, months, school items
Grammar: *tener*; *tú* and *usted*; *hay*; the indefinite article; plurals
Language learning: questions; giving your name, birthday and age; saying what is in your school bag
Pronunciation: alphabet; the letter *c*; vowels
Cultural focus: greetings; *tú* and *usted*; the San Fermín celebrations in Pamplona

Assessment opportunities

Speaking: SB, page 12, activity 4
Reading: SB, page 13, activity 6
Listening: SB, page 15, activity 8
Writing: SB, page 17, Reto

AT1.1

1 Escucha y lee. ¿Qué nombres son de chico y cuáles de chica? ¿Sabes tu nombre o el de algún amigo en español? ¿Qué es diferente en los apellidos españoles?

AT3.1

Students listen to the register being called. They try to identify which are boys'/girls' names. Focus on the two surnames for each Spanish student on the register (note that Adam is different).

Answers: Boys' names: Julián, Adam, Jorge, Jesús, Carlos; girls' names': Berta, Diana, Emilia, María, Pial

The two surnames used in Spanish are the father's surname followed by the mother's maiden name. Both are given in formal situations, but only the first in everyday conversation.
The students are replying that they are 'present'.

 CD 1, track 3   página 11, actividad 1

- Álvarez Diéguez, Berta
- ¡Presente!
- Barros Fernández, Diana
- ¡Presente!
- Díaz Rodríguez, Emilia
- ¡Presente!
- García López, Julián
- ¡Presente!
- Johnson, Adam
- ¡Presente!
- López García, Jorge
- ¡Presente!
- Medina Vidal, Jesús
- ¡Presente!
- Ozores Valdés, María
- ¡Presente!
- Patel, Pial
- ¡Presente!
- Pérez Brito, Carlos
- ¡Presente!

Planner

●●●●●●●●●●●●●●●●●●●●●

1.1 Mis amigos
páginas 12–13

Objectives

▶ Greetings: saying hello, goodbye and asking and answering how someone is

▶ Introduce yourself and ask about others' names

▶ Understand the Spanish alphabet and spell aloud

Resources

Students' Book, pages 12–13
CD 1, tracks 4–6
Uno/Dos Workbooks, page 4

Key language

¡Hola!
¿Cómo te llamas? Me llamo …
Encantado/encantada
¿Cómo se escribe tu nombre?
Buenos días / Buenas tardes / Buenas noches
¿Qué tal? Fenomenal. / Muy bien. / Regular. / Fatal.
¿Y tú?
Adiós / Hasta luego

Programme of Study reference

1a, 1b, 2a, 2b, 2c, 2d, 2e, 3c, 4c, 5a, 5b, 5c

Framework reference

(L) 7W1, 7W6, 7S9, 7T1, 7T2, 7T6, 7C5

●●●●●●●●●●●●●●●●●●●●●

¡A sus marcas!

Mira las fotos. ¿Qué pasa?

Students look at the photos and discuss what is happening.

***Answers**:* Carlos and Fátima are meeting for the first time. Adam is meeting Señora Álvarez, one of his teachers while he is at school in Spain.

AT1.1

AT 3.1/2

1 Escucha, lee y repite.

Students listen, read and repeat the conversations. Focus on the differences between the *tú* and *usted* in the question forms and on the adjective endings.

***Answers**:* The first question is addressed to a friend, whereas the second one is addressed to an older person whom Adam doesn't know. *Encantado* is the masculine form, used by Carlos and Adam; *encantada* is the feminine form used by Fátima and Señora Álvarez.

 CD 1, track 4
página 12, actividad 1

1 – ¡Hola! ¿Cómo te llamas?
   – Me llamo Fátima. ¿Y tú? ¿Cómo te llamas?
   – Me llamo Carlos.
   – Encantada.
   – Encantado.
2 – ¡Hola! ¿Cómo se llama usted?
   – Me llamo Señora Álvarez. Y tú, ¿cómo te llamas?
   – Me llamo Adam.
   – ¿Cómo se escribe?
   – A–D–A–M.
   – Encantada.
   – Encantado.

AT1.1
AT3.1

2 Escucha y lee.

Students listen to a song teaching the alphabet in Spanish.

 CD 1, track 5
página 12, actividad 2

a–b–c … ch–d–e
f–g–h–I … j–k–l–ll
m–n–ñ–o …p–q
r–s–t … u–v–w
x–y–z
a es la letra de avión.
b es la letra de balón.
c es la letra de camión.
El abecedario en español es…

a–b–c … ch–d–e

Todo el mundo en clase canta esta canción
del abecedario en español.

a–be–ce … che–de–e

efe–ge–hache–i … jota–ka–ele–elle
eme–ene–eñe–o … pe–q

ere–ese–te … u–uve–uve doble–
equis–i griega y zeta.

f es la letra de fútbol.
g es la letra de girasol.
i es la letra de ilusión.
e es la letra de Español.

a–b–c … ch–d–e
Todo el mundo en clase canta la canción
del abecedario en español.

Zoom gramática

This section highlights the use of *tú* and *usted*.

AT2.2 **3** Now it's your turn. How would you address your friend's mother? How would you ask a classmate their name?

Answers: You would address your friend's mother as *usted*; *¿Cómo te llamas?*

AT 2.1 **4** Con tu compañero/a haz un diálogo.

In pairs, students make up a conversation following the model between Señora Alvárez and Adam but using their own name and spelling it aloud. They swap roles so that both students practise spelling their name.

AT1.2 **5** Escucha, lee y repite.

AT3.2 Students listen to, read and repeat the comic strip. Focus on the different greetings for the different times of day and encourage students to copy the intonation to show how the people feel.

CD 1, track 6 página 13, actividad 5

1 – ¡Buenos días! ¿Qué tal?
– Fenomenal, ¿y tú?
– Fenomenal. ¡Adiós!
2 – ¡Buenas tardes! ¿Qué tal?
– Muy bien, ¿y tú?
– Muy bien.
3 – Hola, ¿qué tal?
– Regular, ¿y tú?
– Fatal. Cansado … ¡Buenas noches!
– ¡Buenas noches!
– ¡Hasta luego!

AT3.1 **6** Lee. Empareja los símbolos y las palabras.

Students use what they saw and heard in the comic strip to match the symbols with the words.

Answers: a Fenomenal; b Muy bien; c Regular; d Fatal

AT2.1 **7** Con tu compañero/a haz un diálogo.

In pairs, students make up a conversation following the model in exercise 5.

AT3.2 **8** Lee y divide la serpiente.

Students read the conversation and then write it out correctly. Ask volunteers to write a line each on the board for the class to check answers.

Answers:
– ¡Hola! ¿Cómo te llamas?
– Me llamo Marcos. ¿Y tú?
– Me llamo Marina.
– Encantado, Marina.
– Encantado, Marcos.

Reto

AT 4.2/3 Con tu compañero/a haz un diálogo.

In pairs, students make up a conversation using the language from the double-page spread.

Planner

1.2 ¿Cuántos años tienes?
páginas 14–15

Objectives

▶ Count from 1–16

▶ Say how old you are

▶ Ask other people how old they are

Resources

Students' Book, pages 14–15
CD 1, tracks 7–13
Uno/Dos Workbooks, page 5

Key language

uno, dos, tres, cuatro, cinco, seis, siete, ocho, nueve, diez, once, doce, trece, catorce, quince, dieciséis
¿Cuántos años tienes? Tengo… años. Yo también. ¿Cuántos años tiene Marga? Tiene… años.

Programme of Study reference

1a, 1b, 1c, 2a, 2b, 2c, 2d, 3b, 3c, 3e, 4a, 4c, 4d, 5a, 5c, 5d, 5e, 5g, 5i

Framework reference

(L) 7W5, 7S2, 7S4, 7L1, 7C4

¡A sus marcas!

a Empareja las palabras con los dibujos.

Students try to match the numbers with the Spanish words. If they studied any French in Key Stage 2, ask them to look for similar words to help them.

b Escucha y comprueba tus respuestas.

Students listen and check.

 CD 1, track 7 página 14, actividad b

uno dos tres cuatro cinco seis siete ocho nueve diez once doce trece catorce quince dieciséis

| AT1.1 | **1 Escucha la canción.** |

Students listen to a number song. You could ask them to listen out for which numbers are repeated.

 CD 1, track 8 página 14, actividad 1

Uno … dos … tres
Cuatro … cinco … seis
Siete … ocho
Nueve … diez
Nueve … diez, nueve … diez, nueve … diez
Nueve … diez.
Once … doce
Trece … catorce
Quince … dieciséis … dieciséis.

| AT1.1 / AT3.1 | **2 Lee en voz alta.** |

Ask individual students to read the first three words, checking that the class agree with the pronunciation. Students then read the following four numbers to each other in pairs.

| AT1.1 | **3 Escucha y comprueba tus respuestas.** |

Students listen and check. Pause the CD after each number.

 CD 1, track 9 página 14, actividad 3

catorce … cinco … cuatro
once … doce … trece … quince

Se pronuncia así

The first part of this section focuses on the hard and soft pronunciation of *c* in Spanish. Read the rules with the class and make sure that students realize that they can follow these with all new words that they meet in Spanish.

| AT4.1 | **4 Copia y completa.** |

Students copy and complete the sequences.

Answers:

dos, cuatro, seis, ocho, diez, doce, catorce, dieciséis
uno, tres, cinco, siete, nueve, once, trece, quince
dos, cinco, siete, diez, trece, dieciséis
uno, cinco, nueve, trece

| AT2.1 | **5 Now pronounce the words below. Listen and check.** |

Students practise the words, following the rules. (You may want to translate the words too.)

 CD 1, track 10 página 14, actividad 5

cama … cita … cena … cuna … coma

The second part focuses on the pronunciation of diphthongs. Point out that when two vowels come together in Spanish, they are pronounced exactly the same as the two separate sounds. You may want to contrast with diphthongs in English (e.g. *great*, *rain*) or French if the students have studied any (e.g. *neuf*, *beau*).

AT1.1 | **6 Now try these words. Listen and check.**

Students practise the words, giving each vowel its full sound. (You may want to translate the words too.)

 CD 1, track 11   página 14, actividad 6

bueno ... guapo ... cielo

AT1.2 | **7 Escucha y lee.**

AT3.2 | Students listen to and read the photo story.

 CD 1, track 12   página 15, actividad 7

1 – ¿Cuántos años tienes, Jorge?
– Tengo 12 años. ¿Cuántos años tienes, Raquel?
– Tengo 13 años.
2 – ¡Hola, Carlos!
– ¡Hola, Adam! ¿Cuántos años tienes?
– Tengo 12 años.
– ¡Yo también!
3 – ¿Cuántos años tiene Marga?
– Marga tiene 14 años.
– ¿Y tú, Fátima? ¿Cuántos años tienes?
– Tengo 14 también.

AT2.2 | **8 Con tu compañero/a haz un diálogo.**

Students make up a dialogue following the model in exercise 7.

AT1.1 | **9 Escucha. Copia y completa para Marisa, Olga, Antonio y Rubén.**

Students copy the table and complete it with the four names. They then listen and complete it with names and ages.

Answers: Marisa: 15; Olga: 13; Antonio: 13; Rubén 16

 CD 1, track 13   página 15, actividad 9

– Buenas noches, señoras y señores ...¡Aquí están los concursantes! ... Muy bien... ¡Marisa! Bienvenida ....
¿Cuántos años tienes?
– Tengo quince años.
– Muy bien, Marisa ... y la concursante número dos... ¡Olga! Bienvenida...
– Gracias.
– ¿Cuántos años tienes, Olga?
– Tengo trece años.
– Gracias, Olga ... y el concursante número tres es ... Antonio. Buenas noches, Antonio.
– Buenas noches.
– ¿Cuántos años tienes?
– Tengo trece años.
– Muy bien, muy bien ... y ... Rubén. Buenas noches y bienvenido.
– Hola, buenas noches.
– ¿Cuántos años tienes?
– Tengo dieciséis años.
– Muy bien. Perfecto. Y ahora, ¡a concursar!

Zoom gramática

This section focuses on the irregular verb *tener*. Make sure that students understand the use of different forms for different persons and the meanings 'to have' as well as 'to be' for age. (Students will use *tener* to mean 'have' in Unit 2.) Encourage them to find examples in the photo story in exercise 7.

AT 4.1/2 | **10 How would you say 'he is 14'? How would you say 'you are 15 years old'?**

Students call out the answers. Ask volunteers to write them on the board.

Answers: Tiene catorce años; Tienes quince años.

Reto

AT4.1 | Copia y rellena los espacios.

Students copy and complete the note with the words given underneath.

Answers: llamo ... Qué ... gracias ... once ... tú ... tienes

Planner

● ●

1.3 **¿Cuándo es tu cumpleaños?** páginas 16–17

Objectives

▶ Say the months of the year in Spanish

▶ Count from 15–31

▶ Say when your birthday is

▶ Ask other people when their birthday is

Resources

Students' Book, pages 16–17
CD 1, tracks 14–16
Uno/Dos Workbooks, page 6

Key language

¿Cuándo es tu cumpleaños?
Mi cumpleaños es el… primero/dos/tres (etc.) de…
enero, febrero, marzo, abril, mayo, junio, julio, agosto,
septiembre, octubre, noviembre, diciembre

Programme of Study reference

1b, 1c, 2a, 2b, 2c, 2d, 3b, 3c, 3e, 4a, 4c, 4d, 5a, 5d, 5e, 5h, 5i

Framework reference

(L) 7S4

● ●

¡A sus marcas!

AT3.1 | Lee. ¿Cuántos reconoces?

Students work out which months they can recognize in Spanish. Encourage them to look for cognates.

Answers: enero – January; febrero – February; marzo – March; abril – April; mayo – May; junio – June; julio – July; agosto – August; septiembre – September; octubre – October; noviembre – November; diciembre – December.

AT1.1
AT2.1 | **1** Escucha y repite.

Students listen and repeat the months. Pay particular attention to the vowel sounds, pausing the CD as necessary.

 CD 1, track 14 página 16, actividad 1

enero … febrero … marzo … abril … mayo … junio … julio … agosto … septiembre … octubre … noviembre … diciembre

Zoom gramática

Use the *¡A sus marcas!* exercise to support the rule that capital letters are not used for the months of the year. Find out if any students have their birthday on the first day of a month and practise saying it as a class.

AT1.2 | **2** Escucha (1–4). ¿Verdad o mentira?

Students listen and mark whether the given birthdays are correct.

Answers: 1 V; 2 M; 3 M; 4 V

 CD 1, track 15 página 16, actividad 2

1 – Adam, ¿cuándo es tu cumpleaños?
– Mi cumpleaños es el quince de octubre.
2 – Fátima ¿cuándo es tu cumpleaños?
– Mi cumpleaños es el diez de noviembre.
3 – Mohammed, ¿cuándo es tu cumpleaños?
– Mi cumpleaños es el siete de febrero.
4 – Rubén ¿cuándo es tu cumpleaños?
– Mi cumpleaños es el 13 de abril.

Cultura

Discuss the San Fermín celebrations in Pamplona. Ask if the students have ever seen the famous bull run through the streets (on the news or in documentaries). Describe how people sometimes have to clamber up the walls and cling onto balconies or railings to avoid the bulls. Explain that there are sometimes accidents but that the tradition is still very popular.

AT3.1 | **3** Lee los números del 15 al 31.

Students use their knowledge of the lower numbers to complete the series from 15–31. With a weaker group, do *18* and *24* as a whole class and then ask the students to complete the rest by themselves.

AT1.1 | **4** Escucha y comprueba tus respuestas.

Students listen and check. Ask volunteers to write the missing numbers on the board. Point out that *veintiséis*, like *dieciséis* that the students studied in 1.2, needs an accent. (Students will learn more about accents in the Gramática section, p 122.)

 CD 1, track 16 página 17, actividad 4

quince … dieciséis … diecisiete … dieciocho … diecinueve … veinte … veintiuno … veintidós … veintitrés … veinticuatro … veinticinco … veintiséis … veintisiete … veintiocho … veintinueve … treinta … treinta y uno

Zoom gramática

This section highlights the use of question marks in Spanish. Students will by now have seen various Spanish questions in *Amigos 1*. Read the *Zoom gramática* box with the class and encourage the students to find examples in Unit 1 so far.

AT 3.1/2	**5** What would be the question to this answer: *Tengo doce años?*

Students call out the question. Write it on the board missing out the question marks and ask the class to correct it.

Answer: ¿Cuántos años tienes?

AT4.1	**6** Los cumpleaños de la clase. Haz un sondeo.

Ask a few pairs of students to practise the model question and answer across the class. Then divide the class into groups of 5 or 6. In their groups, students ask and take notes of the answers. Compile the results of each group on the board to create a class survey and to find out the most popular month.

Reto

AT4.2	Escribe estos cumpleaños.

Students write out the other three birthdays following the example.

Answers:
El cumpleaños de Luis es el trece de marzo.
El cumpleaños de José es el veinticinco de julio.
El cumpleaños de Pepe es el nueve de septiembre.

Planner

• •

1.4 **¿Qué hay en tu mochila?** páginas 18–19

Objectives

▶ Say what you have in your school bag

▶ Use plurals in Spanish

Resources

Students' Book, pages 18–19
CD 1, track 17
Uno/Dos Workbooks, page 7

Key language

una goma, una regla, una pluma, una agenda, una carpeta, un estuche, unos patines, una revista, un equipo de gimnasia, un i-pod, unas canicas, un diccionario, un cuaderno, un libro, un bolígrafo, un sacapuntas, un lápiz, un móvil, una botella de agua, una bolsa de caramelos, un monopatín
¿Hay?, Hay…, No hay…, Hay un/una/unos/unas…, ¿Qué hay en tu mochila?, ¿Tienes…?, Sí, tengo…, No, no tengo…

Programme of Study reference

1b, 1c, 2a, 2c, 2d, 2e, 3a, 3b, 3c, 3e, 4a, 4c, 4d, 5a, 5c, 5d, 5e, 5f, 5g, 5i

Framework reference

(L) 7W8, 7S5
(R) 7W4

• •

¡A sus marcas!

AT3.1 Mira el vocabulario del ejercicio 1.

Students look for cognates and false friends in the words in exercise 1.

Answers: *fútbol, gimnasia, i-pod, diccionario, móvil* and *botella* are quite similar to English words; *agenda* and *carpeta* look like English but have a different meaning.

AT1.1 **1** Escucha y lee.

AT3.2 Students listen to and read the dialogues. They then match the schoolbags with the correct characters.

Answers: Adam's schoolbag is on the left; Carlos' schoolbag is on the right.

🎧 **CD 1, track 17**   página 18, actividad 1

– Hola, Adam, ¿Qué tal?
– ¡Uf! ¡Fatal! ¿Y tú?
– ¡Uf! ¡Cansado!
– ¡Hola, Adam! ¡Hola, Carlos! ¿Qué tal?
– Uf … bien … bien …
– ¿Bien? Mmm … ¿Qué hay en tu mochila, Adam? ¡Es enorme!
– Pues … en mi mochila hay … una goma, una regla, una pluma, una agenda, una carpeta, un estuche, unos patines, una revista de fútbol, un equipo de gimnasia, un i-pod y unas canicas.
– ¿Y tú, Carlos? ¿Qué hay en tu mochila?
– A ver … un diccionario, un cuaderno, un libro, un bolígrafo, un sacapuntas, un lápiz, un móvil, una botella de agua, una bolsa de caramelos, un monopatín …

AT2.2 **2 Con tu compañero/a, ¿cómo se dice en español?**

Ask several pairs of students to read the model question and answer across the class, using other examples if you prefer. Students then work in pairs asking and answering about items labelled in exercise 1.

AT4.1 **3 Copia y rellena un cuadro.**

Students copy and complete the table with singular and plural masculine and feminine nouns from exercise 1.

Zoom gramática

The first part of this section focuses on the forms of the indefinite article. If the students have not studied a foreign language in Key Stage 2, the concept of gender will probably be new to them. Explain that they will need to learn whether new words are masculine or feminine.
The section then moves on to highlight plurals. With the spelling change of *lápiz – lápices*, remind the students that *c* before *e* is pronounced 'th'. You may want to introduce the spelling rule: For 'th' we use *c* where it **can** be (before *i* and *e*) and *z* where it **must** be (all other vowels or at the end of words).

AT4.1 **4 What are the plurals of *un bolígrafo* and *una agenda*?**

Students call out the plurals.

Answers: unos bolígrafos; unas agendas

Zoom gramática

This next section introduces the negative (*tengo/no tengo* and *hay/no hay*). As well as the negative form, focus too on the silent *h* in *Hay/No hay* in preparation for the pairwork in exercise 5?
Remind students that *Sí* means *Yes* and *No* means *No*.

AT2.2 | **5** Con tu compañero/a. ¿Qué hay en tu mochila?

Ask two students to read the model dialogue. Students then work in pairs asking and answering until each has guessed five objects.

Reto

AT4.1 | Completa las frases.

Students complete the sentences.

Answers: En mi mochila hay dos libros y un cuaderno. No tengo un estuche. Mi amigo Alí tiene un diccionario y tres plumas, y una agenda.

Planner

● ●

1.5 **El calendario maya** páginas 20–21

Resources

Students' Book, pages 20–21
CD 1, tracks 18–19
Uno/Dos Workbooks, page 8

Programme of Study reference

2a, 3b, 3c, 3e, 4a, 4c, 4d, 5d, 5e, 5f, 5g, 5h, 5i

Framework reference

7C3

● ●

AT1.1 **AT3.3** **1 Escucha y lee.**

Students listen to and read the text. Ask the students to identify the different numbers mentioned.

 CD 1, track 18 página 20, actividad 1

Los Mayas son una civilización antigua del sur de Méjico y Guatemala que existió del siglo tres al siglo quince.
Los Mayas tienen cuatro calendarios diferentes. En uno de sus calendarios el año tiene 365 días. Hay dieciocho meses de veinte días y otro mes de cinco días, cinco días de mala suerte.
Ahora vas a aprender los números mayas del uno al diecinueve.

AT3.1 **2 Utiliza las pistas y rellena los espacios con el número maya.**

Students copy and complete the grid and use the clues given.

Answers:
a = ··· ; b = ··· ;
c = <u>··</u> ; d = <u>····</u>

AT3.1 **3 ¿Verdad o mentira? Corrige los dos números falsos.**

Answers:

<u><u>····</u></u> = catorce; <u><u>····</u></u> = diecinueve

AT3.1 **4 Mira esta estela maya. ¿Qué números lees?**

Students work out the numbers.

Answers:
a ocho, siete, siete, ocho, siete
b uno, tres, doce, tres, doce
c trece, dieciocho, dieciséis, trece, diez
d ocho, ocho, ocho, ocho, ocho
e diecisiete, diecisiete, diecisiete, diecisiete, diecisiete

AT1.1 **5 Escucha y lee.**

Students listen to and read about Chichén Itzá.

 CD 1, track 19 página 21, actividad 5

Chichén Itzá es como un calendario enorme. Hay una pirámide que se llama 'El Castillo' y tiene 365 escaleras. Hay curiosidades muy interesantes en todo el lugar.
Por ejemplo, si estás en la pirámide y hablas con tu amigo, la persona que está abajo oye tu conversación perfectamente.
Los mayas eran aficionados a los deportes y el juego de pelota era su deporte favorito. El campo del juego de pelota es muy grande (166 metros), pero un susurro en un lado del campo se oye en el otro lado perfectamente. En el juego de pelota no utilizaban las manos y un juego podía durar varios días.

AT3.3 **6 ¿Verdad o mentira?**

Students read and decide whether the sentences are true or false.

Answers: a M; b V; c M; d V; e M

Repaso página 22

Resources

Students' Book, page 22

Programme of Study reference

1c, 2a, 2c, 2f, 3b, 3e, 4a, 4c, 5d, 5f, 5g, 5h, 5i

AT3.1 **1 Lee y descifra el mensaje secreto.**

Students work out the letter and number code to read the secret message. You may want to write the message on the board to check for the use of Spanish exclamation marks and capital or small letters.

Answers: ¡Hola! Me llamo Pablo. Mi cumpleaños es el dos de enero.

AT4.2 **2 Escribe tú un mensaje secreto. Utiliza el código del ejercicio 1.**

Students write a message for and swap it with a partner. They write out the message that they receive and check answers in pairs.

AT3.2 **3 Empareja las preguntas con las respuestas.**

Students read and match the questions and answers.

Answers: 1c; 2a; 3d; 4e; 5b

AT3.1
AT4.1 **4 Rellena los espacios.**

Students complete the note with the words given underneath.

Answers: ¡Hola! Me llamo Pedro. ¿Qué tal? Yo muy bien. Tengo catorce años. ¿Y tú? ¿Cuántos años tienes? Mi cumpleaños es el quince de septiembre. ¿Cuándo es tu cumpleaños?

Vocabulario
página 23

This page provides a theme-based Spanish–English summary of the key language of this unit. It can be used for reference throughout the unit or as an aid to learning vocabulary.

C5 Copymaster 5 contains a summary of the key language of the unit and can be given to the students at this point to help with revision.

W11 Page 11 of the *Uno/Dos* Workbooks also provides a summary of the key language of the unit.

Ya sé
página 24

The *Ya sé* page provides an end-of-unit checklist of learning objectives. At the foot of the page are activities at three levels of difficulty to extend the work of the unit. Encourage students to select an activity at the most appropriate level.

C6 Copymaster 6 contains a checklist to keep track of the students' progress.

W12 Page 12 of the *Uno/Dos* Workbooks gives an end-of-unit checklist in English, together with activities to keep track of the students' progress.

Unidad 1 Uno
página 96

Objectives
This reinforcement page is intended for those students who need further practice of core language of the unit. It can be used by students who finish other activities early or as alternative class or homework material.

Resources
Students' Book, page 96
CD 1, track 20

Programme of Study reference
1c, 2a, 2c, 2d, 3b, 3c, 3e, 4a, 4c, 5f, 5g, 5i

AT3.2 **1 Escoge y escribe las respuestas.**

Students write the correct answers for each cartoon.

AT1.1 **2 Escucha y comprueba tus respuestas.**

Students listen and check.

Answers: 1e; 2c; 3d; 4b; 5a

 CD 1, track 20   página 98, actividad 2

1 – Hola! ¿qué tal?
  – Muy bien, gracias, ¿y tú?
2 – ¿Cómo te llamas?
  – Me llamo Estrella.
3 – ¿Cómo se escribe tu nombre?
  – A–L–I–C–I–A.
4 – ¿Cuándo es tu cumpleaños?
  – Mi cumpleaños es el 22 de abril.
5 – ¡Adiós!
  – Hasta luego.

AT2.2 **3 Con tu compañero/a, practica los diálogos del ejercicio 1.**

Students practise the dialogues from exercise 1. Encourage them to copy the expression from the CD in order to vary the practice of the core language of the unit.

AT3.1 **4 Busca el plural de estas palabras en la sopa de letras.**

Students find and circle the plurals.

Answers: lápices; reglas; estuches

Unidad 1 Dos página 97

Objectives

This extension page is intended for more able students who are confident with the core language of the unit. It can be used by students who finish other activities quickly or as alternative class or homework material.

Resources

Students' Book, page 97
CD 1, track 21

Programme of Study reference

1c, 2a, 2c, 2e, 2f, 2i, 3b, 3c, 3e, 4a, 4c, 5a, 5b, 5d, 5e, 5g, 5h, 5i

| AT 4.1/2 | **1 Escribe las preguntas.** |

Students read the answer in each cartoon and write the corresponding question.

| AT 1.1/2 | **2 Escucha y comprueba tus respuestas.** |

Students listen and check.

Answers: a ¿Cómo te llamas?; b ¿Cómo se escribe tu nombre?; c ¿Cuántos años tienes?; d ¿Cuándo es tu cumpleaños?

 CD 1, track 21 página 97, actividad 2

a – ¿Cómo te llamas?
– ¡Hola! Me llamo Juan.
b – ¿Cómo se escribe tu nombre?
– P-E-D-R-O.
c – ¿Cuántos años tienes?
– Tengo doce años.
d – ¿Cuándo es tu cumpleaños?
– Mi cumpleaños es el primero de mayo.

| AT2.2 | **3 Con tu compañero/a, practica una conversación.** |

Students use their own personal information to practise the conversation from exercise 1.

| AT3.2 | **4 Lee y contesta a las preguntas en inglés.** |

Students read the text and write *True* or *False* for each sentence.

Answers: a True; b False; c True; d False; e False

Lectura: Unidad 1 Uno página 108

Objectives

This page is to encourage independent reading. Students should attempt it once they are confident with the core language of the unit. It can be used by students who finish other activities early or as alternative class or homework material.

Resources

Students' Book, page 108
CD 1, track 22

Programme of Study reference

2a, 2c, 2f, 3b, 3c, 3e, 4a, 4c, 5d, 5e, 5f, 5g, 5i

| AT 1.1/2 | **1 Escucha y lee. Empareja las personas con los cumpleaños.** |
| AT3.2 | |

Students listen to and read the speech bubbles. They then match each person with their birthday.

Answers: 1d; 2b; 3a; 4c

 CD 1, track 22 página 108, actividad 1

1 – Hola, me llamo Raquel y tengo doce años. Mi cumpleaños es el quince de marzo.
2 – ¿Qué tal? Me llamo David y tengo quince años. Mi cumpleaños es el primero de agosto.
3 – Hola, me llamo Inés y tengo trece años. Mi cumpleaños es el catorce de diciembre.
4 – Hola, me llamo Tomás y tengo dieciséis años. Mi cumpleaños es el nueve de septiembre.

| AT3.2 | **2 Lee. ¿Qué número es?** |

Students read the descriptions and write the correct number in Spanish.

Answers: b quince; c veintiocho; catorce

| AT3.2 | **3 ¿Qué mes es? Lee y escribe.** |

Students read the number of days and letters and write the correct month in Spanish.

Answers: a diciembre; b noviembre; c febrero; d agosto; e mayo

| AT4.3 | **4 Escribe una descripción similar de los otros meses.** |

Students write puzzles like those in exercise 3 about the other months of the year.

Lectura: Unidad 1 Dos   página 109

Copymasters

Objectives

This page is to encourage independent reading. Students should attempt it once they are confident with the core language of the unit. It can be used by students who finish other activities early or as alternative class or homework material.

Resources

Students' Book, page 109
CD 1, track 23

Programme of Study reference

2a, 2c, 2d, 2f, 3b, 4a, 4d, 5c, 5d, 5e, 5g, 5h, 5i

AT3.2 **1 Lee el poema en voz alta y contesta a las preguntas.**

In pairs, students practise reading the poem aloud. They then answer the questions.

Answers: a febrero; b enero, marzo, mayo, julio, agosto, octubre, diciembre; c enero

AT3.2 **2 Escucha y lee. ¿Quién es?**

Students listen to and read the cartoon strip. Tell them to look carefully at the pictures as well. They then write the correct name for each sentence.

Answers: a Marta; b Pedro; c Pedro; d Pedro; e Pedro

 CD 1, track 23   página 109, actividad 2

1 – ¡Hola, Pedro!
   – ¡Hola, Marta!
2 – ¿Qué hay en tu mochila?
   – Tengo un diccionario, un estuche, dos bolígrafos, tres gomas …
   – Aaah …
   – Y cuatro reglas y un móvil y …
3 – Y… ¿Tienes un cuaderno?
   – ¡Oh no! ¡No tengo!
4 – ¡Adiós, Pedro!
   – ¡Adiós, Marta!

AT4.3 **3 Escribe la respuesta o la pregunta.**

Students complete the missing answers or questions. They can use their own ideas for the answers.

Answers: a Es el (student's answer); b (student's answer); c ¿Cómo te llamas?; d (student's answer); e ¿Cuántos años tienes?

Hoja 7 ¡A sus marcas!

This can be used after page 11 of the Students' Book.

AT3.1 **1 Separa los nombres de la serpiente. ¿Cuáles son de chico y cuáles de chica?**

Students separate and group the names in two lists: boys and girls.

Answers:
Boys' names: Antonio; Julio; Pedro; Julián; Jorge. (It would also be correct to add Ángel to this list.)
Girls' names: Andrea; María; Ángela

AT3.1 **2 Une las sumas con los resultados.**

Students draw lines to match the sums with the answers.

Answers:
siete + cinco = doce
ocho + seis = catorce
nueve + dos = once
tres + uno = cuatro
trece + tres = dieciséis
diez + cinco = quince

AT3.1 **3 Une los meses con su traducción en inglés.**

Students draw lines to match the months in Spanish and English

Answers: marzo = March; octubre = October; noviembre = November; julio = July; febrero = February; abril = April; enero = January; septiembre = September; diciembre = December; junio = June; agosto = August; mayo = May

Hoja 8 Reto

This can be used after pages 12–13 of the Students' Book.

AT4.1 **1 Pon las letras en orden.**

Students order the letters and write the correct word to complete the sentence.

Answers: años; trece; llamas; llamo; Fenomenal

AT4.1 **2 Une las mitades.**

Students draw lines to match the halves of the words.

Answers: mochila; bolígrafo; estuche; lápiz; carpeta; regla; libro; cuaderno

AT4.1 **3 Escribe las palabras que faltan.**

Students write the correct word for each question or sentence. Check for the correct use of the accent in questions 1–3.

Answers: 1 Cuándo; 2 Cómo; 3 Qué; 4 Tengo

Hoja 9 Escuchar: uno

This can be used after pages 14–15 of the Students' Book.

AT1.1 **1 Escucha con atención. ¿Qué números faltan?**

Students listen and complete the missing numbers.

Answers: 2 = 81**75**4923; 3 = 234**68**659; 4 = 9**1**4358**2**6

 CD 3, track 1   Hoja 9, uno, actividad 1

1 – Eduardo, ¿cuál es tu número de móvil?
– Mi número es el 6 – 1 – 4 – 3 – 5 – 9 – 8 – 2.
– Ah, gracias.
2 – Pedro, ¿cuál es tu número de móvil?
– Mi número es el 8 – 1 – 7 – 5 – 4 – 9 – 2 – 3.
3 – Lidia, ¿cuál es tu número de móvil?
– Mi teléfono es el 2 – 3 – 4 – 6 – 8 – 6 – 5 – 9.
4 – Paco, ¿cuál es tu número de móvil?
– Es el 9 – 1 – 4 – 3 – 5 – 8 – 2 – 6.

AT1.1 **2 Escucha y pon un círculo en las letras. Descubre el mensaje secreto.**

Students circle the letters they hear. They then read the remaining letters from left to right, top row then bottom row, to find the secret message.

Answers: Me llamo Juan.

 CD 3, track 2   Hoja 9, uno, actividad 2

 b … w … f … g … t … ñ … v … l … c … r

Hoja 9 Escuchar: dos

AT1.1 **3 Escucha. ¿Verdad o mentira?**

AT4.2 Students compare the birthdays on the page with what they hear and mark them with a tick or cross. They then write the correct birthdays for the ones that they crossed.

Answers:
Mario: ✗ Es el 5 de febrero.
Ricardo: ✓
Lorena: ✗ Es el 21 de marzo.
Sonia: ✓

 CD 3, track 3   Hoja 9, Dos, actividad 3

Arturo
– Me llamo Arturo, mi cumpleaños es el 14 de agosto.
Mario
– ¿Cómo te llamas?
– Me llamo Mario.
– ¿Cuándo es tu cumpleaños?
– Es el 5 de febrero.
Ricardo
– Oye, Ricardo, ¿cuándo es tu cumpleaños?
– Mi cumpleaños es el 30 de junio.
Lorena
– Lorena, ¿cuándo es tu cumpleaños?
– Es el 21 de marzo.
Sonia
– Hola, Sonia, ¿cuándo es tu cumpleaños?
– Mi cumpleaños es el 2 de abril.

Hoja 10 Hablar: uno

This can be used after pages 18–19 of the Students' Book.

AT2.1 **1a/b ¿Qué hay en tu mochila? Describe tu mochila a tu compañero/a.**
1a/b Escucha a tu compañero/a y dibuja las diferencias.

Student A describes the school items in their picture. Student B listens and draws the items that they don't already have in their picture. They then swap roles.

Answers: Student B should draw two exercise books, a diary and a pencil. Student A should draw a dictionary, a fountain pen and a ruler.

Hoja 10 Hablar: dos

AT2.1 En mi mochila no hay …

As an extension, students working at the higher level tell their partner what they don't have in their own school bag.

Hoja 11 Leer y escribir: uno

This can be used after pages 16–17 of the Students' Book.

AT3.1 **1 Lee los cumpleaños de estas personas.**

Students read the dates given in figures and find the dates and months in the wordsearch.

Answers:

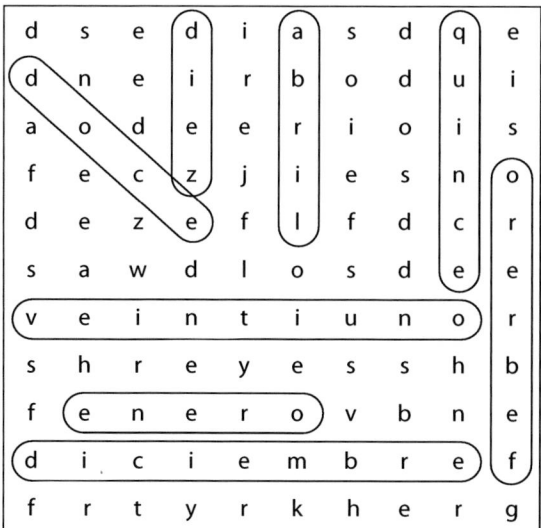

Answers:

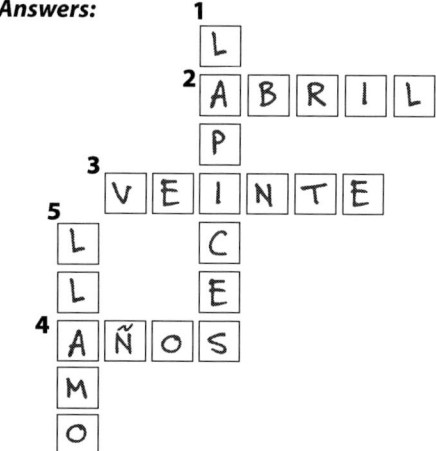

AT
4.2/3 **2 Mira los carnés de identidad. Escribe lo que dicen.**

Students read the identity cards and write a speech bubble as in the example.

Answers:

¡Hola! Me llamo José. Mi cumpleaños es el quince de octubre.

¡Hola! Me llamo Miriam. Mi cumpleaños es el veintidós de diciembre.

¡Hola! Me llamo Alfredo. Mi cumpleaños es el veinticinco de septiembre.

AT4.3 **3 Ahora escribe tu cumpleaños.**

Students write their birthday in the speech bubble in the same way as activity 2.

Hoja 12 Leer y escribir: dos

This can be used after pages 16–17 of the Students' Book.

AT3.2

AT4.1 **1 Rellena el crucigrama con las palabras adecuadas. Hay una palabra que tiene un acento. ¿Cuál es? Escríbela.**

Students complete the crossword and write the word with an accent in the last space.

AT4.3

AT3.2 **2 Lee las respuestas de la entrevista con Fernando y escribe las preguntas.**

Students write the questions for Fernando's answers.

Answers:

¿Cómo te llamas?

¿Cuántos años tienes?

¿Cuándo es tu cumpleaños?

¿Qué tienes en tu mochila?

¿Qué no tienes en tu mochila?

AT4.1 **3 Rellena los espacios con las palabras adecuadas.**

Students complete the text using appropriate words for the context.

Answers: llama; libros; estuche; diccionario; tengo; bolígrafo; goma

Hoja 13 Gramática

This can be used after pages 18–19 of the Students' Book.

AT4.1 **1 ¿Un o una, unos or unas?**

Read the first *¡Recuerda!* box with the class. Students then circle the correct article.

Answers: una goma; un bolígrafo; unas carpetas; unos estuches; unas mochilas; una regla

AT4.1 **2 Haz los plurales de estas palabras. Ponlas en la columna correcta.**

Look at the second *¡Recuerda!* box with the class. Students then work out the plural of each word and then write it in the correct column.

Answers:

-s	-es	-ces
bolígrafos	papeles	lápices
reglas	relojes	

3 Usa un diccionario. Busca una palabra que termine en una consonante y otra que termine en z, y haz los plurales.

Students use a dictionary or the Glosario in the Students' Book to find a word ending in a consonant and another ending in *-z*. They form the relevant plurals in *-es* and *-ces*.

Hoja 14 Técnica

This can be used after pages 18–19 of the Students' Book.

1 Now try some of these styles of learning. Make up a tune to help you learn the names of things in your school bag. Or draw some items and label them in Spanish.

Discuss the page with the class. You may like to ask the students to prepare something as homework for the next lesson to share their ideas.

Hoja 15 Cultura

This can be used after pages 20–21 of the Students' Book.

AT 3.3/4 **1** Lee las siguientes descripciones de las fiestas en España.

Students read the texts and use the different colours to show words that they find difficult to guess and closer cognates that they can guess. Answers will vary, but will form the basis for a useful class discussion.

AT4.1 **2** Ahora une las palabras en inglés con su traducción al español.

Students match the Spanish words with the English translations.

Answers: los niños – children; ganadores – winners; los reyes – kings; largo – long; hogueras – bonfires; casa – house; el número ganador – the winning number; los regalos – presents

Hoja 16 Se pronuncia así

This can be used after pages 14–15 of the Students' Book.

AT4.1 **1** You have come cross many words with the sounds 'ca', 'ce', 'ci', 'co' and 'cu'. Write out these numbers, then listen to their pronunciation.

Students write out the numbers and then listen to them on the CD to remind themselves of the pronunciation.

Answers: catorce; trece; doce; cinco; cuatro

 CD 3, track 4   Hoja 16, actividad 1

catorce ... trece ... doce ... cinco ... cuatro

AT2.1 **2** Work out how to say these words, then listen to check.

Students use the pronunciation rules to work out how to say the words and then listen to check.

 CD 3, track 5   Hoja 16, actividad 2

quince ... cine ... color ... cuna ... cama ... cena ... comida ... cocina

AT1.1 **3** Now try these tongue-twisters, then listen to check.

Students again use the pronunciation rules to work out how to say the tongue-twisters, and then listen to check.

 CD 3, track 6   Hoja 16, actividad 3

Carmen come carne en la cocina de Carlos.
Doce y trece son veinticinco.
Cuando cocino la comida, como con Cecilia.

AT4.1 **4** You have also come across two vowels together. Write out these words, then say them, following the pronunciation rules in the box below.

Students write out the numbers and practise saying them giving each vowel its full value. Make sure that they still keep each vowel sound short, and that the *o* sound is never a diphthong as in English.

Answers: veinte; siete; dieciocho; cuatro; nueve

AT2.1 **5** How would you pronounce 'dieciséis'? Remember the pronunciation for 'ci' too!

Practise saying *dieciséis* as a class. Divide up each syllable but make sure that the students keep each vowel sound short. It can also be useful to start from the end of the word and build up, like this:
séis
iséis
dieciséis

AT2.1 **6** Now try to pronounce these words, then listen to check.

Students combine all the rules they have been studying on the page to practise saying the words. Explain the meaning of any new words. They then listen and compare with the CD.

 CD 3, track 7   Hoja 16, actividad 6

cien ... cuarenta ... puerta ... miel ... pierna ... reino ... peine

Control Unidad 1

Resources
Copymasters 17–22
CD 3, tracks 8–11

Hoja 17 Escuchar: uno

AT1.1 **1** Escribe el orden de los objetos que oyes.

Students number the pictures.

Answers: 1 pencil; 2 diary; 3 pencil sharpener; 4 folder; 5 school bag; 6 ruler

Notes on mark scheme:

Each of the four language skills (Listening, Speaking, Reading and Writing) in the *Amigos* Copymaster tests is marked out of 25.

There are separate Reading and Writing tests at levels *uno* and *dos* which you can choose to use with different levels. The available marks for the test have been calculated to give a mark out of 25.

The Listening and Speaking Copymasters can be copied for groups at either level and then used as follows:

Listening: Less confident students need only tackle the first one or two activities of the Listening test, under the heading *uno*, but the marks available for them have been calculated to give a mark out of 25 as well. Students working at a higher level should complete all the activities on the page, and the marks available for them have been redistributed to give a mark out of 25.

Speaking: There is usually some differentiation between the Speaking test for less confident and stronger students. Sometimes the stronger students are given more questions to ask on the same topic, and sometimes they have an additional follow-up activity. However, the available marks for the test at each level have been calculated to give a *mark out of 25*.

Mark scheme: Students who attempt *uno* only: 2 marks for each correct answer = 12 marks.

Students who attempt *uno* and *dos*: 1 mark for each correct answer = 6 marks.

Assessment criteria: Students who identify five or six objects correctly show evidence of performance at AT 1.1.

 CD 3, track 8 Hoja 17, actividad 1

1 – un lápiz
2 – una agenda
3 – un sacapuntas
4 – una carpeta
5 – una mochila
6 – una regla

AT4.1 **2** Escribe los cumpleaños de estas personas.

Students listen and write the birthdays in words.

Answers: Ana: el once de marzo; Nagore: el nueve de diciembre; Patricia: el siete de octubre; Julián: el quince de agosto.

Mark scheme: Students who attempt *uno* only: 3 marks for each correct answer: 2 marks for the correct word; 1 mark for the correct spelling. Award an extra mark for the correct use of lower case for the months. = 13 marks

Students who attempt *uno* and *dos*: 1 mark for each correct answer. Award an extra mark for the correct use of lower case for the months. = 5 marks

Assessment criteria: Students who communicate three or four birthdays correctly show evidence of performance at AT 4.1.

 CD 3, track 9 Hoja 17, actividad 2

– Ana, ¿cuándo es tu cumpleaños?
– El once de marzo.
– Nagore, tu cumpleaños?
– Mi cumpleaños es el nueve de diciembre.
– Soy Patricia. Mi cumpleaños es el siete de octubre.
– Soy Julián. Mi cumpleaños es el quince de agosto.

Hoja 17 Escuchar: dos

AT1.1 **3** Escucha y escribe lo que hay (✓) y lo que no hay (✗) en la mochila.
AT4.1

Students listen and complete the columns with what Pedro does and doesn't have in his school bag.

Answers: ✓: un libro; un cuaderno; una carpeta
✗: un diccionario; un móvil

Mark scheme: 1 mark for each correct answer = 5 marks. (Half a mark for the correct word; half a mark for the correct spelling)

Assessment criteria: Students who score 2 or more show evidence of performance at AT 1.1. Students who score 4 or more show evidence of performance at AT 4.1.

 CD 3, track 10 Hoja 17, actividad 3

– Pedro, ¿qué hay en tu mochila?
– Bueno, hay muchas cosas. Hay un libro, un cuaderno, una carpeta … pero no hay un diccionario o un móvil.

AT 4.1/2

4 Escribe la información sobre estas personas en el cuadro.

Students listen and complete the table. They can use figures for the dates as this is a listening test.

Answers:

Ana	20/4	cuaderno; lápiz
Iago	15/8	estuche; carpeta
Pedro	25/12	goma; libro

Mark scheme: 1 mark for each correct answer = 9 marks

Assessment criteria: Students who communicate accurately with some spelling errors show evidence of performance at AT 4.1. Students who spell everything correctly are performing at AT 4.2.

CD 3, track 11 Hoja 17, actividad 4

1 – Me llamo Ana.
   – ¿Cómo se escribe?
   – A–N–A.
   – ¿Cuándo es tu cumpleaños?
   – Es el 20 de abril.
   – ¿Qué hay en tu mochila?
   – Hay un cuaderno y un lápiz.
2 – Me llamo Iago.
   – ¿Cómo se escribe?
   – I–A–G–O. Mi cumpleaños es el 15 de agosto.
   – ¿Y qué hay en tu mochila, Iago?
   – Hay un estuche y una carpeta.
3 – ¿Cómo te llamas?
   – Me llamo Pedro.
   – ¿Cómo se escribe?
   – P–E–D–R–O.
   – ¿Cuándo es tu cumpleaños, Pedro?
   – Pues es el veinticinco de diciembre.
   – ¿Qué hay en tu mochila?
   – Hay una goma y un libro.

Hoja 18 Hablar: uno

AT2.3

1 Haz preguntas a tu compañero/a.

2 Responde a las preguntas.

Students work in pairs on the speaking test. A asks questions first for B to answer with the information given, and then they swap roles.

Mark scheme: 6 marks (2 each) for the correct questions; 15 marks (5 each) for the correct answers; 4 marks for communicative fluency and accent = 25 marks

Assessment criteria: Students who score 17 or more show evidence of performance at AT 2.3.

Answers: A – Bruno; doce abril; quince años. B – Lola; diez marzo; cuatorce años.

Hoja 18 Hablar: dos

AT2.3

1 Haz preguntas a tu compañero/a.

2 Responde a las preguntas.

Students working at a higher level ask the additional questions.

Mark scheme: 5 marks (1 each) for the correct questions; 15 marks (3 each) for the correct answers; 5 marks for communicative fluency and accent = 25 marks

Assessment criteria: Students who score 17 or more show evidence of performance at AT 2.3.

Answers: A (✓) dos lápices; un cuaderno; (✗) una carpeta; un diccionario. B (✓) una regla; dos libros; (✗) un bolígrafo; un estuche

Hoja 19 Leer: uno

AT3.2

1 Une las personas con su tarta de cumpleaños.

Students draw lines to match the people with their birthday cakes.

Answers: Pepe 12; Alfredo 14; Sonia 13; Isabel 15

Mark scheme: 2 marks for each correct answer = 8 marks

Assessment criteria: Students who match three or four correctly show evidence of performance at AT 3.2.

AT3.2

2 ¿Verdad (V) o Mentira (M)?

Students read the speech bubbles and mark whether the birthdays are correct or not.

Answers: Katrina V; Julio M; Sebastián M; Gerardo V

Mark scheme: 3 marks for each correct answer = 9 marks

Assessment criteria: Students who mark two or three correctly show evidence of performance at AT 3.2.

AT3.3

3 ¿De quién es la mochila? Escribe el nombre. ¡Cuidado! Hay una descripción extra...

Students look at what is in the two school bags and match the names with two of the descriptions.

Answers: 1 Ramón; 3 Raquel

Mark scheme: 4 marks for each correct answer = 8 marks

Assessment criteria: Students who match both correctly show evidence of performance at AT 3.3.

Hoja 20 Leer: dos

AT3.2   **1** Lee los mensajes electrónicos y escribe el nombre de la persona adecuada.

Students read the emails and write the correct name for each sentence.

Answers: a Martín; b Elena; c María, d Martín; e Andrea

Mark scheme: 2 marks for each correct answer = 10 marks

Assessment criteria: Students who write four or five names correctly show evidence of performance at AT 3.2.

AT3.2   **2** Une las preguntas con las respuestas.

Students match the questions with the answers.

Answers: 1e; 2d; 3a; 4b; 5c

Mark scheme: 3 marks for each correct answer = 15 marks

Assessment criteria: Students who match four or five correctly show evidence of performance at AT 3.2.

Hoja 21 Escribir: uno

AT4.1   **1** Rellena los espacios con las palabras adecuadas de abajo.

Students complete the text.

Answers: Me llamo; tal; quince; mochila; lápices; regla; cuaderno

Mark scheme: 1 mark for each correct answer = 7 marks

Assessment criteria: Students who complete six or seven gaps correctly show evidence of performance at AT 4.1.

AT4.3   **2** Escribe una presentación sobre ti. Cambia los detalles del ejercicio 1.

Students write a text about themselves similar to the one in exercise 1.

Mark scheme: 6 marks for communication; 4 marks for grammatical accuracy = 10 marks

Assessment criteria: Students who score 7 or more show evidence of performance at AT 4.3.

AT4.1   **3** Escribe el número y el plural de estas palabras.

Students write the number (as a word) and the correct plural form of the objects in the pictures using the words in the box to help them.

Answers: tres bolígrafos; seis estuches; nueve diccionarios; diez móviles

Mark scheme: 2 marks for each correct answer = 8 marks

Assessment criteria: Students who score 6 or more show evidence of performance at AT 4.1.

Hoja 22 Escribir: dos

AT3.2   **1** Lee la información y responde a las preguntas.

Students read the information and answer the questions.

Answers: Antonio; el 15/quince de julio; un libro, un bolígrafo y un cuaderno; un diccionario y una agenda

Mark scheme: 2 marks for each correct answer = 8 marks

Assessment criteria: Students who answer three or four correctly show evidence of performance at AT 3.2.

AT4.1   **2** Rellena la carta con la información que falta.

Students complete the letter.

Answers: Me llamo; Qué; Tengo; cumpleaños; tengo

Mark scheme: 2 marks for each correct answer = 10 marks

Assessment criteria: Students who complete four or five gaps correctly show evidence of performance at AT 4.1.

AT4.1   **3** Escribe los plurales de estas palabras.

Students write the number (as a word) and the correct plural form of the item shown in the picture.

Answers: cinco móviles; tres lápices; cuatro reglas

Mark scheme: 2 marks each for *móviles / reglas*; 3 marks for *lápices* = 7 marks

Assessment criteria: Students who score 5 or more show evidence of performance at AT 4.1

Uno Workbook

Página 4 (1.1)

This page can be used with pages 12–13 of the Students' Book.

AT3.1   **1** ¿Cómo estás? Escoge la palabra apropiada.

Students write the correct word on the line according to the expression in the picture.

Answers: 2 muy bien; 3 regular; 4 bien

AT4.1   **2** Pon estos nombres españoles en orden alfabético.

Students write the names in alphabetical order next to the numbers.

AT4.1   **Answers:** 2 Beatriz; 3 Charo; 4 Diego; 5 Enrique; 6 Felipe; 7 Gema; 8 Iñaki; 9 Joaquín; 10 Laura; 11 Manuel; 12 Nacho; 13 Óscar; 14 Pepa; 15 Pilar; 16 Ramón; 17 Silvia; 18 Teresa; 19 Úrsula; 20 Víctor

AT3.1 **3** Escribe las frases apropiadas en los globos.

Students complete the speech bubbles.

Answers:
Me llamo Montse. ¿Y tú?
Encantado

Página 5 (1.2)

This page can be used with pages 14–15 of the Students' Book.

AT4.1 **1** Escribe las vocales que faltan.

Students complete the numbers 1–16 with the correct vowels.

Answers: 1 uno; 2 dos; 3 tres; 4 cuatro; 5 cinco; 6 seis; 7 siete; 8 ocho; 9 nueve; 10 diez; 11 once; 12 doce; 13 trece; 14 catorce; 15 quince; 16 dieciséis

AT3.1 **2** Une los puntos en orden correcto para descubrir el dibujo.

Students join the dots to reveal the hidden picture.

Answers: a car

AT3.2 **3** ¿Qué contestan estos chicos?

Students look at the pictures and complete the answers with the correct ages from the box.

Answers: b un; c dieciséis; d tres; e catorce; f ocho

AT4.2 **4** ¿Cuántos años tienes tú?

Students write their age on page 13, the spare page for writing at the end of the unit.

Answers: Tengo once / doce / trece años.

Página 6 (1.3)

This page can be used with pages 16–17 of the Students' Book.

AT3.1 **1** Busca los meses del año.

Students find the months in the wordsearch.

Answers:

AT3.2 **2** Une cada fecha con su forma abreviada.

Students match the full forms of the dates with the abbreviated forms.

Answers: 2 c; 3 f; 4 e; 5 a; 6 d

AT3.2 **3** Escoge la frase correcta.

Students tick the correct sentence according to the dates shown.

Answers: 2 a; 3 b; 4 a

AT4.2 **4** ¿Cuándo es tu cumpleaños?

Students write out their birthday on page 13, using the same format as exercise 3.

Página 7 (1.4)

This page can be used with pages 18–19 of the Students' Book.

AT3.1 **1** ¿Cuántos artículos puedes encontrar en esta serpiente? Hay diez.

Students find ten items in the wordsnake.

Answers: un cuaderno; un estuche; una carpeta; un lápiz; una regla; una goma; una botella de agua; un móvil; un bolígrafo; una mochila

AT4.1 **2** Utiliza algunas de estas palabras para nombrar estos artículos.

Students some of the words from exercise 1 to label the pictures.

Answers: b una botella de agua; c un estuche; d una carpeta; e un móvil; f un bolígrafo / una pluma; g una regla; h una goma

AT3.2 **3 ¿Quién habla? Escribe P (Pepe), M (Marisa) o los dos.**

Students look at the picture, read the sentences and mark the sentences P, M or P, M.

Answers: b M; c P; d P; e M; f P, M

Página 8 (1.5)

This page can be used with pages 20–21 of the Students' Book.

AT4.1 **1 Escribe el número maya que falta. Escribe los números en español.**

Students write the missing Mayan number in each sequence and then write it in Spanish. They will need access to the Students' Book for this.

Answers:

a	—	cinco
b	═	diez
c	··	diecisiete
d	⠶	dos

AT4.1 **2 Rompe el código y descubre el mensaje secreto.**

Students crack the code and write out the secret message.

Answer: Siete millones de mayas viven en México y Centro América.

AT4.1 **3 Escribe un mensaje secreto.**

Students use the Mayan code to write their own secret message.

Página 9 Gramática

This page can be used with pages 18–19 of the Students' Book.
It revises indefinite articles and gender, and the forms of *llamarse* and *tener* that the students have met so far.

AT3.1 **1 Género y número: Traduce la palabra y escríbela en la columna apropiada.**

Students translate the words and write them in the correct column of the table.

Answers:

Masculino	Femenino
un cuaderno	una carpeta
un estuche	una regla
un diccionario	una goma
un sacapuntas	una agenda
un lápiz	una botella de agua
un móvil	una pluma
un bolígrafo	una mochila

AT3.2 **2 Verbos: tacha las frases incorrectas.**

Students cross out the incorrect sentences.

Answers: The **correct** sentences are:
b ¿Cómo te llamas?
c Me llamo José.
d Tiene trece años.
e Tienes un móvil.
f Se llama Pedro.

AT4.2 **3 Verbos: escribe en español.**

Students translate the sentences into Spanish.

Answers:
a Te llamas Charo.
b Se llama Pablo.
c Se llama Arantxa.
d Tengo una pluma.
e Tienes diez años.
f Tiene una goma.

Página 10 Reto

This page can be used with page 22 of the Students' Book.

AT4.1 **1 Escribe una palabra que has aprendido que empieza con estas letras.**

Students write a word starting with each of the given letters. They can look back through their work, the *Vocabulario* page in the Workbook and the Students' Book to help them. Answers will vary.
Possible Answers:
B bolígrafo = biro; C carpeta = folder; D dos = two;
E estuche = pencil case; F febrero = February;
H Hola = Hello; J junio = June; L lápiz = pencil;
M móvil = mobile phone; N nueve = nine; O once = eleven;
S sacapuntas = pencil sharpener; T tengo = I have;
U uno = one; V veinte = twenty

AT3.1 **2 Encuentra la respuesta correcta.**

Students work out the numbers and match the sums with the correct answers.

Answers: 2 b; 3 c; 4 f; 5 d; 6 a; 7 g

AT4.2 **3 Aquí está la Familia Real Española. ¿Cuándo son sus cumpleaños?**

Students look at the information and write sentences following the example.

Answers:
b El cumpleaños de la Reina Doña Sofía es el dos de noviembre.
c El cumpleaños del Príncipe Felipe es el treinta de enero.
d El cumpleaños de la Princesa Doña Leticia es el quince de septiembre.
e El cumpleaños de la Infanta Doña Elena es el veinte de diciembre.
f El cumpleaños de la Infanta Doña Cristina es el trece de junio.

Dos Workbook

Página 4 (1.1)
This page can be used with pages 12–13 of the Students' Book.

AT3.1 | **1** ¿Cómo estás? Escoge la palabra apropiada para cada dibujo.

Students look at pictures 1–4 and choose the correct word from the box to express the feeling shown.

Answers: 2 muy bien; 3 regular; 4 bien

AT4.1 | **2** Pon estos nombres españoles en orden alfabético.

Students write out the Spanish names in alphabetical order.

Answers: 2 Arantxa; 3 Charo; 4 Diego; 5 Enrique; 6 Enriqueta; 7 Fátima; 8 Felipe; 9 Gema; 10 Isabel; 11 Javier; 12 Joaquín; 13 Jorge; 14 Josefa; 15 Manuel; 16 María; 17 Montserrat; 18 Pilar; 19 Sandra; 20 Silvia

AT3.1 | **3** Escribe las frases apropiadas en los globos.
AT4.1 |

Students look at the pictures and write the sentences into the correct speech bubbles to complete the conversation.

Answers:
¡Hola! ¿Cómo te llamas?
Me llamo Montse. ¿Y tú? ¿Cómo te llamas?
Me llamo Asier.
Encantado.
Encantada.

Página 5 (1.2)
This page can be used with pages 14–15 of the Students' Book.

AT3.1 | **1** Une los puntos en orden correcto para descubrir el dibujo.

Students follow the numbers to join the dots to reveal the hidden picture.

Answer: a car

AT3.1 | **2** Empareja las frases con los dibujos.

Students match the sentences with the pictures.

Answers: a 2; b 6; d 3; e 5; f 4

AT3.2 | **3** Contesta las preguntas. Utiliza la forma correcta del verbo *tener*.
AT4.2 |

Students answer the questions using the correct person of the verb *tener*.

Answers:
1 Pedro tiene siete años.
2 Nuria tiene dos años.
3 Tengo nueve años.
4 Florentina tiene ocho años.
5 Tengo cuatro años.
6 José Luís tiene diez años.

Página 6 (1.3)
This page can be used with pages 16–17 of the Students' Book.

AT3.1 | **1** Busca los meses del año. Escríbelos en orden.
AT4.1 |

Students find the months of the year in the wordsearch, then write them out in order.

Answers: enero; febrero, marzo, abril, mayo, junio, julio, agosto, septiembre, octubre, noviembre, diciembre

E	N	E	R	O	Y	J	U	N	I	O	B
B	N	A	E	C	O	E	U	I	L	G	S
M	M	E	N	T	U	A	T	L	V	W	A
O	A	R	E	U	K	M	T	V	I	N	N
G	R	B	R	B	B	A	A	H	G	O	U
A	Z	M	S	R	G	B	R	Y	H	V	T
B	O	E	F	E	B	R	E	R	O	I	C
B	Z	I	N	M	H	I	G	A	E	E	O
N	L	T	B	P	R	L	S	M	R	M	F
S	E	P	K	O	C	T	U	T	S	B	D
G	T	E	D	I	C	I	E	M	B	R	E
O	T	S	O	G	A	M	E	I	O	E	F

AT3.2 **2a** ¿Es verdad o mentira?

Students look at the pictures and decide if statements a–e are true or false.

Answers: b V; c M; d M; e M

AT3.2 **2b** Corrige las frases incorrectas del ejercicio 2a.

AT4.2

Students write out the incorrect answers from 2a correctly.

Answers:

c El cumpleaños del Príncipe William es el veintiuno de junio.

d El cumpleaños del Príncipe Harry es el quince de septiembre.

AT4.2 **3** ¿Cuándo es tu cumpleaños? Contesta la pregunta. Sigue el ejemplo.

Students answer the question as if each date were their birthday.

Answers:

b Mi cumpleaños es el cinco de octubre.

c Mi cumpleaños es el seis de julio.

d Mi cumpleaños es el diez de abril.

e Mi cumpleaños es el diecisiete de junio.

Página 7 (1.4)

This page can be used with pages 18–19 of the Students' Book.

AT3.2 **1** Escoge la mochila correcta para cada personaje.

Students read the descriptions of the school bags and write the correct name for each picture..

Answers: Raúl; Marisa; Yolanda; Pepe

AT3.2 **2** Juan ha hecho una lista. Mira la lista y contesta a las preguntas.

AT4.2

Students read Juan's list and answer the questions.

Answers:

b Sí, tengo una agenda.

c Sí, tengo un libro.

d Sí, tengo un cuaderno.

e Sí, tengo una carpeta.

f No, no tengo un equipo de gimnasia.

Página 8 (1.5)

This page can be used with pages 20–21 of the Students' Book.

AT4.1 **1** Escribe el número maya que falta. Escribe los números en español.

Students write the missing Mayan number in each sequence and then write it in Spanish. They will need access to the Students' Book for this.

Answers:

a — cinco

b ═

      diez

c •• diecisiete

d •• dos

AT4.1 **2** Rompe el código y descubre el mensaje secreto.

Students crack the code and write out the secret message.

Answer: Siete millones de mayas viven en México y Centro América.

AT4.1 **3** Escribe un mensaje secreto.

Students use the Mayan code to write their own secret message in Spanish.

Página 9 Gramática

This page can be used with pages 18–19 of the Students' Book.

The aim of this page is to practise gender and number of nouns, and the different parts of the verbs *tener* and *llamarse*.

I have	You have	He/she has	You (Sir/Madam) have
	tienes		
My name is	**Your name is**	**His/her name is**	**Your name (Sir/Madam) is**
			Se llama

AT4.2 **1** Género y número: Traduce la palabra y escríbela en la columna apropiada.

Students complete the grid by putting the Spanish word in the correct column. (For *pen*, students may choose *bolígrafo* or *pluma* as long as they list it in the correct column.)

Answers:

Masculino singular: un monopatín; un estuche; un móvil; un sacapuntas; un agenda; un equipo de gimnasia; (un bolígrafo); un i-pod; un cuaderno

Femenino singular: una carpeta; una goma; una botella de agua; una revista de fútbol; una bolsa de caramelos; una regla; (una pluma)

Masculino plural: unos patines

Femenino plural: unas canicas

AT3.2 | **2 Verbos: Tacha las frases incorrectas dejando la frase correcta.**

Students read the English sentences and cross out the incorrect translation in Spanish.

Answers: The correct answers are: 1 a; 2 a; 3 b; 4 b; 5 b; 6 a

AT4.2 | **3 Verbos: Escribe en español.**

Students complete the verb table.

Answers: Reading across the rows:
tengo; tienes; **tiene**; tiene
Me llamo; **Te llamas**; **Se llama**; Se llama

Página 10 Reto

This page can be used with page 24 of the Students' Book.

AT4.1 | **1 Escribe una palabra que has aprendido en esta unidad que empieza con estas letras.**

Students write a word starting with each of the given letters. They can look back through their work, the *Vocabulario* page in the Workbook and the Students' Book to help them. Answers will vary.

Possible Answers:
B bolígrafo = biro; C carpeta = folder; D dos = two;
E estuche = pencil case; F febrero = February; H Hola = Hello;
J junio = June; L lápiz = pencil; M móvil = mobile phone;
N nueve = nine; O once = eleven; S sacapuntas = pencil
sharpener; T tengo = I have; U uno = one; V veinte = twenty

AT3.1 | **2 Completa.**

Students work out the sums and write the answers in Spanish.

Answers: b catorce; c setenta y cinco; d veintiséis; e diez;
f cuarenta y siete; g cuarenta y tres; h tres; i veintisiete;
j treinta y siete

AT4.2 | **3 Aquí está la Famila Real Española.¿Cuándo son sus cumpleaños?**

Students write out the Spanish Royal Family's birthdays in month order.

Answers:
2 El cumpleaños del Príncipe Felipe es el treinta de enero.
3 El cumpleaños de la Infanta Doña Cristina es el trece de junio.
4 El cumpleaños de la Princesa Doña Leticia es el quince de septiembre.
5 El cumpleaños de la Reina Doña Sofía es el dos de noviembre.

6 El cumpleaños de la Infanta Doña Elena es el veinte de diciembre.

AT4.3 | **4 Escoge un miembro de la Famila Real y escribe una entrevista.**

Students choose a member of the Spanish Royal Family and write a short interview with them following the guidelines given on page 13, the spare page for writing at the end of the unit.

Possible answer:
¡Hola! ¿Qué tal?
Muy bien, gracias.
¿Cómo se llama usted?
Me llamo la Princesa Doña Leticia.
¿Cuántos años tiene usted?
Tengo treinta y cuatro años.
Gracias. Adiós.
Adiós.

Pages/Contexts/ Cultural focus	Objectives	Grammar	Skills and Pronunciation	Key language	Framework	National Curriculum PoS	AT level
26–27 **2.1 ¿De dónde eres?** Countries; nationalities; languages	Name countries and say where you are from; say what your nationality is and ask others theirs; say what languages you speak	*ser*: its use for nationalities and saying where you are from	–	*Inglaterra, Escocia, Gales, Irlanda, España, Francia, Portugal, Alemania, Italia, Estados Unidos, inglés/inglesa, americano/americana, australiano/australiana, escocés/escocesa, portugués/portuguesa, alemán/alemana, italiano/italiana*	(L) 7S3, 7L2 (R) 7W5, 7W8, 7T2	1b, 1c, 2a, 2c, 2d, 2e, 2f, 3b, 3c, 3e, 4a, 4c, 4d, 5a, 5b, 5c, 5d, 5f, 5h, 5i	1.1–3, 2.3, 3.2–3, 4.1–2
28–29 **2.2 ¿Tienes hermanos?** Family members	Talk about your family; say how many brothers and sisters you have and what they are called; ask about other people's families	*llamarse* *mi/mis, tu/tus, su/sus*	–	*¿Tienes hermanos? Sí, tengo…, una hermana/un hermano, dos hermanos, dos hermanas, Soy hijo único/hija única, un tío/una tía, los tíos, un padre, una madre, los padres, ¿Cómo se llama?, Se llama…, ¿Cómo se llaman? Se llaman…*	(L) 7W2 (R) 7T6	1a, 1b, 1c, 2a, 2b, 2c, 2d, 3b, 3c, 3e, 4a, 4c, 4d, 5a, 5d, 5e, 5f, 5g, 5i	1.3–4, 2.1–4, 3.1–3, 4.1–3
30–31 **2.3 ¿Tienes un animal doméstico?** Pets; colours	Talk about your pets; say what colour they are; ask other people about their pets	Agreements and plurals	–	*¿De qué color es? Es blanco/a, rojo/a, negro/a, amarillo/a, verde, azul, gris, marrón*	(L) 7S1, 7S8 (R) 7W4, 7C4	1a, 1c, 2a, 2b, 2c, 2d, 2f, 2i, 3b, 3c, 3e, 4a, 4c, 4d, 5a, 5d, 5e, 5f, 5g, 5i	1.1–4, 2.2, 3.1–3, 4.1–3
32–33 **2.4 ¿Cómo eres?** Descriptions; hair and eye colour; comparisons	Describe yourself; describe your hair and eye colour; compare people	Comparative	–	*Tengo/tienes/tiene el pelo rubio, castaño, rizado, liso, largo, corto, los ojos verdes, los ojos azules, los ojos castaños, los ojos negros, la piel negra, la piel blanca, la piel morena. Soy calvo/a, alto/alta, bajo/baja. Lleva barba, lleva bigote, lleva gafas, soy/eres/es un poco, muy, bastante alto/a, bajo/a.*	(L) 7T3, 7T5 (R) 7W3	1a, 1b, 1c, 2a, 2c, 2d, 2f, 2i, 3b, 3c, 3e, 4a, 4c, 4d, 5a, 5d, 5e, 5f, 5g, 5i	1.3, 2.3–4, 3.1–3, 4.2–4
34–35 **2.5 Entre amigos** Formula 1 champion	Use the language and structures learnt in the unit in a different context	–	–	–	(R) 7C3	1c, 2a, 2c, 2d, 2f, 2i, 3b, 3c, 3e, 4a, 4c, 4d, 5d, 5e, 5g, 5h, 5i	3.3–4, 4.1–2

AMIGOS 1 UNIT 2 MEDIUM TERM PLAN

About this unit: In this unit students talk about their family members, their pets, countries and their nationality. They learn adjectives of colour to describe pets, and the adjective forms for masculine and feminine singular and plural. Students learn how to ask questions so that they can engage in independent talk with their partners. Learning is demonstrated by students adapting texts for their own spoken/written work and by responding to a range of prompts in order to produce sentences and short descriptive paragraphs.

Framework objectives (launch)	Teaching and learning	Week-by-week overview (assuming 6 weeks' work or approx. 10–12.5 hours)
7W2: high-frequency words	*mi/mis, tu/tus, su/sus*	**Week 1**
7S1: typical word order	Adjectival agreement and nouns, e.g. *unos gatos blancos*	Students learn to name countries and say where they are from; say what nationality they are and say what languages they speak
7S3: adapting sentences	Alter the conversation on p. 27 about what languages you speak	
7S8: punctuation	Separating words in the wordsnake on p. 31 to show understanding of adjectival agreement	**Week 2**
7L2: following speech	Dialogue between Carlos and Adam on p. 28	Talk about family; say how many brothers and sisters you have and what they are called; ask about other people's families
7T3: appraise texts	Physical descriptions	**Week 3**
7T5: assemble short texts	Students write a description of themselves	Talk about your pets and say what colour they are; ask other people about their pets
7T7: check written work	Copymasters: checking adjectival agreements	**Week 4**
Framework objectives (reinforce)		Describe yourself, your hair and eye colour; comparing people
7W3: classroom words	*muy, bastante, un poco*	**Week 5**
7W4: gender and plural	Making masculine and feminine agreements in the singular and plural, when talking about colours and animals, e.g. *una araña roja*	Students apply the language and structures learnt in this unit to reading and answering questions on longer texts which focus on an aspect of Spanish or Latin American culture
7W5: verbs present (+ past)	Use of *ser* to refer to nationality (*soy, eres, es*)	
7W8: finding meanings	Using cognates to work out the meaning of country names	**Week 6**
7T2: read aloud simple texts	Students read aloud a conversation with their partner	Recycle language of the unit via *Uno, Dos* and *Lectura* pages; students check their progress via the *Ya sé...* self-assessment checklist in the Students' Book and on Hoja 24.
7T6: respond to prompts	Answer questions on family members and their age	
7C3: authentic materials	Students learn about Fernando Alfonso, Formula 1 champion	
7C4: stories and songs:	Song about animals on p. 30	
Teaching and learning (additional)		
	Spain, other countries and their capital cities	

Me presento

2

Unit objectives

Contexts: nationalities, countries, family members, pets, colours
Grammar: *ser*, adjectival agreement with colours and nationalities, possessive adjectives, the comparative
Language learning: questions
Pronunciation: *c*, *rr* and *ñ*
Cultural focus: Fernando Alonso Díaz, a Formula 1 champion

Assessment opportunities

Speaking: SB, page 27, activity 8
Reading: SB, page 33, activity 7
Listening: SB, page 30, activity 2
Writing: SB, page 29, Reto

AT3.1 **1 Mira las banderas. ¿A qué países pertenecen?**

Students name the countries by using their world knowledge of flags and by looking at the names on the T-shirts. Many country names are close cognates so they will be able to work them out from this.

Answers: France; Germany; Spain; Ireland; Portugal; United States; Italy

Planner

• •

2.1 **¿De dónde eres?** páginas 26–27

Objectives

► Name countries and say where you are from

► Say what your nationality is and ask others theirs

► Say what languages you speak

Resources

Students' Book, pages 26–27
CD 1, tracks 24–26
Uno/Dos Workbooks, page 14

Key language

Inglaterra, Escocia, Gales, Irlanda, España, Francia, Portugal, Alemania, Italia, Estados Unidos
inglés/inglesa, americano/americana, australiano/australiana, escocés/escocesa, portugués/portuguesa, alemán/alemana, italiano/italiana

Programme of Study reference

1b, 1c, 2a, 2c, 2d, 2e, 2f, 3b, 3c, 3e, 4a, 4c, 4d, 5a, 5b, 5c, 5d, 5f, 5h, 5i

Framework reference

(L) 7S3, 7L2
(R) 7W5, 7W8, 7T2

• •

¡A sus marcas!

AT3.1 ¿Cómo se dicen en inglés los países del mapa?

Students look at the map and make sentences in Spanish as in the example to give the English name for each country.

Answers:

1	Inglaterra	England
2	Escocia	Scotland
3	Gales	Wales
4	Irlanda	Ireland
5	España	Spain
6	Francia	France
7	Portugal	Portugal
8	Alemania	Germany
9	Italia	Italy
10	Estados Unidos	the USA

AT3.2 **1** ¿Qué país es? Empareja la descripción con el país adecuado.

Students read the descriptions and match them with the countries. Encourage them to read both sentences as in the example, making a clear distinction between the pronunciation of the country in Spanish and in English.

Answers: 1 a; 2 g; 3 j; 4 b; 5 i; 6 d; 7 f; 8 c; 9 h; 10 e

AT1.1 **2** Escucha a Carlos y Fátima.

Students listen to Carlos and Fátima discussing the puzzle in exercise 1. You may like to pause the recording after each country for students to repeat.

 CD 1, track 24 página 26, actividad 2

– Mmm … a… bueno, a … la capital es Londres, que es la capital olímpica. Obviamente … ¡Inglaterra!
– ¿Y el b?
– Dublín es la capital … ¡Irlanda!
– Perfecto … y c … la capital es Berlín … obviamente Alemania.
– Muy bien … y d … la capital es París …es un país …
– ¡Francia!
– Sí …
– Y la letra e … hay muchos estados diferentes… pues ya lo dice el nombre …¡Estados Unidos!
– f … la capital es Lisboa … muy fácil. Es Portugal.
– g … la capital es Edimburgo… obviamente es Escocia.
– ¿Y h? Pues es fácil. Roma es la capital de Italia.
– Y Madrid es la capital de España.
– Y la de Gales es Cardiff.
– Pues muy bien, ¡perfecto!

AT1.2
AT2.3 **3** Escucha y lee. Con tu compañero/a, haz un diálogo.

Students listen to the model and practise in pairs. If you have students in class from countries not covered in the preceding activities, you will need to supply vocabulary.

 CD 1, track 25 página 26, actividad 3

– ¿De dónde eres?
– Soy de Escocia. ¿Y tú? ¿De dónde eres?
– Soy de Francia.

Zoom gramática

This section presents the use of *ser* for the various uses covered by this spread (saying where you are from and giving your nationality). The second part of the section covers adjective agreement.

AT4.1 | **4 Fill in the gap in the following sentence.**

Students complete the sentence with the correct form of *ser*.

Answers: a Soy; b es

AT4.1 | **5 Look at this example, then have a go at the other two nationalities.**

Students use the rules they have discussed in the *Zoom gramática* box to form feminine adjectives.

Answers: americana; australiana

AT4.1 | **6 If a masculine nationality has an accent on the last vowel, when you make it feminine the accent disappears. Here is one example. Can you do the rest?**

Students use the rules about adjectives with accents to make feminine forms. Ask volunteers to write them on the board to check that no accents have been used.

Answers: escocesa; galesa; portuguesa; alemana

AT1.3 | **7 Escucha (1–3). Copia y rellena el cuadro.**

Students copy the grid. They then listen and complete it with countries and nationalities. Complete the grid on the board for students to check answers, paying particular attention to whether capital letters and accents are needed.

Answers: Jenny: Irlanda, irlandesa; Karl: Alemania, alemán; Bianca: Italia, italiana

---

 CD 1, track 26   página 27, actividad 7

– ¡Hola Jenny! ¿De dónde eres?
– Soy de Irlanda.
– ¿Cuál es tu nacionalidad?
– Soy irlandesa.
– Muy bien, gracias, ¡adiós!

– Hola, Karl. ¿De dónde eres?
– Soy de Alemania.
– Ah … eres alemán.
– Sí, soy alemán.

– Hola, me llamo Bianca y soy de Italia. Soy italiana.

AT2.3 | **8 Lee y con tu compañero/a haz un diálogo.**

Model the dialogue with a confident student reading the questions while you answer. The student then reads the last bubble too. You could then practise a simple question and answer again, this time giving real information about the languages you speak. Students then work in pairs making up a dialogue in the same way.

Reto

AT4.1 | **Escribe las nacionalidades.**

Students make a list of the close cognates amongst the nationality words that they have studied. They could highlight or use a different colour for the differences.

Planner

2.2 ¿Tienes hermanos?

páginas 28–29

Objectives

▶ Talk about your family

▶ Say how many brothers and sisters you have and what they are called

▶ Ask about other people's families

Resources

Students' Book, pages 28–29
CD 1, track 27
Uno/Dos Workbooks, page 15

Key language

¿Tienes hermanos? Sí, tengo…
una hermana/un hermano
dos hermanos/dos hermanas
Soy hijo/a único/a
un tío/una tía, los tíos
un padre/una madre, los padres
¿Cómo se llama? Se llama…
¿Cómo se llaman? Se llaman…

Programme of Study reference

1a, 1b, 1c, 2a, 2b, 2c, 2d, 3b, 3c, 3e, 4a, 4c, 4d, 5a, 5d, 5e, 5f, 5g, 5i

Framework reference

(L) 7W2
(R) 7T6

¡A sus marcas!

AT2.1 | Explica las frases clave a tu compañero/a.

Students work in pairs discussing the family vocabulary. They identify masculine and feminine words by their endings and work out in what way Spanish is different when asking about brothers or sisters.

Answers: Spanish uses the plural form *hermanos* to refer to both brothers and sisters. (You may also want to highlight the use of *padres* and *tíos* in the same way.)

AT 1.3/4 | **1** Escucha y lee.

Students listen to and read the dialogue. You could ask them to identify all the family words that are used.

CD 1, track 27 página 28, actividad 1

– Hola, Carlos, ¿qué tal?
– Hola Adam. Mira, yo estoy con mi familia en Ecuador.
– ¡Ah! ¿Tienes hermanos?
– Sí, tengo dos hermanos y una hermana.
– ¿Cómo se llaman tus hermanos?
– Se llaman José y Benjamín. Son gemelos.
– ¿Y tu hermana?
– Se llama Lita.
– ¿Cuántos años tiene Lita?
– Lita tiene diez años. Y tú, Adam, ¿tienes hermanos?
– No, soy hijo único.

Zoom gramática

In this section, students add to their knowledge of the verb *llamarse*, studying questions and answers in the third person singular and plural. They also learn the relative pronoun *que* to introduce the specific context of giving a name.

AT4.1 | **2** Fill in the gaps in the sentences.

Students complete the sentences.

Answers: a se llama; b Se llaman; c Me llamo

AT 2.3/4 | **3** Con tu compañero/a, haz un diálogo.

Students make up a dialogue following the model in exercise 1. If relevant in your class, ask students to work out the meaning of *gemelos* (twins), explain that twin girls would be called *gemelas*, and that if twins are a boy and girl, Spanish uses a completely different word, *mellizos*.

AT3.3 | **4** Lee y haz una encuesta en clase.
AT 2.2/3 |

Students read the bubbles. To do the survey, divide the class into small groups. In groups, students ask and answer in Spanish to make notes about how many people there are in their families. Bring the class together and combine the results on the board.

Zoom gramática

This section highlights the possessive adjectives *mi/mis*, *tu/tus* and *su/sus*. If the students have studied any French, they may notice that there is no gender agreement in these particular forms. You may like to explain that they will learn other forms which do agree (*nuestro/a/os/as*, *vuestro/a/os/as*) later in their Spanish studies.

AT3.1 | **5** Can you complete these translations?

Students supply the missing possessive adjectives.

Answers: a Tu; b Su

AT2.4 | **6** Con tu compañero/a, haz un diálogo.

In pairs students choose a character from exercise 4 and make up a dialogue asking about the names of the people in the family. They can invent names where they are not sure.

Reto

AT 4.1/2 | Completa las preguntas.

Students complete the questions about the Addams family to match the given answers. They also complete the name of Wednesday's brother.

Answers: a te llamas; b hermanos; c se llama, Pugsley; d Se llama

Planner

● ●

2.3 ¿Tienes un animal doméstico?

páginas 30–31

Objectives

▶ Talk about your pets

▶ Say what colour they are

▶ Ask other people about their pets

Resources

Students' Book, pages 30–31
CD 1, tracks 28–31
Uno/Dos Workbooks, page 16

Key language

¿De qué color es?
Es blanco/a, rojo/a, negro/a, amarillo/a, verde, azul, gris, marrón

Programme of Study reference

1a, 1c, 2a, 2b, 2c, 2d, 2f, 2i, 3b, 3c, 3e, 4a, 4c, 4d, 5a, 5d, 5e, 5f, 5g, 5i

Framework reference

(L) 7S1, 7S8
(R) 7W4, 7C4

● ●

¡A sus marcas!

AT3.1 ¿Qué animales son?

Students read the animal noises in Spanish and work out which animal makes each noise.

Answers: a un perro: ¡guau guau! b un gato: ¡miau! ¡miau! c una rana cro- cro- cro d un caballo ¡Hiii! e un pájaro ¡pío! ¡pío! f un cerdo ¡oink! ¡oink! g un gallo ¡quiquiriquí!

AT1.1 **1 Escucha la canción y canta.**

Students listen to a song about animals. The first time they hear it, you could ask them to close their books and note down the order of the animals in the song. Students then open their books and read the lyrics to check their answers. You may want to explain that *bichos* is a very informal word for 'animals'.

 CD 1, track 28 página 30, actividad 1

En la vieja factoría, ía ía oooo.
Con los bichos de Tobías, ía, ía oooo
Con el perro – ¡guau guau!
Perro – ¡guau guau!
Pe- pe- perro
Con el gato – ¡Miau!
Gato - ¡Miau!
Ga- ga- gato ...
Con la rana – cro-cro
Rana- cro-cro
Ra, ra, rana …

AT 1.1/2 **2 Escucha y rellena. ¿Qué animales tienen?**

Students listen and complete the grid.

Answers:
Susana: perro, gato; Ana: caballo, pájaro; Roberto: cerdo, caballo; Tomás: perro, gato, pájaro

 CD 1, track 29 página 30, actividad 2

1 – Me llamo Susana. Tengo un perro y un gato.
2 – Me llamo Ana. Tengo un caballo y un pájaro.
3 – Me llamo Roberto. Tengo un cerdo y un caballo.
4 – Me llamo Tomás. Tengo un perro, un gato y un pájaro.

AT1.2 **3 Escucha y repite.**

Students look at the pictures and repeat the phrases.

 CD 1, track 30 página 30, actividad 3

un conejo blanco
un loro amarillo
un hámster marrón
una tortuga verde
un ratón gris
una araña negra
una serpiente azul
un pez rojo

AT1.4 **4 Escucha. ¿Qué animales tiene Marta? ¿De qué color son?**

Students listen and note down in Spanish what pets Marta has and what colour they are, as in the example.

Answers: un gato gris; un loro amarillo; un caballo marrón

CD 1, track 31   página 30, actividad 4

– Tengo un perro blanco. Tengo un gato que es gris y se llama Micho. Tengo un loro que es amarillo y que se llama Pepe, y tengo un caballo que es marrón y se llama Furia.

AT3.3 **5** Lee. ¿Verdad o mentira?

Students read the text and decide whether the sentences a–d are true or false.

Answers: a V; b M; c M; d M

Zoom gramática

This section covers adjective agreement and plural formation. You may want to compare the adjective endings with the indefinite article forms that the students studied earlier. Similarly you can compare the use of the accent in *ratón–ratones* with the rule studied in 2.1 (e.g. *portugués–portuguesa*) and use the opportunity to remind students about word stress in Spanish.

AT4.2 **6** How would you say 'a black mouse' in Spanish? And what about 'some white snakes'?

Students use the rules to help them translate the phrases.

Answers: un ratón negro; unas serpientes blancas

AT2.2 **7** Haz un sondeo. ¿Tienes un animal doméstico? ¿Cómo se llama?

Ask two students to read the model dialogue for the class. To do the survey, divide the class into small groups to ask and answer about pets. Bring the class together and combine the results on the board. You could also make this into a class poster.

Reto

AT3.1 Trabaja con tu compañero/a.

Students find noun + colour phrases in the word snake.

Answers: un perro blanco; unas serpientes azules; un gato negro; un caballo marrón; unos pájaros amarillos; unas tortugas verdes

Planner

2.4 ¿Cómo eres?

páginas 32–33

Objectives

► Describe yourself

► Describe your hair and eye colour

► Compare people

Resources

Students' Book, pages 32–33
CD 1, tracks 32–33
Uno/Dos Workbooks, page 17

Key language

Tengo/Tienes/Tiene…
… el pelo rubio/castaño/rizado/liso/largo/corto
… los ojos verdes/azules/castaños/negros
… la piel negra/blanca/morena
Soy calvo/a.
Lleva barba/bigote/gafas.
Soy/Eres/Es…
muy/bastante/un poco…
… alto/a, bajo/a

Programme of Study reference

1a, 1b, 1c, 2a, 2c, 2d, 2f, 2i, 3b, 3c, 3e, 4a, 4c, 4d, 5a, 5d, 5e, 5f, 5g, 5i

Framework reference

(L) 7T3, 7T5, 7T7
(R) 7W3

¡A sus marcas!

AT3.1 Mira los dibujos.

Students look at the pictures and skim read the speech bubbles in exercise 1 to help them work out the meaning of the new words for describing people.

Answers: *ojos*: eyes; *pelo*: hair; *piel*: skin

AT3.3 **1** Escucha y lee (1–5). Empareja las descripciones con las personas.

Students listen to and read the bubbles. They match the descriptions with the people.

Answers: 1 b; 2 e; 3 d; 4 a; 5 c

 CD 1, track 32   página 32, actividad 1

1 – Me llamo Gonzalo y tengo los ojos castaños y el pelo pelirrojo y corto. Tengo la piel blanca.
2 – Hola, me llamo Mateo y tengo los ojos azules y el pelo rubio y largo. Tengo la piel blanca.
3 – Me llamo Nerea y tengo los ojos verdes y el pelo castaño y rizado. Tengo la piel morena.
4 – Me llamo Nuria y tengo los ojos negros y el pelo negro y ondulado. Tengo la piel negra.
5 – ¡Hola, me llamo Suso! Tengo los ojos azules y no tengo pelo. ¡Soy calvo!

AT1.3 **2** Escucha y mira las fotos. ¿Quién es?

Students listen and decide which of the characters is being described.

Answers: 1 Jorge; 2 Adam; 3 Fátima

 CD 1, track 33   página 32, actividad 2

1 – Tiene los ojos castaños y el pelo castaño, corto y liso. Tiene la piel blanca.
2 – Tiene los ojos verdes y el pelo rubio, corto y liso. Tiene la piel blanca.
3 – Tiene los ojos castaños y el pelo rizado, castaño y largo. Tiene la piel morena.

AT2.3 **3** Con tu compañero/a, describe a un miembro de la clase.

Discuss the *Frases clave* box before dividing the class into pairs. Students then take it in turns to describe someone in the class for their partner to guess.

AT 2.3/4 **4** Describe a dos de las personas.

Students describe two of the people in the pictures as in the model.

Answers:
Raquel: Tiene los ojos castaños y el pelo castaño y largo. Tiene la piel blanca. Es baja.
Elisa: Tiene los ojos verdes y el pelo pelirrojo, corto y rizado. Tiene la piel blanca. Es muy alta.
Pedro: Tiene los ojos verdes y el pelo negro, corto y liso. Tiene la piel blanca. Es muy bajo.
Miriam: Tiene los ojos negros y el pelo negro, largo y rizado. Tiene la piel negra. Es bastante alta.

AT4.4 | **5** Escribe una descripción de tus amigos.

Students describe one or more of their friends following the model.

Zoom gramática

This section introduces the comparative. If the students have studied French, you may want to compare the two languages, particularly the pronunciation of *que* in Spanish.

AT4.4 | **6** How would you say 'Fran is shorter than Alicia'?

Students use the rule to translate the sentence.

Answer: Fran es más baja que Alicia.

AT3.2 | **7** Mira atentamente a las personas del ejercicio 4. ¿Quién es?

Students read the sentences and look at the people in exercise 4. They write the correct name for each sentence. Do the first example with the class to make sure that the students focus on the masculine or feminine form of the adjectives *alto* and *bajo* where relevant.

Answers: a Manuel; b Raquel; c Miriam; d Pedro; e Elisa; f Raquel

Reto

AT4.4 | Escribe una descripción de ti mismo.

Check that everyone understands which form of *ser* and *tener* to use when talking about yourself. Refer back to exercise 1 if necessary. Students then write a description comparing themselves with others in the class.
Ask students to check over their writing, making sure that they have used the correct verb form and adjectival agreement.

Planner

• •

2.5 **Entre amigos:**
Fernando Alonso páginas 34–35

Resources
Students' Book, pages 34–35
CD 1, track 34
Uno/Dos Workbooks, page 18

Programme of Study reference
1c, 2a, 2c, 2d, 2f, 2i, 3b, 3c, 3e, 4a, 4c, 4d, 5d, 5e, 5g, 5h, 5i

Framework reference
(R) 7C3

• •

AT3.3 | **1** Escucha y lee.

Students listen to and read the interview with Fernando Alonso.

 CD 1, track 34 página 34, actividad 1

– ¡Hola, Fernando! ¿Qué tal?
– Bien, gracias, ¿y tú?
– Muy bien. Te llamas Fernando, pero ¿cuáles son tus apellidos?
– Mis apellidos son Alonso Díaz.
– ¿Cuándo es tu cumpleaños?
– Mi cumpleaños es el veintinueve de julio.
– ¿Cuántos años tienes?
– Tengo veinticinco años.
– ¿De dónde eres?
– Soy de Oviedo, una ciudad en el norte de España.
– ¿Y tu horóscopo?
– Soy Leo.
– ¿Tienes hermanos?
– Sí, tengo una hermana que se llama Lorena.
– ¿Cuántos años tiene?
– Tiene cinco años más que yo. Soy el benjamín de la familia.
– ¿Cómo se llama tu padre?
– Se llama José Luis Alonso y es mecánico. Su pasión es la Fórmula 1.
– ¿Cuál es tu color favorito?
– El negro.
– ¿Tienes animales?
– No, ¡no tengo animales porque no tengo tiempo para cuidarlos con las competiciones!
– Gracias, Fernando.
– De nada.

AT3.4 | **2** Contesta a las preguntas.

Students answers the questions in English.

Answers: a 29 July; b 25; c Oviedo (in the north); d Yes, one sister (Lorena); e older; f he's a mechanic; g No, because he doesn't have time to look after them with all his races.

AT4.2 | **3** Copia y rellena los espacios. ¿Cómo llaman a Fernando su familia y amigos?

Students complete the crossword to find the nickname.

Answer: Nano

ªF	E	R	N	A	N	D	O
			ᵇA	Ñ	O	S	
ᶜH	E	R	M	A	N	A	
	ᵈN	E	G	R	O		

AT3.3 | **4** Lee la ficha personal de Fernando Alonso. ¿Cómo se dicen en inglés las palabras a–e?

Students read the profile and work out the meanings of the words a–e. They use their world knowledge and English–Spanish cognates to help them.

Answers: a height; b weight; c sport; d food; e quality

AT4.1 | **5** Ordena las letras de las frases.

Students solve the anagrams and write the complete sentences.

Answers:
a Fernando Alonso es piloto.
b Es el benjamín de la familia.
c Tiene el pelo rizado.
d Sus apellidos son Alonso Díaz.

Repaso página 36

Resources
Students' Book, page 36

Programme of Study reference
1c, 2a, 2c, 2f, 3b, 3c, 3e, 4a, 4c, 5d, 5e, 5f, 5g, 5h, 5i

AT3.2 | **1** Lee. ¿Quién es el dueño?

Students read the owner's descriptions 1–4 and match them with the pets a–d.

Answers: 1 c; 2 a; 3 d; 4 b

AT4.1 **2 Escribe. ¿Qué animal es?**

Students identify the animals in exercise 1 as in the example.

Answers: El número dos es un pez. El número tres es un gato. El número cuatro es un conejo.

AT 3.2/3 **3 ¡Los Grammy Latinos! ¿Quién es quién?**

Students read and match the pictures 1–5 with the descriptions a–e.

Answers: 1 a Ágata López; 2 d David Vicente; 3 c Jessica Rodríguez; 4 e Montserrat Perea; 5 b DJ Solo

Vocabulario

página 37

This page provides a theme-based Spanish–English summary of the key language of this unit. It can be used for reference throughout the unit or as an aid to learning vocabulary.

C23 Copymaster 23 contains a summary of the key language of the unit and can be given to the students at this point to help with revision.

W21 Page 21 of the *Uno/Dos* Workbooks also provides a summary of the key language of the unit.

Ya sé

página 38

The *Ya sé* page provides an end-of-unit checklist of learning objectives. At the foot of the page are activities at three levels of difficulty to extend the work of the unit. Encourage students to select an activity at the most appropriate level.

C24 Copymaster 24 contains a checklist and activities to keep track of the students' progress.

W22 Page 22 of the *Uno/Dos* Workbooks gives an end-of-unit checklist together with activities to keep track of the students' progress.

Unidad 2 Uno

página 98

Objectives

This reinforcement page is intended for those students who need further practice of core language of the unit. It can be used by students who finish other activities early or as alternative class or homework material.

Resources

Students' Book, page 98

Programme of Study reference

1c, 2a, 2c, 2h, 2i, 3b, 3c, 3e, 4a, 4c, 5a, 5c, 5d, 5e, 5f, 5g, 5i

AT3.1 **1 Pilla al intruso.**

Students find the odd one out in each of the four examples, using the glossary to check for meaning if necessary.

Answers: a perro; b alto; c pelo; d español

AT3.2 **2 Lee y empareja las descripciones.**

Students read the descriptions a–f and match them with the pictures of Antonio, Andrea and Curro.

Answers: Antonio c, f; Andrea b, e; Curro a, d

AT3.2 **3 Mira el dibujo. ¿Verdad o mentira?**

Students look at the pictures and decide if the four statements are true or false.

Answers: a M; b V; c V; d M

AT4.2 **4 Escribe las frases falsas correctamente.**

Students write out correctly the statements from exercise 3 that were false.

Unidad 2 Dos

página 99

Objectives

This extension page is intended for more able students who are confident with the core language of the unit. It can be used by students who finish other activities quickly or as alternative class or homework material.

Resources

Students' Book, page 99
CD 1, track 35

Programme of Study reference

1c, 2a, 2c, 2f, 3b, 3c, 3e, 4a, 5a, 5d, 5e, 5g, 5i

AT 3.2/3 **1 ¿Quién soy yo? Lee y escribe los nombres.**

Students match the short texts with the pictures.
Answers: a 5 Gonzalo; b 2 Nacho; c 3 Adela; d 4 Amaya; e 1 Susana

AT4.3 **2** Escribe una descripción de Susana.

Students write a description of Susana using her photo to help them.

AT1.3 **3** Escucha. Copia y rellena el cuadro.

Students listen and complete the grid with the nationalities of the speakers and the languages they speak.

Answers: Francisco inglés: español, inglés, italiano; Claudia francesa: francés, español; Luis alemán: alemán, español, italiano

 CD 1, track 35   página 99, actividad 3

1 – ¿Cuál es tu nacionalidad, Francisco?
  – Soy inglés.
  – ¿Qué idiomas hablas?
  – Hablo español, inglés y también italiano.
2 – Claudia, ¿cuál es tu nacionalidad?
  – Soy francesa.
  – ¿Qué idiomas hablas?
  – Hablo francés y español porque mi madre es española. Soy bilingüe.
3 – Luis, ¿cuál es tu nacionalidad?
  – Vivo en Italia pero soy alemán.
  – ¿Qué idiomas hablas?
  – Hablo alemán perfectamente y español, pero también hablo italiano en el colegio.

Unidad 2 Lectura: uno   página 110

Objectives

This page is to encourage independent reading. Students should attempt it once they are confident with the core language of the unit. It can be used by students who finish other activities early or as alternative class or homework material.

Resources

Students' Book, page 110
CD 1, track 36

Programme of Study reference

1c, 2a, 2c, 2d, 2i, 3b, 3c, 3e, 4a, 5a, 5e, 5f, 5g, 5i

AT1.2 **AT 3.2/3** **1** Lee y rellena los espacios. Escucha y comprueba tus respuestas.

Students read the texts and fill in the spaces with the correct family words, then students listen and check their answers.

Answers: Nano hermano; Pío tío; Mariana hermana

 CD 1, track 36   página 110, actividad 1

– Es la madre de mi madre
  Se llama Adela;
  Tiene el pelo blanco
  Y es mi abuela.
– Es el hijo de mi madre
  Se llama Nano;
  Tiene el pelo pelirrojo
  Y es mi hermano.
– Es el hermano de mi padre
  Y se llama Pío;
  Tiene gafas y el pelo rubio
  Y es mi tío.
– Es la hija de mi madre
  Y se llama Mariana;
  Tiene el pelo largo y castaño
  Y es mi hermana.

AT1.2 **AT 3.2/3** **2** ¿Quién habla? Empareja las descripciones y los animales.

Students read the speech bubbles. They then match each bubble with a photo/picture.

Answers: a 4; b 2; c 1; d 3

AT4.4 **3** Ahora escribe una descripción de un animal. Tu compañero/a tiene que adivinar qué animal es.

Students work in pairs. One student writes a brief description of an animal in a speech bubble and the other has to guess which animal it is.

Unidad 2 Lectura: dos   página 111

Objectives

This page is to encourage independent reading. Students should attempt it once they are confident with the core language of the unit. It can be used by students who finish other activities early or as alternative class or homework material.

Resources

Students' Book, page 111
CD 1, tracks 37–38

Programme of Study reference

1c, 2a, 2c, 2d, 2i, 3b, 3c, 3e, 4a, 5a, 5e, 5f, 5g, 5i

1 Escucha y lee. ¿Qué es? Escoge la opción adecuada.

Students listen to and read the riddles. Tell them to look carefully at the pictures as well. They then choose the correct answer from the choice below each riddle.

Answers: b mi abuela; c Francia; d el elefante

CD 1, track 37 página 111, actividad 1

a Son hijos de tus abuelos
 De tus padres hermanos son
 Tus hermanos con tus hijos
 Tienen esa relación.
b Es como mi madre
 Pero es mayor
 Tiene otros hijos:
 Mis tíos son.
c Su bandera es azul, blanca y roja
 Y tiene la torre Eiffel.
 ¿Qué país es?
d Tiene mucha memoria
 Tiene gris la piel
 Es grande y es de África.
 ¿Qué animal es?

AT3.4 **2** Escucha y lee. Empareja los dibujos y las descripciones.

Students listen to and read the descriptions. Tell them to look carefully at the pictures as well. They then match each picture with a description.

Answers: a 1; b 3; c 4; d 2

CD 1, track 38 página 111, actividad 2

1 – Es un animal pequeño y agresivo. Vive en zonas tropicales.
2 – Es un animal negro que tiene mucho pelo y es muy independiente ¡y tiene bigotes!
3 – Es un animal curioso, activo, rápido y pequeño. Es marrón.
4 – Es un pez blanco muy grande, más grande que la piraña.

AT4.1
AT4.4 **3** Which new words are there in the text whose meaning you can work out?

Students list any words in the texts that are new to them, and try to work out the meaning. They can use the glossary to check if necessary. They then draw their own animal card and write an appropriate description.

Copymasters

Hoja 25 ¡A sus marcas!

This can be used after pages 26–27 in the Students' Book.

AT3.1 **1** Empareja las dos mitades.

Students match 1–7 with a–g to find the country names.

Answers: 1 b Italia; 2 d España; 3 a Francia; 4 c Rusia; 5 f China; 6 e Alemania; 7 g Inglaterra

AT3.1 **2** Con tu compañero/a dice un animal y tú lo encuentras.

In pairs, students take it in turns to say an animal for their partner to point to.

AT3.1 **3** Elige el adjetivo adecuado.

Students choose the correct adjective for each sentence.

Answers: 1 rubio; 2 azules; 3 inglesa; 4 morena

AT4.1 **4** Rellena los espacios con las letras adecuadas.

Students complete the animal words.

Answers: 1 perro; 2 caballo; 3 tortuga; 4 pájaro; 5 gato

Hoja 26 Reto

This can be used after pages 26–27 in the Students' Book.

AT4.1 **1** Rellena los espacios con la información adecuada.

Students complete the gaps with a suitable word.

Answers: 1 alemán, alemán; 2 Francia, francés; 3 Italia

2 ¡Ahora tú! Escribe tu propia carta.

Students use the ideas in exercise 1 to write a similar letter of introduction. They should write their name first but the other details can be in any order.

Answers: The students' answers should include:
Me llamo … Vivo en (city / country) *Soy* (nationality) *Hablo …*

AT4.3 **3** Pon en orden estas frases.

Students write the sentences correctly.

Answers:
1 Tengo un perro blanco.
2 Soy de España y hablo español. / Hablo español y soy de España.
3 Tengo los ojos azules.
4 Mi hermana es muy alta.

Hoja 27 Escuchar: uno

This can be used after pages 26–27 in the Students' Book.

AT1.2 | **1 Escucha. Empareja las descripciones con los dibujos.**

Students listen and write the correct number 1–4 in the boxes.

Answers: a 4; b 3; c 2; d 1

 CD 1, track 12   Hoja 27, actividad 1

1 – Hola, me llamo Susana. Tengo la piel blanca y los ojos verdes. Tengo el pelo negro y corto.
2 – Hola, me llamo Leticia. Tengo la piel negra y los ojos negros. Tengo el pelo corto y castaño.
3 – Hola, me llamo Rodrigo. Tengo la piel morena y los ojos marrones. No tengo pelo y ¡llevo gafas!
4 – Me llamo Fernando y tengo la piel blanca y los ojos azules. Tengo el pelo largo y rubio.

AT1.2 | **2 ¿Qué animales tienen estas personas? Escribe el número en la casilla correcta.**

Students listen and write the correct number 1–5 in the boxes.

Answers: a 5; b 3; c 2; d 1; e 4

 CD 3, track 13   Hoja 27, actividad 2

1 – Tengo una tortuga. Es verde y muy vieja.
2 – Tengo dos ratones blancos y pequeños.
3 – Tengo un hámster. Es marrón.
4 – Tengo un perro negro.
5 – Tengo un conejo gris.

Hoja 27 Escuchar: dos

AT1.3 | **3 Escucha. ¿Verdad o mentira? Corrige las afirmaciones falsas.**

Students listen and check whether the descriptions on the CD match the pictures. Where there are mistakes, they write the correct information.

Answers:
1 M – Carlos tiene dos hermanas.
2 V
3 M – Marcos tiene dos hermanos (pequeños).
4 M – Blanca es hija única. Tienen dos caballos.

 CD 3, track 14   Hoja 27, actividad 3

1 – Tengo un amigo que se llama Carlos. En su familia hay un padre, una madre y una hermana. Carlos tiene un abuelo y tiene un animal en casa: un perro grande y negro.
2 – Mi amiga Sonia vive con su padre, su madre y su gato. No tiene hermanos; es hija única.
3 – Marcos vive con su padre, su madre y su hermano pequeño. Tiene un animal en casa: un hámster.
4 – Blanca vive con su madre y con su hermano mayor. Tienen tres caballos.

Hoja 28 Hablar: uno

This can be used after pages 28–29 in the Students' Book.

AT2.2 | **1 Responde a las preguntas.**

2 Haz preguntas a tu compañero/a.

In pairs, students ask and answer questions about the people in the pictures.

Answers: A – (a) francés; rubio/corto; (b) española; rizado; negro. B – (c) alemán; largo; castaño; (d) china; corto/liso; negro

Hoja 28 Hablar: dos

AT2.3 | **3 Describe dos personas a tu compañero/a.**

Students take it in turns to describe two of the people in the pictures. Encourage them to talk about the ones that they asked about earlier, not the ones that they answered about, so that they practise all the language.

Hoja 29 Leer y escribir: uno

This can be used after pages 28–29 in the Students' Book.

AT3.2 | **1 Mira los dibujos y lee las descripciones. ¿Quién es quién?**

Students look at the picture of the alien family and write the correct animal, family member or name for each sentence.

Answers: 1 d; 2 a; 3 f; 4 e; 5 g; 6 b

AT3.2 | **2 Une las descripciones con los dibujos.**

Students match the descriptions with the pictures and then colour them.

Answers: 1 c; 2 b; 3 a; 4 d

Hoja 30 Leer y escribir: dos

This can be used after pages 28–29 in the Students' Book.

AT 3.3/4 **1 Lee las cartas y las descripciones. ¿Quién es quién?**

Students read the three letters and then write the correct name for each sentence.

Answers: 1 Harry; 2 Hermione; 3 Ron; 4 Hermione; 5 Harry; 6 Harry

AT3.3 **2 ¿Verdad o mentira?**

1 V; 2 M; 3 M; 4 M; 5 M; 6 V; 7 V; 8 V

Hoja 31 Gramática

This can be used after pages 30–31 in the Students' Book.

AT3.2 **1 ¿Masculino o femenino? ¿Singular o plural? Elige la opción adecuada.**

Read the first *¡Recuerda!* box with the class. Students then choose the correct form according to gender and number.

Answers: 1 pequeño; 2 baja; 3 largo, negros; 4 blancas; 5 corto, rojas; 6 alto

AT4.1 **2 Rellena los espacios con la palabra adecuada.**

Students complete the sentences with the correct form of the adjectives in brackets.

Answers: 1 blancas, negras; 2 negros; 3 blanco, marrón; 4 negros, verdes

AT 4.1/2 **3 ¿Tengo, tienes o tiene?**

Look at the second *¡Recuerda!* box with the class. Students then complete the sentences with the correct form of tener.

Answers: 1 Tengo; 2 Tiene; 3 Tienes; 4 tengo

AT3.2 **4 Utiliza la palabra correcta.**

Students choose the correct form to complete the sentences.

Answers: 1 francés; 2 español; 3 italiano; 4 los Estados Unidos

Hoja 32 Técnica

This can be used after pages 32–33 in the Students' Book.

AT3.3 **1 Read the text below. What's the Spanish for 'and', 'but' and 'also'?**

Students read the text and work out the translations of *and*, *but* and *also*.

Answers: and = y; but = pero; also = también

AT4.1 **2 Now read these sentences and write one of the three words in each gap.**

Students complete the sentences with the correct word from exercise 1.

Answers: 1 pero; 2 y; 3 también

AT3.3 **3 Read the text and underline the cognates in green and the false friends in red.**

Discuss the *¡Recuerda!* box with the class. Students then read and underline the cognates and false friends. (Students who have studied some French may feel that words such as *quince*, *doce* and *años* are cognates. Accept their answers, but explain that cognate is usually a word that is similar to your own language.) Answers may vary but use any discrepancies as an opportunity for class discussion about the language.

Answers:
Cognates: *mi, diciembre, familia, miembros, rápido, agresivo, secretaria, inteligentes*
False friends: *profesor, agenda, carpeta*

AT4.1 **4 Now write lists of false friends and cognates in the box below.**

Students complete the table with cognates and false friends.

Answers:

False friends in Spanish	Meaning in English
profesor	teacher
agenda	diary
carpeta	folder

Cognates: mi = my; diciembre = December; familia = family; miembros = members; rápido = rapid/fast; agresivo = aggressive; secretaria = secretary; inteligente = intelligent

Hoja 33 Cultura

This can be used after pages 34–35 in the Students' Book.

AT3.4

1 Lee el texto.

Students read the text and underline any new words that are possible cognates.

Answers: importante; famosa; internacionalmente; honor; santo; celebraciones; movimiento; personas; caótica; accidentes

AT4.1

2 Escribe las palabras españolas.

Students complete the table with the words they underlined in the text in exercise 1.

Answers:

español	inglés
importante	important
famosa	famous
internacionalmente	internationally
honor	honour
santo	saint
celebraciones	celebrations
movimiento	movement
personas	persons (people)
caótica	chaotic
accidents	accidents

AT 4.3/4

3 Answer these questions on the text in English.

Students answer in English.

Answers:

Sanfermines last for six days.
It's dangerous because bulls and people run in the streets.
It starts on 6 July.

AT4.3

4 Diseña un póster para los Sanfermines. Incluye el día y la ciudad.

Students design a poster for the Sanfermines in Pamplona. They should include the date and Pamplona.

Hoja 34 Se pronuncia así

This can be used after pages 28–29 in the Students' Book.

AT3.3

1 There are letters in Spanish which don't exist in the English alphabet. Can you think of any?

Students list the letters that are different in the Spanish alphabet.

Answers: ch, ll, ñ, rr

AT2.2

2 As you know, the letter 'c' looks the same in Spanish but is pronounced differently. Read these words aloud, then listen to check.

Students use their knowledge of the pronunciation rules for *c* to practise reading the words aloud. They then listen and check.

 CD 3, track 15   Hoja 34, actividad 2

caballo – conejo – blanco – Francia – cerdo – castaño – cuántos

AT2.2

3 In Spanish, 'b' and 'v' are both pronounced like an English 'b'. Read these words aloud, then listen to check.

Students practise reading the words making sure that they pronounce 'b' and 'v' the same. They then listen and check.
To emphasize the point, you might like to explain that Spanish children starting to write have to learn which words are written with 'b' and which with 'v' because they sound so similar to them. With a stronger group, you could also model the difference between the very plosive initial sound and the more relaxed sound in *abuelo, calvo, llevo*.

 CD 3, track 16   Hoja 34, actividad 3

blanco – verde – abuelo – caballo – calvo – llevo – bigote

AT2.2

4 The letter 'h' is not pronounced in Spanish! Read these word aloud, then listen to check.

Students practise reading the words. They are all familiar words, so it is a good opportunity to focus on accurate pronunciation of all the sounds, not just the silent 'h'. Make sure for example that the students are pronouncing 'hay' as in English 'eye' and not as in the English letter 'a'. They listen and check with the CD.

 CD 3, track 17   Hoja 34, actividad 4

hola – hermano – hay – hablo

AT1.3

5 Listen and circle the word which is said each time.

Discuss the *¡Recuerda!* box with the class. Students then listen carefully to the r / rr minimal pairs and circle the word they hear.

 CD 3, track 18   Hoja 34, actividad 5

pera/perra – pero/perro – caro/carro

6 Read these words aloud, then listen to check.

Students read the new words aloud, making a distinction between *r* and *rr*. They then listen and check.

 CD 3, track 19   Hoja 34, actividad 6

cero – cerro – Teresa – terreno

 7 Try this tongue-twister, then listen to check.

Students practise saying the tongue-twister and then listen and check.

 CD 3, track 20   Hoja 34, actividad 7

R con R guitarra,
R con R barril,
Rápido corren los trenes
Cargados de azúcar al ferrocarril.

Control Unidad 2

Resources

Copymasters 35–40
CD 3, tracks 21–24

Hoja 35 Escuchar: uno

 1 Escucha y pon el número en las descripciones correctas.

Students listen and number the pictures.

Answers: a 2; b 5; c 4; d 3; e 6; f 1

Mark scheme:
Students who attempt *uno* only: 2 marks for each correct answer = 12 marks. 1 extra mark for accuracy.
Students who attempt *uno* and *dos*: 1 mark for each correct answer = 6 marks.

Assessment criteria: Students who number five or six pictures correctly show evidence of performance at AT 1.1.

 CD 3, track 21   Hoja 35, actividad 1

Ejemplo – Tiene el pelo negro, corto y rizado.
1 – Tiene el pelo corto, rubio y rizado. Tiene pecas.
2 – Tiene el pelo largo, liso y rubio.
3 – Tiene el pelo muy corto y rubio. Tiene gafas.
4 – Tiene la piel negra y el pelo negro, rizado y largo.
5 – Tiene el pelo negro, corto y rizado.
6 – Tiene una barba larga, gafas y el pelo blanco.

 2 Une la persona con su nacionalidad.

Students listen and match each person with the correct picture according to their nationality.

Answers: 1 d; 2 c; 3 a; 4 b

Mark scheme:
Students who attempt *uno* only: 3 marks for each correct answer = 12 marks.
Students who attempt *uno* and *dos*: 1 mark for each correct answer = 4 marks.

Assessment criteria: Students who match three or four correctly show evidence of performance at AT 1.1.

 CD 3, track 22   Hoja 35, actividad 2

– Lorena, ¿de qué nacionalidad eres?
– Soy italiana.
– Elisa, ¿de qué nacionalidad eres?
– Soy española.
– Paul, ¿de qué nacionalidad eres?
– Soy inglés.
– Fred, ¿de qué nacionalidad eres?
– Soy francés.

Hoja 35 Escuchar: dos

3 Escucha y rellena la ficha.

Students listen and complete the grid.

Answers:
Paolo: italiano, castaños, castaño, 2 hermanos, 0
Axel: alemán, verdes, rizado, 1 hermana, un gato
Chloé: francesa, negros, corto y liso, 2 hermanas, un hámster
Raquel: española, azules, pelirrojo, 1 hermano, dos ratones

Mark scheme: Half a mark for each correct answer = 10 marks.

Assessment criteria: Students who score 8 or more show evidence of performance at AT 1.1.

 CD 3, track 23   Hoja 35, actividad 3

Ejemplo:
– Hola, me llamo Antonio y soy español. Tengo los ojos azules y el pelo rubio. Tengo un hermano y un perro.
– Hola, me llamo Paolo. Soy italiano. Tengo los ojos castaños y el pelo castaño. Tengo dos hermanos y no tengo animales.
– Hola, me llamo Axel. Soy alemán. Tengo los ojos verdes y el pelo rizado. Tengo una hermana y tengo un animal en casa, un gato.
– Hola, me llamo Chloé. Soy francesa. Tengo los ojos negros y el pelo corto y liso. Tengo dos hermanas y tengo un hámster.
– Hola, soy Raquel. Soy española. Tengo los ojos azules y tengo el pelo pelirrojo. Tengo un hermano y tengo dos animales: dos ratones.

4 Escucha y escribe las 4 diferencias.

Students look at the picture as they listen carefully. They correct the three remaining mistakes in the descriptions.

Answers:
2 Gerardo tiene la piel blanca.
3 Benjamín tiene el pelo corto.
4 Benjamín tiene el pelo liso.

Mark scheme: 1 mark for each correct answer = 3 marks. 2 extra marks for grammatical accuracy.

Assessment criteria: Students who convey all the correct ideas show evidence of performance at AT 1.3. Students who use the correct verb form and place the adjectives correctly after the nouns show evidence of performance at AT 4.3.

 CD 3, track 24   Hoja 35, actividad 4

– Gerardo es **bajo** y tiene el pelo largo y rizado. Tiene la piel **blanca** y lleva gafas.
Benjamín es bajo. Tiene el pelo **largo y rizado**, y tiene pecas.

Hoja 36 Hablar: uno

1 Haz preguntas a tu compañero/a.

2 Responde a tu compañero/a.

In pairs, students ask and answer. They then complete the pictures by drawing on the hair and colouring the eyes.

Mark scheme:
Students who attempt uno only:
2 marks for each correct question asked = 8 marks.
3 marks for each correct answer and drawing = 12 marks.
5 marks for communicative fluency and accent
Students who attempt uno and dos:
2 marks for each correct question asked = 8 marks.
2 marks for each correct answer and drawing = 8 marks.

Assessment criteria: Students who score 80% of the marks for their level show evidence of performance at AT 2.4.

Answers: Santiago – español; negros; largo y rizado; castaño
Isabel – italiana; verdes; corto y liso; negro
Sebasián – inglés; castaños; corto y rizado; rubio
Lucía – francesca; azules; largo y liso; castaño

Hoja 36 Hablar: dos

3 Describe dos personas a tu compañero/a.

Students take it in turns to describe two of the people in the pictures. Encourage them to talk about the ones that they asked about earlier, not the ones that they answered about, so that they practise all the language.

Mark scheme:
6 marks for communicative fluency; 3 marks for accuracy and variety = 9 marks

Assessment criteria: Students who score 6–7 show evidence of performance at AT 2.2. Students who score 8–9 with a good range of language are performing at AT 2.3.

Hoja 37 Leer: uno

1 Lee los textos y emparéjalos con los dibujos.

Students read the texts and match them with the pictures.

Answers: 1 d; 2 c; 3 a; 4 b

Mark scheme: 3 marks for each correct answer = 12 marks

Assessment criteria: Students who match three or four correctly show evidence of performance at AT 3.2.

2 ¿Qué persona es? ¡Cuidado!

Students read the texts and the sentences underneath. They write the correct name for each sentence.

Answers: 1 Julián; 2 Julián; 3 Susi; 4 Susi, Claudia; 5 Susi; 6 Susi

Mark scheme: 2 marks for each correct answer with 3 marks for sentence 4 = 13 marks

Assessment criteria: Students who score 8 or more show evidence of performance at AT 3.4.

Hoja 38 Leer: dos

1 Empareja las frases.

Students match the sentences that have a similar meaning.

Answers: 1 c; 2 a; 3 e; 4 b; 5 d

Mark scheme: 1 mark for each correct answer = 5 marks

Assessment criteria: Students who match four or five correctly show evidence of performance at AT 3.2.

2 Escribe el nombre de los miembros de la familia.

Students read the sentences and write the correct family member.

Answers: 2 Mi tío; 3 Mi primo; 4 Mi madre

Mark scheme: 1 mark for each correct answer = 3 marks

Assessment criteria: Students who name two or three correctly show evidence of performance at AT 4.3.

3 ¿Verdad, mentira o no se menciona (?)?

Students read the text and mark the sentences to show whether they are true, false, or that the information is not given.

Answers: 1 V; 2 V; 3 M; 4 M; 5 V; 6 V; 7 ?

Mark scheme: 1 mark for each correct answer = 7 marks

Assessment criteria: Students who score 5 or more show evidence of performance at AT 3.3.

AT4.4 | **4 Corrige las afirmaciones falsas.**

Students correct the incorrect statements from exercise 3.

Answers:
Genoveva tiene dos hermanas.
Tiene tres animales en casa.

Mark scheme: 6 marks for communicating the correct ideas; 4 marks for grammatical accuracy = 10 marks

Assessment criteria: Students who score 8 or more show evidence of performance at AT 4.4.

Hoja 39 Escribir: uno

AT4.2 | **1 Rellena el árbol genealógico de Lorena.**

Students complete Lorena's family tree.

Answers: mi abuela; mi abuelo; mi madre; mi padre; yo

Mark scheme: 2 marks for each correct answer = 10 marks

Assessment criteria: Students who name four or five family members correctly show evidence of performance at AT 4.2.

AT4.2 | **2 Escribe los colores de estos animales.**

Students write the correct colours.

Answers: 2 blanco, negro (or *vice versa*); 3 verde; 4 gris

Mark scheme: 1 mark for each correct colour = 4 marks

Assessment criteria: Students who name three or four colour correctly show evidence of performance at AT 4.2.

AT4.3 | **3 Lee la carta. Contesta a las preguntas.**

Students read the letter. They then write a reply answering the questions that they have been asked.

Mark scheme: 7 marks for communication (1 mark for opening, answering each question, and closing); 4 marks for grammatical accuracy = 11 marks

Assessment criteria: Students who score 9 or more show evidence of performance at AT 4.3. Students who communicate the answers to the questions but lack accuracy are performing at AT 4.2.

Hoja 40 Escribir: dos

AT4.3 | **1 Describe los futbolistas del equipo 1. Escribe las diferencias de los futbolistas del equipo 2.**

Students complete the Team 1 column with a description of each player's hair. They then compare the players with the same number in Team 2 and write what is different about them.

Answers:
Team 1
2 Tiene el pelo negro, corto y rizado.
3 Es calvo.
4 Tiene el pelo rubio y corto.
5 Tiene el pelo rubio, largo y rizado.
6 Tiene el pelo negro, corto y rizado.
Team 2
2 Tiene el pelo largo.
3 Lleva bigote.
4 Lleva barba.
5 Tiene pecas.
6 Lleva gafas.

Mark scheme: 1 mark for each correct answer = 10 marks. (Half a mark for the correct idea; half a mark for the correct form and spelling)

Assessment criteria: Students who score 8 or more show evidence of performance at AT 4.3.

AT 4.3/4 | **2 Rosa busca un/a amigo/a por correspondencia. Escríbele una respuesta.**

Students read Rosa's email and write an answer. To gain full marks for communication, they should cover their name, their nationality and where they live, what languages they speak, whether they have any pets, and some information about their family.

Mark scheme: 10 marks for communication; 5 marks for accuracy and variety = 15 marks

Assessment criteria: Students who score 9–12 show evidence of performance at AT 4.3. Students who score 13–15 are performing at AT 4.4

Uno Workbook

Página 14 (2.1)
This page can be used with pages 26–27 of the Students' Book.

AT4.1 | **1 Identifica el país.**

Students label the outlines with the country names in the box.

Answers: b Estados Unidos; c Escocia; d Alemania; e España; f Inglaterra

AT3.2 | **2 Escribe el diálogo en el orden correcto.**

Students write the letters in the boxes to order the dialogue.

Answers: 1 c; 2 d; 3 a; 4 b

| AT3.3 | **3** Lee. ¿Verdad o mentira?

Students read the text and mark the sentences true or false.

Answers: b ✓; c ✓; d ✗

| AT4.2 | **4** Escribe tres frases sobre ti en la página 23.

Using the language given, students write three sentences about themselves on page 23, the spare page for writing at the end of the unit.

Página 15 (2.2)

This page can be used with pages 28–29 of the Students' Book.

| AT3.3 | **1** Empareja las frases con las familias.

Students match the sentences with the pictures.

Answers: 2 a; 3 d; 4 b

| AT3.3 | **2** Completa el email.

Students choose the correct words.

Answers: llaman; años; año; mi; familia; mis; tu; personas; hermanos

| AT4.3 | **3** Describe a la familia en la página 23.

Students look at the family tree and describe the family on page 23. They use the language in the box.

Answers:
En mi familia hay seis personas. Mi madre se llama Marta y mi padre se llama José. Tengo tres hermanos. Mi hermana tiene 16 años. Mis hermanos tienen 9 y 6 años.

Página 16 (2.3)

This page can be used with pages 30–31 of the Students' Book.

| AT3.3 | **1a** ¿Qué animales tienen? Escoge las palabras correctas.

Students look at the pictures and circle the correct option in each sentence.

Answers: a dos perros; b tiene un gato; c un pájaro; d no tiene ningún animal; e cuatro peces

| AT4.1 | **1b** Escribe los nombres de los animales de 1a en orden alfabético.

Students write the animals from exercise 1a in alphabetical order.

Answers: gato; pájaro; peces; perro

| AT3.3 | **2** Empareja las preguntas con las respuestas.

Students match the questions with the answers.

Answers: 1 c; 2 d; 3 a; 4 b

| AT3.3 | **3** ¿Qué animales tiene Juan?

Students look at Juan's pets' passports and choose the correct words.

Answers: marrón; llama; rojos, verdes; llaman; negras, llaman

Página 17 (2.4)

This page can be used with pages 32–33 of the Students' Book.

| AT3.2 | **1** Lee las frases y dibuja las caras.

Students read the descriptions and then draw and colour the corresponding features.

Answers: a blue eyes, chestnut hair; b bald, blue eyes; c black hair, hazel eyes; d blond, green eyes and moustache

| AT3.3 | **2** Lee y mira las fotos. ¿Qué chico es: a, b o c? Pon una señal.

Students read the text and then tick the picture which matches it.

Answers: Picture c

| AT3.2 | **3** Lee las frases. ¿Verdad o mentira?

Students look at the pictures and mark the sentences at the side true or false.

Answers: a V; b V; c M; d M

| AT4.2 | **4** Completa lo que dice Lucía.

Students complete Lucía's description of her boyfriend.

Answers: castaño/corto; castaños; blanca

Página 18 (2.5)

This page can be used with pages 34–35 of the Students' Book.

| AT3.3 | **1** Lee la entrevista y pon los dibujos en el orden correcto.

Students read the interview and number the pictures 1–5.

Answers: Reading down the page: 3, 2, 5, 4, 1

AT4.1 **2 Escribe dos preguntas más.**

Students write two more questions that they would like to ask Fernando Alonso. They could refer to the Vocabulary pages in the Students' book, Workbook or Copymasters for ideas. Answers will vary.

AT4.2 **3 Completa una ficha personal para tu deportista favorito/a.**

Students complete the form with information about their favourite sports star (or other celebrity, if they wish).

Answers: Students' own answers

Página 19 Gramática

This page can be used with page 28 of the Students' Book. The aim of this page is to revise the main verbs that students have learnt in the unit and to go over adjective agreement.

AT3.3 **1 Completa la carta de Blanca con los verbos apropiados.**

Remind the students of verb forms in the *Flashback* box. Students then choose the correct words to complete Blanca's letter.

Answers: llamo; soy; Tengo; Tengo; llaman; tiene; es; soy; llama; Es; eres; es

AT3.2 **2 Escoge el adjetivo correcto.**

Look at the *Flashback* box with the class. Students then choose the correct adjective form for each phrase.

Answers: a negro; b grises; c marrones; d blancos

AT4.2 **3 ¿Qué animales hay?**

Students look at the pet rescue notice and complete the list of animals looking for a home.

Answers: blanco; perros; gris; dos; blancos

Página 20 Reto

This page can be used with page 36 of the Students' Book.

AT3.1 **1a Busca las nacionalidades. Mira el ejemplo.**

Students circle four more nationalities in the wordsearch.

Answers:

I	S	É	C	R	A	N	F
J	T	V	O	H	C	A	R
U	G	A	L	É	S	L	A
G	Y	N	L	R	F	E	N
S	A	P	I	I	M	M	C
L	B	N	W	T	A	Á	E
E	N	M	I	P	D	N	S
E	S	C	O	C	E	S	A

AT4.1 **1b Escribe las otras formas.**

Students complete the table with the masculine and feminine forms of the adjectives in exercise 1a.

Answers:

masculine	femenino
galés	galesa
escocés	escocesa
alemán	alemana
francés	francesa
italiano	italiana

AT3.2 **2 Completa las preguntas.**

Students draw lines to make six more different questions, using each word or group of words only once.

Answers:
¿Cuántos años tienes?
¿Qué idiomas hablas?
¿Cómo se llaman tus hermanos?
¿De dónde eres?
¿Cuántas personas hay en tu familia?
¿Tienes animales?

AT4.2 **3 Escribe tres frases sobre tu major amigo/a en la página 23.**

Using the language given, students write three sentences about their best friend on page 23.

Dos Workbook

Página 14 (2.1)

This page can be used with pages 26–27 of the Students' Book.

AT4.1 | **1 Identifica el país**

Students label the outlines with the country names in the box.

Answers: a Italia; b Estados Unidos; c Escocia; d Alemania; e España; f Inglaterra

AT3.2 | **2 Escribe el diálogo en el orden correcto.**

Students write the letters in the boxes to order the dialogue.

Answers: 1 f; 2 d; 3 b; 4 e; 5 a; 6 c

AT3.3 | **3a Lee. ¿Verdad o mentira?**

Students read the text and mark the sentences true or false.

Answers: 2 ✓; 3 ✓; 4 ✗

AT4.2 | **3b Corrige las frases falsas en la página 23.**

Students correct the false sentences from exercise 3a on page 23, the spare page for writing at the end of the unit.

Answers:
1 Juan es de Zaragoza.
4 Habla tres idiomas.

AT3.3 | **4 Escribe unas frases sobre ti en la página 23.**

Using the language given, students write three sentences about themselves on page 23.

Página 15 (2.2)

This page can be used with pages 28–29 of the Students' Book.

AT3.2 | **1 Empareja las frases con las familias.**

Students match the sentences with the pictures shown.

Answers: d, a, c, b, e

AT3.3 | **2 Completa el email.**

Students complete the email from Jorge using the words given in the box.

Answers: llaman; años; mi; familia; mis; tu; personas; hermanos; hijo

AT4.3 | **3 Describe a la familia en la página 23.**

Students look at the family tree and describe the family on page 23 using the support language given.

Página 16 (2.3)

This page can be used with pages 30–31 of the Students' Book.

AT3.2 | **1 ¿Qué animales tienen? Completa las frases según el dibujo.**

Students look at the pictures and complete the sentences.

Answers: 1 perros; 2 un gato; 3 un pájaro; 4 caballo; 5 tiene tres hámsters; 6 tiene cuatro peces

AT3.2 | **2 Empareja las preguntas con las respuestas.**

Students match the questions and the answers.

Answers: 1 c; 2 d; 3 a; 4 b

AT4.3 | **3 ¿Qué animales tiene Juan?**

Students look at Juan's pets' passports and write sentences about what pets he has.

Answers:
b Tiene dos pájaros rojos y verdes. Se llaman Cirilo y Olga.
c Tiene dos arañas negras. Se llaman Harold y Arturo.
d Tiene una serpiente amarilla. Se llama Julia.

Página 17 (2.4)

This page can be used with pages 32–33 of the Students' Book.

AT3.2 | **1 Lee las frases y dibuja las caras.**

Students read the descriptions and then draw and colour the corresponding features.

Answers: 1 blue eyes, long curly hair, glasses; 2 no hair, beard, green eyes; 3 straight black hair, hazel eyes; 4 very short blond hair, a moustache

AT3.3 | **2 Lee y mira la foto. Corrige los errores.**

Students read the text and look at the picture, then correct any mistakes in the text.

Answers: Tengo la piel **blanca** y **no** llevo bigote **ni** gafas. Tengo el pelo **corto** y **rizado**.

AT4.3 | **3 Escribe frases.**

Students write sentences in Spanish to describe the people in the pictures.

Answers:
1　Elena es más alta que Isabel.
2　Jaimito es más bajo que Jaime.
3　Yo soy más bajo que mi hermano.
4　El pelo de Julia es más largo que el pelo de Daniela.

Página 18 (2.5)

This page can be used with pages 34–35 of the Students' Book.

AT3.4 | **1 Lee la entrevista y pon los dibujos en el orden correcto.**

Students read the interview and number the pictures.

Answers: Reading down the page: 2; 3; 1; 4

AT4.2 | **2 Completa una ficha personal para tu deportista favorito/a.**

Students complete the form with information about their favourite sports star (or other celebrity, if they wish).

Answers: Students' own answers

Página 19 Gramática

This page can be used with pages 28–29 of the Students' Book.
The aim of this page is to revise the main verbs that students have learnt in the unit and to go over adjective agreement.

AT3.3 | **1 Completa la carta de Blanca con los verbos apropiados.**

Remind the students of verb forms in the *Flashback* box. Students then complete Blanca's letter using the verb forms in the word box.

Answers: Soy; soy; Tengo; Tengo; llaman; tiene; es; soy; llama; Es; eres; es

AT4.1 | **2 Escribe el adjetivo correcto.**

Look at the *Flashback* box with the class. Students then write the colour adjective correctly in Spanish, matching number and gender.

Answers: 1 negro; 2 grises; 3 marrones; 4 blancos

AT4.2 | **3 Qué animales hay?**

Students look at the pet rescue notice and complete the list of animals looking for a home.

Answers: un ratón blanco; tres perros negros; un caballo gris; dos conejos negros y blancos

Página 20 Reto

This page can be used with page 38 of the Students' Book.

AT3.1 | **1a Busca las nacionalidades.**

Students circle five nationalities in the wordsearch.

Answers:

I	S	É	C	R	A	N	F
J	T	V	O	H	C	A	R
U	G	A	L	É	S	L	A
G	Y	N	L	R	F	E	N
S	A	P	I	I	M	M	C
L	B	N	W	T	A	Á	E
E	N	M	I	P	D	N	S
E	S	C	O	C	E	S	A

AT4.1 | **1b Escribe las otras formas.**

Students complete the table with the masculine and feminine forms of the adjectives in exercise 1a.

Answers:

masculine	femenino
galés	galesa
escocés	escocesa
alemán	alemana
francés	francesa
italiano	italiana

AT4.2 | **2 Escribe las preguntas.**

Students use the words given to write as many questions as possible. They could refer to the Vocabulary pages in the Students' book, Workbook or Copymasters for ideas. Answers will vary.

AT4.3 | **3 Describe a tu mejor amigo/a en la página 23.**

Students write a description of their best friend on page 23.

Unit 3 Overview grid					National Curriculum		
Pages/Contexts/ Cultural focus	Objectives	Grammar	Skills and Pronunciation	Key language	Framework	PoS	AT level
40–41 **3.1 ¿Adónde vas?** Places in town; where you are going	Talking about places in town; Say where you are going; Ask somebody where he/she is going	*ir* (present tense)	–	*el restaurante, el cine, el parque, el café, el centro comercial, el estadio, el polideportivo, el supermercado, el hospital, el colegio, la playa, la estación de autobuses/trenes/RENFE*	(L) 7S7 (R) 7W5, 7S2, 7S9	1a, 1b, 1c, 2a, 2b, 2c, 2d, 2f, 2i, 3b, 3c, 3e, 4a, 4c, 4d, 5a, 5c, 5d, 5e, 5f, 5g 5i	1.1–2, 2.2, 3.1–3, 4.1–4
42–43 **3.2 ¿Dónde está...?** Directions	Understand basic directions; Give basic directions in Spanish	Imperatives	–	*¿Dónde está el colegio? Está a la derecha. Está a la izquierda. el mercado, la estación de autobuses, el café Internet, la biblioteca, la casa de X, la tienda, el hospital, el colegio Está cerca, lejos, a diez minutos andando, bastante, muy, a diez kilómetros en coche*	(R) 7S3, 7C5	1a, 1b, 1c, 2a, 2b, 2c, 2d, 2f, 3b, 3c, 3e, 4a, 4c, 4e, 5a, 5d, 5e, 5f, 5g, 5i	1.1, 2.1–3, 3.2–3, 4.3–4
44–45 **3.3 ¿Por dónde se va a... ?** Directions; places in town	Say where places are in town; Give more detailed directions	*del/de la*	–	*Cruza, cruce, sube, suba, baja, baje, dobla, doble, tuerce, tuerza ¿Por dónde se va al/a la ...? ¿Dónde está... ? Está al final de, al lado de, delante de, enfrente de... Baja la calle. Sube la calle. Dobla la calle. Cruza la calle.*	(L) 7L3 (R) 7S1	1a, 1b, 1c, 2a, 2b, 2c, 2d, 2f, 2g, 2h, 2i, 3b, 3c, 3d, 3e, 4a, 4c, 4d, 5a, 5c, 5d, 5e, 5f, 5g, 5i	1.1–2, 2.3, 3.1–4, 4.1–4
46–47 **3.4 ¿Cómo es tu ciudad?** Home town; weather; points of the compass	Describe your home town; Say what the weather is like; Name the points of the compass	*muy* and *mucho/a/os/as*	–	*¿Qué tiempo hace? Hace sol, hace calor, hace viento, hace frío, hace buen tiempo norte, sur, oeste, este Vivo en una ciudad bonita, histórica, ruidosa, industrial, interesante, moderna. Hay mucho tráfico, Hay muchos museos.*	(L) 7L6 (R) 7S4, 7T5, 7T6, 7C1	1a, 1c, 2a, 2b, 2c, 2d, 2e, 2f, 3a, 3b, 3c, 3d, 3e, 4a, 4d, 5a, 5b, 5e, 5g, 5i	1.1–3, 2.1–2, 3.1–4, 4.1–4
48–49 **3.5 Entre amigos** Valencia	–	–	–	–	(R) 7C3	1c, 2a, 2c, 2f, 2h, 2i, 3b, 3c, 3e, 4a, 4c, 4d, 5d, 5e, 5g, 5h, 5i	1.1, 2.3, 3.2–4, 4.5

AMIGOS 1 UNIT 3 MEDIUM TERM PLAN

About this unit: In this unit students learn about and use a range of new language in the context of places about town, directions and the weather. They develop their knowledge of words through awareness of both topic vocabulary and high-frequency words. More sentences for everyday use are acquired, and emphasis is placed upon correct spelling. Students use prior learning to formulate sentences of their own, and they are introduced to *estar* with directions. Throughout the unit there is a strong emphasis on student response.

Framework objectives (launch)	Teaching and learning	Week-by-week overview (assuming **6 weeks' work** or approx. **10–12.5 hours**)
7S7: time phrases and past and future events	Learning about the present tense of *ir* and how to use *ir + a*	**Week 1**
7L3: gist and detail	Listen for basic things, e.g. directions on p. 44	Talk about places in town; say where you are going and ask somebody where he/she is going
7L6: improving speech	Listen and check weather pronunciation on p. 47	**Week 2**
Framework objectives (reinforce)	**Teaching and learning (additional)**	Understand basic directions and give basic directions in Spanish
7W5: verbs present (+ past)	*ir* (all parts); imperatives	**Week 3**
7S1: typical word order	*Está muy cerca* (where you put *muy*); *del/de la*; *Voy al/a la*; *¿Por dónde se va a...?*	Say where places are in town and give more detailed directions
7S2: sentence gist	*Al/a la* both meaning 'to'	**Week 4**
7S3: adapting sentences	Draw map. Give directions to 5 places near your home, following model on p. 43	Describe your home town; say what the weather is like and name the points of the compass
7S4: simple questions	Asking questions about the weather in various towns	**Week 5**
7S9: simple sentences for routine communication	Writing text about where you go, with whom and when	Students apply the language and structures learnt in this unit to reading and answering questions on longer texts which focus on an aspect of Spanish or Latin American culture
7T2: read aloud simple texts	Reading aloud descriptions of towns	**Week 6**
7T5: assemble short texts	Writing a description of the weather	Recycle language of the unit via *Uno, Dos* and *Lectura* pages; students check their progress via the *Ya sé...* self-assessment checklist in the Students' Book and on Hoja 42.
7T6: respond to prompts	Write about the weather on map on p. 47, following the model	
7T7: check written work	Copymasters: checking writing for genders, agreements, accents, word order and correct verbs	
7C1: geographical facts	Weather in Spain	
7C3: authentic materials	Students read a web page about Valencia	
7C5: social/linguistic conventions	Imperatives: *tú* and *usted* forms	
	Teaching and learning (additional)	
	Weather in Spain	

3 En el pueblo

Unit objectives

Contexts: places in town, directions, weather
Grammar: *ir*; *estar*; imperatives; *de*; *muy* and *mucho*
Language learning: spelling; using *estar* with directions
Cultural focus: weather in Spain

Assessment opportunities

Speaking: SB, page 42, activity 2
Reading: SB, page 41, activity 5
Listening: SB, page 44, activity 4
Writing: SB, page 43, Reto

AT3.1 **1 Mira las fotografías. ¿Cuáles te gustan?**

Students discuss in English the places shown in the photographs and say which ones they like.

AT3.1 **2 Which words could you work out from the English?**

Students identify the meaning of the words from English cognates.

Answers: Students will probably not recognize *la plaza de toros*–bullring, but should be able to work out the others: *cine*–cinema; *parque*–park; *café*–café; *restaurante*–restaurant; *café Internet*–Internet café; *discoteca*–disco

Planner

• •

 3.1 **¿Adónde vas?**   páginas 40–41

Objectives

▶ Talk about places in town

▶ Say where you are going

▶ Ask somebody where he/she is going

Resources

Students' Book, pages 40–41
CD 1, tracks 39–41
Uno/Dos Workbooks, page 24

Key language

voy, vas, va, vamos, vais, van…
al, a la…
el restaurante, el cine, el parque, el café, el centro comercial, el estadio, el polideportivo, el supermercado, el hospital, el colegio, la playa, la estación de autobuses

Programme of Study reference

1a, 1b, 1c, 2a, 2b, 2c, 2d, 2f, 2i, 3b, 3c, 3e, 4a, 4c, 4d, 5a, 5c, 5d, 5e, 5f, 5g, 5i

Framework reference

(L) 7S7
(R) 7W5, 7S2, 7S9, 7T7

• •

¡A sus marcas!

AT3.1 | Escucha (a–h) y escribe en inglés. Mira la lista. ¿Qué número es?

Students listen to the recording and make a list of places in English. They then give the correct picture number.

Answers: a park 3; b café 4/restaurant 5; c beach 11; d railway station 13; e disco 15; f school 10; g bullring 14; h hospital 9

 CD 1, track 39   página 40, ¡A sus marcas!

a sound of park
 – el parque
b sounds of crockery
 – el café
c sound of sea and seagulls
 – la playa
d sound of a train
 – la estación de RENFE
e sound of pop music
 – la discoteca
f sound of school bell and desks closing
 – el colegío
g sound of trumpet, clapping and a voice Olé
 – la plaza de toros
h sound of an ambulance siren
 – el hospital

AT1.1 | **1** Escucha y repite.

Students repeat the new town vocabulary.

 CD 1, track 40   página 40, actividad 1

1 el centro comercial
2 el cine
3 el parque
4 el café
5 el restaurante
6 el estadio
7 el polideportivo
8 el supermercado
9 el hospital
10 el colegio
11 la playa
12 la estación de autobuses
13 la estación de trenes/la estación de RENFE
14 la plaza de toros
15 la discoteca

Zoom gramática

This section introduces all forms of the irregular verb *ir* together with the preposition *a* and the formation of *al*. Although *ir* is irregular, you may want to point out some of the similarities in verb endings with other verbs that the students have met, for example *-s* for the *tú* form, to help them remember.

AT 3.1/2 | **2** Choose the correct option in these examples.

Students identify the correct prepositional form depending on the gender of the noun.

Answers: a a la; b al; c a la

AT1.2 **3 Escucha y lee. Continúa el juego.**

AT2.2

Students first listen to the model and then play a chain game, with each successive student adding a new place to the sequence. The students will be concentrating most on remembering the nouns, but it is important to pay attention to the correct use of prepositions. To give the activity a competitive edge, anyone who makes a mistake in the order or the preposition is 'out'.

  CD 1, track 41   página 40, actividad 3

- ¿Adónde vas?
- Voy al polideportivo.
- Y tú, ¿adónde vas?
- Voy al polideportivo y al cine.

AT4.1 **4 Completa las frases.**

Students complete the sentences with the correct form of *ir*.

Answers: 1 Vamos; 2 Van; 3 Voy; 4 Va

AT3.3 **5 Lee el texto. ¿Verdad o mentira?**

Students read about Roberto's family and decide whether the sentences are true or false.

Answers: a V; b M; c M; d V; e M

AT4.4 **6 Cambia las palabras. Escribe tu propia composición.**

Students change the highlighted words to write a short paragraph about themselves and their families.

Reto

AT4.4 Diseña un póster.

Students make a poster showing the places in town where they and their family go and don't go. They can draw pictures or cut them out of magazines and label with appropriate sentences. To show where they don't go, they may want to cross out the buildings as well as writing negative sentences.

Ask students to check over their written work, paying particular attention to *a* and verb forms.

Planner

● ●

3.2 **¿Dónde está?** páginas 42–43

Objectives

▶ Understand basic directions

▶ Give basic directions in Spanish

Resources

Students' Book, pages 42–43
CD 1, track 42
Uno/Dos Workbooks, page 25

Key language

¿Dónde está el colegio?
Está a la derecha.
Está a la izquierda.
el mercado, la estación de autobuses, el café Internet, la biblioteca, la casa de X, la tienda, el hospital, el colegio
Está cerca, lejos, a diez minutos andando, bastante, muy, a diez kilómetros en coche

Programme of Study reference

1a, 1b, 1c, 2a, 2b, 2c, 2d, 2f, 3b, 3c, 3e, 4a, 4c, 4e, 5a, 5d, 5e, 5f, 5g, 5i

Framework reference

(R) 7S3, 7C5

● ●

¡A sus marcas!

AT2.1 ¡A contrarreloj! ¿Cuántos lugares recuerdas del principio de la unidad?

Students time themselves and name as much of the town vocabulary as they can in one minute. You could also do this by bringing pairs of students out to the front and timing a minute whilst they take it in turns to say a place in town.

AT1.1 **1** Escucha y lee. ¿Cuántas palabras conoces?

Students listen to Fátima's description of her neighbourhood. Afterwards they say everything that they can remember about it in English using the pictures to help them.

Answers: On the left, there's a market, a railway station and a bus station. Straight on, there's an Internet café, a cinema and a library. On the right, there's a shop, a hospital and school.

 CD 1, track 42 página 42, actividad 1

– Fátima, ¿qué hay en tu barrio?
– A la izquierda, hay un mercado, una estación de trenes y una estación de autobuses. Todo recto, hay un café Internet, un cine y una biblioteca. A la derecha, hay una tienda, un hospital y un colegio.

AT 2.2/3 **2** Mira los dibujos. Con tu compañero/a, haz diálogos.

Before students work in pairs, check the pronunciation of the direction phrases, particularly *izquierda* which students may find difficult. Students then use the pictures and symbols at the bottom of the page to make up dialogues as in the example.

Answers: ¿Dónde está…
a la estación de autobuses? Está a la izquierda.
b el cine? Está todo derecho.
c el hospital? Está a la derecha.
d el mercado? Está a la izquierda.

Zoom gramática

This section introduces imperatives in the context of giving directions. Both the *tú* and *usted* forms are introduced, which provides a good opportunity to remind students about these ways of saying 'you' which they studied in Unit 1. It also introduces more directions language.

AT3.2 **3** Lee el mapa.

Students look at the symbols and the map. Make sure that they all understand the symbols for the new directions language that they learnt in the *Zoom gramática* box. Ask students to name as many places on the map as they can in Spanish.

Answers: Students should know *parque, cine, colegio, café Internet* and *supermercado*. The other place on the map, *la oficina de turismo*, will be new at this stage.

AT 2.2/3 **4** Con tu compañero/a, haz preguntas.

Read the model dialogue with the class. Check that students understand which form of the imperative Raquel uses, and why. In pairs, students then make up similar dialogues about the places a–c.

Answers:

a ¿Dónde está el estadio?

¡Está muy cerca! Está a cien metros.

b ¿Dónde está la estación de trenes?

¡Está bastante lejos! Está a un kilómetro.

c ¿Dónde está el hospital?

¡Está muy lejos! Está a tres kilómetros.

Reto

AT4.3 **Dibuja un mapa de tu barrio. Da direcciones para cinco lugares.**

Students draw a plan of their neighbourhood, labelling the buildings in Spanish. They label a 'You are here' spot (or you may like to introduce *Estás aquí* which students will meet again in 3.3). They then write directions in Spanish in the *tú* form from this point to five places shown on the map.

Planner

●●●●●●●●●●●●●●●●●●●●●●●●●

 3.3 **¿Por dónde se va a ...?**   páginas 44–45

Objectives

▶ Say where places are in town

▶ Give more detailed directions

Resources

Students' Book, pages 44–45
CD 1, tracks 43–44
Uno/Dos Workbooks, page 26

Key language

cruza/cruce, sube/suba, baja/baje, dobla/doble, tuerce/tuerza
¿Por dónde se va al…/a la…?
¿Dónde está…? Está…
… al final de/al lado de/delante de/enfrente de
Baja la calle. Sube la calle. Dobla la calle. Cruza la calle.

Programme of Study reference

1a, 1b, 1c, 2a, 2b, 2c, 2d, 2f, 2g, 2h, 2i, 3b, 3c, 3d, 3e, 4a,
4c, 4d, 5a, 5c, 5d, 5e, 5f, 5g, 5i

Framework reference

(L) 7L3
(R) 7S1

●●●●●●●●●●●●●●●●●●●●●●●●●

¡A sus marcas!

AT3.1 | Mira los dibujos. ¿Cómo se dicen en inglés 1–4?

Students look at the diagrams and work out what the
directions mean.

Answers: 1 Go down the road. 2 Go up the road. 3 Go round
the corner. 4 Cross the road.

AT1.2 | **1** Escucha y repite las direcciones.

Students listen to and repeat the new language. You could
divide the class in half and ask one side to repeat the
question and the other to answer it, then swap roles.

 CD 1, track 43   página 44, actividad 1

1 – ¿Por dónde se va a la discoteca?
   Baja la calle.
2 – ¿Por dónde se va al colegio?
   Sube la calle.
3 – ¿Por dónde se va al mercado?
   Dobla la calle.
4 – ¿Por dónde se va a la biblioteca?
   Cruza la calle.

AT3.2 | **2** Empareja los dibujos con las direcciones.

Students match the arrows with the new verbs.

Answers: a sube; b baja; c cruza; d dobla

AT2.3 | **3** Con tu compañero/a, completa las frases para hacer un
diálogo.

Students make up short dialogues substituting the pictures
with words.

Answers:
a   ¿Por dónde se va al cine?
   Cruza la calle.
b   ¿Por dónde se va al café?
   Baja la calle.
c   ¿Por dónde se va a la estación de trenes/RENFE?
   Dobla/Tuerce la calle.

AT1.1 | **4** Escucha las direcciones (a–e) e indícalas con la mano.

Before playing the CD, agree with the class how you will
show the four directions (*cruza/sube/baja/dobla*) with hand
movements. Then practise the activity by calling out the
four verbs in random order for students to do the correct
movement. Students then listen to directions a–e on the
CD and do the correct hand movements. Ask them what
they think the last person says ('I'm lost').

 CD 1, track 44   página 44, actividad 4

a – ¿Por dónde se va al mercado?
   Sube la calle.
b – ¿Por dónde se va a la discoteca?
   Cruza la calle.
c – ¿Por dónde se va a la plaza de toros?
   Baja la calle.
d – ¿Por dónde se va al estadio?
   Dobla la calle.
e – ¿Por dónde se va al mercado?
   Sube la calle … baja la calle …¡no! Dobla la calle … ¡Uf!
   No sé … ¡estoy perdido!

AT3.2 | **5** Lee las direcciones y adivina los lugares.

Look first at the *Frases clave* box with the class. Students
then read the directions and find the places on the map.

Answers: a El parque; b La oficina de turismo; c La tienda

Zoom gramática

This section builds on the previous work on *a + el*,
introducing *de + el = del*. Once students have answered
exercise 6, ask if they can think of a similar rule that they
have studied.

AT3.1

6 Look closely at these two sentences. When do you use *del* and when do you use *de la*?

Students work out the rule.

Answers: We use *del* if the noun is masculine and *de la* if the noun is feminine.

AT3.1

7 Now choose the correct option in these sentences.

Students choose the correct form for sentences a–d.

Answers: a de la; b del; c de la; d del

AT2.3

8 Con tu compañero/a. Mira el mapa y da direcciones para los lugares.

In pairs, students work out directions for the other three places, as in the example.

Answers:
¿Dónde está el hospital?
Está enfrente del colegio.
¿Dónde está el restaurante?
Está enfrente del centro comercial.
¿Dónde está la tienda?
Está delante de la estación.
¿Dónde está la oficina de turismo?
Está al final de la calle Cuba.

Reto

AT4.1

Copia y rellena la carta de Jorge con las palabras adecuadas.

Students copy and complete the letter with language from the unit so far.

Answers: cerca; recto; primera; izquierda; lado; discoteca; lejos; segunda; derecha

Planner

•••••••••••••••••••••••••

3.4 **¿Cómo es tu ciudad?** páginas 46–47

Objectives

▶ Describe your home town

▶ Say what the weather is like

▶ Name the points of the compass

Resources

Students' Book, pages 46–47
CD 1, tracks 45–47
Uno/Dos Workbooks, page 27

Key language

¿Qué tiempo hace?, Hace sol, hace calor, hace viento, hace frío, hace buen tiempo
norte, sur, oeste, este
Vivo en una ciudad bonita, histórica, ruidosa, industrial, interesante, moderna.
Hay mucho tráfico. Hay muchos museos.

Programme of Study reference

1a, 1c, 2a, 2b, 2c, 2d, 2e, 2f, 3a, 3b, 3c, 3d, 3e, 4a, 4d, 5a, 5b, 5e, 5g, 5i

Framework reference

(L) 7L6
(R) 7S4, 7T2, 7T5, 7T6, 7C1

•••••••••••••••••••••••••

¡A sus marcas!

AT3.1 Mira las fotografías de las ciudades españolas. ¿Qué adjetivos conoces?

Students look at the photos and read the bubbles quickly. They use English–Spanish cognates to work out which adjectives they recognize. As they call them out, encourage them to use Spanish pronunciation, not English.

Answers: Students should recognize *histórica, industrial, moderna* and *interesante*.

AT1.3 **1** Escucha y lee. ¿Cómo es tu ciudad?

Students listen to and read the captions. Ask them to guess the other adjectives (*bonita, ruidosa, grande*) by looking at the pictures and thinking about what other words we might use to talk about cities.
You could also ask students to read the texts aloud for pronunciation practice.

 CD 1, track 45 página 46, actividad 1

1 – Vivo en una ciudad bonita e histórica que se llama Salamanca. ¡Me gusta mucho!
2 – Vivo en una ciudad industrial pero muy bonita. Se llama Bilbao. ¡Me encanta!
3 – Vivo en una ciudad histórica y ruidosa. Se llama Madrid. ¡Es la capital de España!
d – Vivo en una ciudad moderna e interesante que se llama Barcelona. ¡Es muy grande!

AT3.2 **2** Empareja las descripciones con las fotografías del ejercicio 1.

Students read a–d and match them with the photos in exercise 1. Encourage them not to worry about new words, but to guess them if they can.

Answers: a 4; b 3; c 2; d 1

Zoom gramática

This section presents *muy* and *mucho/as/os/as*. Ensure that students understand the terms 'adjective' and 'noun' in order to use this grammar effectively. Ask them to find examples in the captions in exercise 1 (but not exercise 2 as they use this in the following activity).

AT2.2 **3** Con tu compañero/a, pregunta y contesta: ¿Cómo es tu ciudad?

In pairs, students ask and answer about where they live. Students can answer about the nearest city even if they live in a more rural area.

AT4.1 **4** Copia y rellena el cuadro con las palabras del ejercicio 2.

Students copy and complete the table with adjectives and nouns from exercise 2.

Answers: Muy: famoso, famosa, grande; mucho: tráfico; mucha: cultura; muchos: monumentos; muchas: playas

AT2.1 **5** Mira los dibujos. Con tu compañero/a, pronuncia el vocabulario nuevo.

In pairs, students pool their knowledge of Spanish pronunciation to practise saying the new weather words. You may like to monitor to make sure that everyone is pronouncing *hace* correctly from the start of the lesson as it is a high frequency term.

AT 1.1/2 **6** Escucha y compara tu pronunciación. Repite.

Students listen to each phrase to check their pronunciation and then repeat the model.

CD 1, track 46   página 47, actividad 6

a – hace sol
b – hace calor
c – hace viento
d – hace frío
e – hace buen tiempo
f – hace mal tiempo
g – llueve
h – nieva
i – hay niebla
j – hay tormenta

AT
3.1/2

7 Lee las frases. Cambia el dibujo por las palabras apropiadas.

Students replace the symbols with the correct weather phrases.

Answers: a En Cáceres, hace sol. b En Orense, llueve. c En Soria, nieva.

AT1.1

8 ¿Qué tiempo hace en estas ciudades? Escucha y mira el mapa. ¿Verdad o mentira?

Students look at the weather symbols on the map and listen to the weather forecast. They decide whether the forecast corresponds with the symbols or not.

Answers: La Coruña M; Oviedo V; Bilbao V; Madrid M; Almería V

CD 1, track 47   página 47, actividad 8

– Buenos días, señoras y señores ... el tiempo ... En el norte ... y en el oeste ... bueno... en La Coruña ...hace calor.
En el norte ... en Oviedo ... hay niebla y hay tormentas.
En el país Vasco, en Bilbao, hace viento.
En el centro... en Madrid... hace calor.
En el sur, en Almería, hace mucho calor y mucho sol.

AT2.1

9 Con tu compañero/a, haz y contesta a las preguntas.

In pairs, students make up dialogues as in the example.

Answers: See transcript for exercise 8.

Reto

AT
4.3/4

Escribe una descripción del tiempo de cuatro ciudades en el mapa.

Students describe the weather in four of the cities shown on the map.

Answers: See transcript for exercise 8.

Planner

● ●

3.5 ## Entre amigos:
Ven a Valencia

páginas 48–49

Resources
Students' Book, pages 48–49
CD 1, track 48
Uno/Dos Workbooks, page 28

Programme of Study reference
1c, 2a, 2c, 2f, 2h, 2i, 3b, 3c, 3e, 4a, 4c, 4d, 5d, 5e, 5g, 5h, 5i

Framework reference
(R) 7C3

● ●

| AT1.1 | Escucha y lee. |

| AT3.4 | Students listen to and read the web page about Valencia. |

CD 1, track 48 página 48, actividad 1

¡Valencia es la ciudad ideal para las turistas!
¿Dónde está Valencia?
Valencia es una ciudad que está en el sureste de España. Está cerca de Denia y de Alicante.
¿Cómo es Valencia?
Es una ciudad antigua y moderna y hay siempre muchos turistas porque hay museos muy interesantes y playas muy bonitas.
¿Qué tiempo hace en Valencia?
Hace buen tiempo durante todo el año. A veces llueve pero normalmente hace sol y calor. ¡Perfecto!
¿Qué idiomas hablan en Valencia?
Hablan español y valenciano, que es la lengua de la región.
¿Qué hay de interés en Valencia?
Hay una zona antigua y tradicional muy tranquila, pero Valencia es también una ciudad muy moderna.
Visita … las playas – se llaman 'Las arenas' y 'La Malvarrosa'.
Y en la ciudad de las artes y las ciencias:
L'Hemisfèric – un planetario para ver planetas, galaxias.
L'Oceanogràfic – es el acuario más grande de Europa. Tiene 42 millones de litros de agua (¡el equivalente de quince piscinas olímpicas!) y más de 500 especies. Hay cinco piscinas diferentes y ¡un restaurante submarino!
Y muchos museos: el museo de arte moderno, el museo de las ciencias.
¿Qué celebraciones hay en Valencia?
La fiesta más famosa son las Fallas (12–19 de marzo). Hay estatuas que se llaman 'ninots' que queman a las 12 de la noche el día 19.

Todos los días hay fuegos artificiales, 'la mascletá' a las dos de la tarde durante 10 minutos.
Y cerca de Valencia … en Benidorm hay un parque temático fenomenal.

| AT2.3 | **2** Con tu compañero/a, haz y contesta a las preguntas. |

In pairs, students answer the questions.

Answers:
a Está en el sur-oeste de España, cerca de Denia y de Alicante.
b Valencia es un ciudad antigua y moderna.
c Hay museos muy interesantes y playas muy bonitas.
d Llueve.
e Normalmente hace sol y calor.
f Se hablan español y valenciano.
g Hay unas playas, un planetario, un acuario y muchos museos.
h Es el acuario más grande de Europa.
i Las Fallas.

| AT3.2 | **3** Busca en el crucigrama el nombre de un parque temático fenomenal. |

Students read the sentences and complete the clues in the crossword to reveal the name of the theme park in Benidorm.

Answers: Terra Mítica

	ᵃT	I	E	M	P	O				
ᵇL'	O	C	E	A	N	O	G	R	A	F	I	C
	ᶜE	U	R	O	P	A				
ᵈM	O	D	E	R	N	A				
	ᵉP	L	A	Y	A					
	ᶠM	U	S	E	O					
	ᵍN	I	N	O	T	S				
ʰE	S	T	A	C	I	O	N			
	ⁱF	I	E	S	T	A				
ʲC	I	E	N	C	I	A	S			
	ᵏV	A	L	E	N	C	I	A	N	O

| AT4.5 | **4** Haz un póster sobre la ciudad de Valencia. |

Students use the information on the web page to make a poster about Valencia.

Repaso

página 50

Resources

Students' Book, page 50

Programme of Study reference

1c, 2a, 2c, 2e, 2f, 2i, 3b, 3c, 3e, 4a, 4c, 4d, 5d, 5f, 5g, 5h, 5i

AT 1.2/3

1 Escucha y sigue el mapa. ¿Qué lugares son?

Students listen and follow on the museum plan. Stop the CD after each sentence for students to call out where they have reached in the museum. Help students with the pronunciation of the new words. Remind them to move their finger back to the entrance of the museum to follow the route for b and c.

Answers: a la serpiente dorada; b la estatua egipcia; c el diamante azul

 CD 1, track 49 página 50, actividad 1

a – Sigue todo recto, y toma la primera a la derecha.
b – Sigue todo recto. Es la segunda a la izquierda.
c – Sigue todo recto y está al final del pasillo.

AT 4.1/2

2 Copia y completa las frases.

Students copy and complete the directions using the plan of the museum to help them.

Answers: a recto, segunda; b izquierda; c toma, segunda, izquierda

AT3.4

3 El rap de las direcciones. Lee y rapea con tu compañero/a. Dibuja el mapa.

In pairs, students take it in turns to read the question and answer roles in the rap. They then draw a simple map to show where the places are.

Answers:

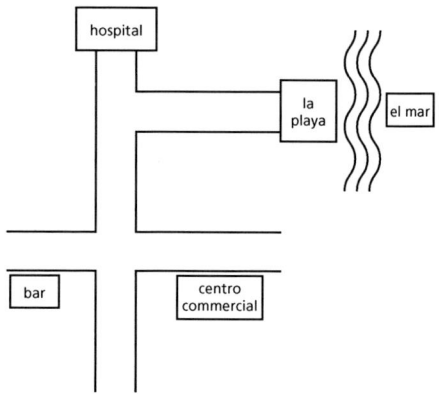

AT4.4

4 Escribe tu propio rap. Cambia las palabras en azul.

Students write their own rap substituting different directions and places.

Vocabulario

página 51

This page provides a theme-based Spanish–English summary of the key language of this unit. It can be used for reference throughout the unit or as an aid to learning vocabulary.

C41

Copymaster 41 contains a summary of the key language of the unit and can be given to the students at this point to help with revision.

W31

Page 31 of the *Uno/Dos* Workbooks also provides a summary of the key language of the unit.

Ya sé

página 52

The **Ya sé** page provides an end-of-unit checklist of learning objectives. At the foot of the page are activities at three levels of difficulty to extend the work of the unit. Encourage students to select an activity at the most appropriate level.

C42

Copymaster 42 contains a checklist and activities to keep track of the students' progress.

W32

Page 32 of the *Uno/Dos* Workbooks gives an end-of-unit checklist in Spanish and English, together with activities to keep track of the students' progress.

Unidad 3 Uno

página 100

Objectives

This reinforcement page is intended for those students who need further practice of core language of the unit. It can be used by students who finish other activities early or as alternative class or homework material.

Resources

Students' Book, page 100
CD 1, track 50–51

Programme of Study reference

1c, 2a, 2c, 2f, 3b, 3c, 3e, 4a, 5d, 5e, 5f, 5g, 5h, 5i

AT3.1

1 Pon las palabras en orden.

Students re-order the letters to make directions phrases.

Answers: a todo recto; b a la derecha; c a la izquierda; d cruza la calle

AT1.1 | **2 Escucha y comprueba tus respuestas.**

Students listen and check.

CD 1, track 50   página 100, actividad 2

a – todo recto
b – a la derecha
c – a la izquierda
d – cruza la calle

AT3.2 | **3 Empareja las direcciones con las frases.**

Students match up the directions drawings with the four phrases.

Answers: a 2; b 4; c 1; d 3

AT 1.1/2 | **4 Escucha. ¿Dónde está?**

Students listen and choose the correct direction to each place shown in the pictures.

Answers: 1 b; 2 d; 3 a; 4 c

CD 1, track 51   página 100, actividad 4

1 – ¿Dónde está la piscina?
  – Sigue todo recto y toma la primera a la derecha.
2 – ¿Dónde está el colegio?
  – Sigue todo recto y toma la segunda a la izquierda.
3 – ¿Dónde está el hotel?
  – Sigue todo recto.
4 – ¿Dónde está el restaurante?
  – Sigue todo recto y toma la primera a la izquierda.

AT2.3 | **5 Con tu compañero/a, practica las conversaciones.**

Students practise the conversations like the example, using the information supplied.

Unidad 3 Dos   página 101

Objectives

This extension page is intended for more able students who are confident with the core language of the unit. It can be used by students who finish other activities quickly or as alternative class or homework material.

Resources

Students' Book, page 101
CD 1, track 52

Programme of Study reference

1c, 2a, 2c, 2d, 2e, 3b, 3c, 3e, 4a, 5d, 5g, 5h, 5i

AT3.3 | **1 Lee y completa las direcciones.**

Students read the directions. Using the pictures to work out what the directions should be, students write out again any directions that are incorrect.

Answers:
a   el restaurante, el hotel, izquierda;
b   recto, a la izquierda, está el polideportivo;
c   el hotel, el hospital, derecha

AT1.3 | **2 Escucha. Copia y rellena el cuadro.**

Students listen and complete the grid with the places and the directions.

Answers:
2 estadio; sigue todo recto
3 colegio; segunda, izquierda

CD 1, track 52   página 101, actividad 2

1 – Buenos días, señor. ¿Dónde está el museo?
  – Está bastante cerca. Toma la primera a la derecha.
2 – Perdón, ¿dónde está el estadio?
  – Está cerca. Sigue todo recto.
3 – Buenas tardes, señora. ¿Dónde está el colegio?
  – Está lejos. Toma la segunda a la izquierda y toma un autobús.

AT3.3 | **3 Lee los dos textos. ¿Qué ciudad es?**

Students read the two texts and decide to which one each of the statements is referring.

Answers: b Bilbao; c Ávila; d Bilbao; e Bilbao

Unidad 3 Lectura: uno   página 112

Objectives

This page is to encourage independent reading. Students should attempt it once they are confident with the core language of the unit. It can be used by students who finish other activities early or as alternative class or homework material.

Resources

Students' Book, page 112

Programme of Study reference

1c, 2a, 2c, 2d, 2i, 3b, 3c, 3e, 4a, 5a, 5e, 5f, 5g, 5i

AT3.2 | **1 Mira el mapa y lee. Rellena los espacios. ¿Qué ciudades son?**

Students look at the map and read the sentences. They then complete them with the correct place names.

Answers: b Mallorca, Valencia; c Málaga, Algeciras; d Santander or Bilbao; Mérida or Badajoz

AT4.3 | **2 Describe las ciudades restantes.**

Students write brief descriptions of the remaining towns following the example in exercise 1.

AT3.3 | **3 Lee el texto. Copia y rellena el cuadro.**

Students read and complete the grid with the weather in each place.

Answers: Santander a, f; Madrid b; Cádiz d; Málaga c; Salamanca e

AT3.2 | **4 Mira las fotos de estas ciudades. ¿Verdad o mentira?**

Students look at the photos of the four towns and decide if the statements about them are true or false.

Answers: a V; b M; c V; d V

Unidad 3 Lectura: dos   página 113

Objectives

This page is to encourage independent reading. Students should attempt it once they are confident with the core language of the unit. It can be used by students who finish other activities early or as alternative class or homework material.

Resources

Students' Book, page 113

Programme of Study reference

1c, 2a, 2c, 2d, 2i, 3b, 3c, 3e, 4a, 5a, 5e, 5f, 5g, 5i

AT3.3 | **1 ¡Visita Méjico! César habla de su ciudad. Lee y escoge la opción correcta: ¿verdad o mentira o no se menciona?**

Students read the text about Mexico City and decide if statements a–h are true, false or it does not say (NS).

Answers: a V; b NS; c M; d NS; e M, f NS; g V; h NS (but accept V by deduction)

AT3.1 **AT4.1** | **2 What new words are there in exercise 1 whose meaning you can work out?**

Students list any words in the texts that are new to them, but they think they can work out the meaning of. They can use a glossary to check if necessary.

AT3.2 | **3 Lee y pon las frases en orden.**

Students re-order the words to make sentences and then write out the whole conversation with the sentences in the correct order.

Answers:
¿Adónde vas, Antonio?
Voy a la biblioteca.
Dónde está la biblioteca?
Toma la primera calle a la derecha.
Está muy cerca?
No, está lejos.
¿Está al lado del centro comercial?
No, está delante del café.

AT4.4 | **4 Escribe una conversación similar. Cambia los detalles.**

Students write a similar conversation changing the details. Using a map of their home town would make the task seem more 'real'.

Copymasters

Hoja 43 ¡A sus marcas!

This can be used after pages 40–41 in the Students' Book.

AT4.1 | **1 Trata de unir las partes de las palabras.**

Students match the halves to make words

Answers: estación; centro comercial; hospital; restaurante; hotel; café; cine; estadio; parque; discoteca

AT2.1 | **2 Lee y recuerda el número. ¿Qué lugar es?**

Students memorize the six numbered places. In pairs, they take it in turns to throw a die. They race each other to see who can name the place first.

AT3.1 | **3 Une estos adjetivos con su traducción al inglés.**

Students match the Spanish with the English.

Answers: 1 f; 2 d; 3 e; 4 b; 5 c; 6 a

AT2.1 **4** Tu compañero/a dice la palabra en inglés y tú tienes que decirla en español.

In pairs, students test each other on the new adjectives in activity 3.

Hoja 44 Reto

This can be used after pages 40–41 in the Students' Book.

AT4.2 **1** Haz frases con las siguientes partes.

Students construct as many grammatically correct sentences as they can from the words in the box.

Answers: Students may use any of the verb forms, but the preposition and noun collocations should be:
al: polideportivo, hotel, cine
a los: parques
a la: playa
a las: discotecas

AT3.3 **2** Empareja las preguntas y las respuestas

Students match the questions and the answers.

Answers: 1 b; 2 c; 3 d; 4 a

AT3.2 **3** Une las frases en español con su equivalente en inglés.

Students match the Spanish sentences with the English translation.

Answers: 1 c; 2 d; 3 a; 4 b

Hoja 45 Escuchar: uno

This can be used after pages 42–43 in the Students' Book.

AT1.1 **1** Escucha y encuentra las palabras que faltan.

Students listen and complete the text with the words in the box.

Answers: bonita; interesante; monumentos; parque; museo; izquierda

 CD 3, track 25   Hoja 45, actividad 1

– Mi ciudad es bonita y muy interesante. En mi ciudad hay muchos monumentos y un parque que está al lado del museo. El cine está a la izquierda.

AT1.1 **2** Escucha y pon la información en orden según la oyes.

Students listen and number the pictures.

Answers: a 1; b 3; c 2; d 5; e 4

 CD 3, track 26   Hoja 45, actividad 2

1 – ¿Dónde está el estadio?
– Sigue todo recto.
2 – ¡Está lejos! A treinta kilómetros …
3 – Toma la primera a la izquierda.
4 – En mi ciudad hay un cine.
5 – Toma la segunda a la derecha.

Hoja 45 Escuchar: dos

AT1.1 **3** ¿Quién habla?

Students listen and write the correct name under each picture.

Answers: a Laura; b Luis; c José; d Olga; e Fran

 CD 3, track 27   Hoja 45, actividad 3

1 – Olga, ¿cómo es tu ciudad?
– En mi ciudad hay un problema con la polución … hay mucho tráfico.
2 – Soy Laura. En mi ciudad hay muchos monumentos y museos, es una ciudad histórica.
3 – Soy José. Mi ciudad es muy industrial, hay muchas fábricas.
4 – Soy Luis. Mi ciudad es muy bonita y hay muchos turistas.
5 – Soy Fran. Mi ciudad es tranquila. Voy al parque a menudo.

Hoja 46 Hablar: uno

This can be used after pages 44–45 in the Students' Book.

AT2.4 **1** Haz preguntas a tu compañero/a.

2 Responde a las preguntas.

In pairs, students ask and answer using the prompts given on the page. You may want to check that students understand the correct article use for question 2 before they begin.

Hoja 46 Hablar: dos

AT2.4 **3** Ahora haz una presentación de tu ciudad. Utiliza las preguntas de la ficha.

Students working at a higher level can prepare an oral presentation of their town or city, covering in particular questions 1 and 3. Encourage the rest of the class to ask follow-up questions using *¿Dónde está el/la …?*

Hoja 47 Leer y escribir: uno

This can be used after pages 40–41 in the Students' Book.

| AT3.1 |
| AT4.1 |

1 Mira el mapa y rellena los espacios.

Students look at the map and complete the sentences.

Answers: 1 museo; 2 colegio; 3 parque; 4 hospital; 5 cine

| AT4.2 |

2 ¿Verdad o mentira? Corrige las afirmaciones falsas.

Students look at the weather map and mark the sentences true or false. They then correct the false sentences.

Answers: 1 M – Hay niebla; 2 V; 3 M – Hace sol; 4 V; 5 V

| AT4.3 |

3 Describe la ciudad del dibujo.

Students use the words in the boxes to write about the city in the picture. Encourage them to use negative sentences, as well as saying what they can see in the picture, in order to make the description more interesting.

Hoja 48 Leer y escribir: dos

This can be used after pages 40–41 in the Students' Book.

| AT3.4 |

1 Lee la carta de Manuela y responde a las preguntas.

Students read the text and decide whether the sentences are true, false or whether the information isn't given.

Answers: 1 ? 2 V; 3 ?; 4 M; 5 M; 6 ?; 7 V

| AT4.4 |

2 Ahora escribe una carta como la de Manuela. Utiliza la información de abajo.

Students write a letter like the one in exercise 1 but using the information given about Málaga. Answers will vary a great deal, but you may like to prepare a sample text for discussion as an overhead or on a projector. Encourage the students to vary their sentence structure, to link sentences with the connectors that they have studied, and to use adjectives.

Sample answer:
¡Hola! Me llamo ... y vivo en Málaga, una ciudad que está en el sur de España. Es una ciudad turística y tiene muchas playas y muchos cafés y restaurantes. Hay una catedral y un museo de arte que se llama la Fundación Picasso. Málaga tiene también un teatro romano y un museo arqueológico. El museo es fascinante pero mi monumento favorito es el Castillo de Gibralfaro que es muy antiguo. Me gusta ir también al parque natural.

| AT4.1 |

3 Lee el texto y completa las palabras que faltan.

Students complete the text.

Answers: histórica; museos; ciudad; frío; calor; sol; tráfico

Hoja 49 Gramática

This can be used after pages 42–43 in the Students' Book.

| AT4.1 |

1 Decide whether you'd use *ser* or *estar* for each sentence and write the letters next to the correct verb.

Look at the ¡Recuerda! box with the class to remind them of the verb forms. To work on usage, students then match a–e with *ser* or *estar*.

Answers:
ser: a; b; d; e
estar: c

| AT4.1 |

2 Now choose the right verb. *¿Ser o estar?*

Students choose the correct verb for each sentence.

Answers: 1 está; 2 es; 3 Estoy; 4 Soy; 5 Es; 6 Somos; 7 es; 8 son

Hoja 50 Técnica

This can be used after pages 46–47 in the Students' Book.

| AT4.1 |

1 Find the 6 mistakes in this text and correct them.

Look at the first ¡Recuerda! box with the class and talk about recent writing tasks that they have done. Did they check their work in this way? To practise, students then read the text and identify six mistakes.

Answers: The correct forms should be: *española, vivo, personas, se llama, blanco, azules.*

| AT4.1 |

2a Write *pero, también* or *porque* into the gaps.

Look at the second ¡Recuerda! box with the class and discuss the examples. Students then complete the text with the high frequency words covered in the box.

Answers: también; porque; pero

| AT4.3 |

2b Add something to each sentence: describe the cat and the museum.

Students complete the sentences with adjectives to describe the cat and the museum. Answers will vary but they should use the masculine singular form of an adjective that makes sense in the context.

Hoja 51 Cultura

This can be used after pages 48–49 in the Students' Book.

AT3.2 **1 ¿Cuánto sabes de España? Responde a las preguntas.**

Students do the quiz.

Answers: 1 V; 2 V; 3 V; 4 V; 5 V; 6 M; 7 M; 8 V; 9 V; 10 V

Hoja 52 Se pronuncia así

This can be used after pages 40–41 in the Students' Book.

AT2.1 **1 Say these words aloud, then listen to check.**

Read the *¡Recuerda!* box with the class. Students then use the rules to help them read the words. They listen and check.

CD 3, track 28	Hoja 52, actividad 1

rojo – lejos – colegio – hijo – baja

AT2.1 **2 Match the tongue twisters to the pictures, then try to say them. Listen to check.**

Students read the tongue twisters and match them with the pictures. They then try saying them and listen to check their pronunciation with the recording.

Answers: Jaime y Juan = picture a; Gabriel García = picture c; Julia = picture b

CD 3, track 29	Hoja 52, actividad 2

– Jaime y Juan juegan al ajedrez en el jardín.
– Gabriel García es guapo y gordo y vive en Gibraltar.
– Julia juega junto a Jorge.

Control Unidad 3

Resources

Copymasters 53–58
CD 3, tracks 30–33

Hoja 53 Escuchar: uno

AT1.2 **1 Une el tiempo con la persona adecuada.**

Students listen and write the correct letter for the weather picture next to each name.

Answers: 1 Luis a; 2 Fernando c; 3 Nico e; 4 Olga b; 5 Gloria d; 6 Carlos f

Mark scheme: Students who attempt *uno* only: 2 marks for each correct answer = 10 marks.
Students who attempt *uno* and *dos*: 1 mark for each correct answer = 5 marks.

Assessment criteria: Students who match four or five weather pictures correctly show evidence of performance at AT 1.2.

CD 3, track 30	Hoja 53, actividad 1

Ejemplo
– Luis, ¿qué tiempo hace en tu ciudad?
– Hace sol.
– Fernando, ¿qué tiempo hace en tu ciudad?
– Hace frío normalmente.
– Nico, ¿qué tiempo hace en tu ciudad?
– Llueve mucho …
– Olga, ¿qué tiempo hace en tu ciudad?
– Hace calor. ¡Es fenomenal!
– Gloria, ¿qué tiempo hace en tu ciudad?
– Nieva mucho …
– Carlos, ¿qué tiempo hace en tu ciudad?
– ¡Normalmente hace viento!

AT1.2 **2 ¿Verdad o mentira? Corrige las frases falsas.**

Students listen and mark whether the directions match the pictures or not. They correct the directions that are wrong.

Answers:
1 M – (El parque) Está al final de la calle.
2 V
3 M – (La tienda) Está a la izquierda. (You don't have to turn left into a street – it's **on** your left.)
4 V

Mark scheme: Students who attempt *uno* only: 3 marks for each correct answer; 3 marks (1.5 each) for correcting the two false sentences = 15 marks
Students who attempt *uno* and *dos*: 1 mark for each correct answer; 3 marks (1.5 each) for correcting the two false sentences = 7 marks

Assessment criteria: Students who mark three or four sentences correctly and can communicate the correct idea for the corrected sentences (even if there are some spelling errors) show evidence of performance at AT 1.2.

CD 3, track 31	Hoja 53, actividad 2

1 – El parque está a la izquierda.
2 – El centro comercial está al final de la calle.
3 – La tienda está en la primera calle a la izquierda.
4 – El polideportivo está en la segunda calle a la derecha.

Hoja 53 Escuchar: dos

AT1.1 **3 Escucha. Rellena las palabras que faltan.**

Students listen and complete the weather forecast.

Answers: calor; sol; buen; llueve; niebla; hace viento; nieva

Mark scheme: 1 mark for each correct answer = 7 marks

Assessment criteria: Students who complete five or more gaps correctly show evidence of performance at AT 1.1.

 CD 3, track 32 Hoja 53, actividad 3

– ¡Buenos días señoras y señores! Hoy en Santander hace calor y sol. En Pontevedra hace buen tiempo pero en Madrid llueve. En Alicante hay niebla y en Barcelona hace viento. En los Pirineos nieva.

AT1.2 **4 Escucha y escribe tres puntos de información.**

Students listen and complete the table about where Belén and Ana live.

Answers:

Belén: Palma; hace (mucho) calor; la playa
Ana: Oviedo, llueve (un poco); cafés, monumentos

Mark scheme: 1 mark for each correct answer = 6 marks

Assessment criteria: Students who complete four or more gaps correctly show evidence of performance at AT 1.2.

 CD 3, track 33 Hoja 53, actividad 4

1 – Hola, Fátima. ¿Cómo se llama tu ciudad?
 – Se llama Toledo.
 – ¿Cómo se escribe?
 – T – O – L – E – D – O.
 – ¿Qué tiempo hace?
 – Hace buen tiempo.
 – ¿Qué hay de interesante en Toledo?
 – Bueno… la catedral es preciosa.
2 – Belén, ¿Dónde vives?
 – Vivo en Palma.
 – ¿Cómo se escribe?
 – P – A – L – M – A.
 – ¿Qué tiempo hace?
 – El tiempo es maravilloso: hace mucho calor.
 – ¿Qué hay de interesante en Palma?
 – ¿Lugares interesantes? La playa …
3 – Ana, ¿cómo se llama tu ciudad?
 – Se llama Oviedo.
 – ¿Cómo se escribe?
 – O – V – I – E – D – O.
 – ¿Qué tiempo hace?
 – Pues bueno… llueve un poco.
 – ¿Qué es interesante en Oviedo?
 – Pues los cafés y los monumentos.

Hoja 54 Hablar

AT 2.2/3 **1 Pregunta a tu compañero/a y toma notas de lo que dice.**

2 Responde a las preguntas.

Students ask and answer the questions using the picture prompts.

Mark scheme: 1 mark for each correct question; 2 marks for each correct drawing on the map = 10 marks
9 marks for communicating the correct ideas in the answers; 6 marks for accuracy and accent = 15 marks

Assessment criteria: Students who score 17–20 show evidence of performance at AT 2.2. Students who score 21 or more are performing at AT 2.3

Hoja 55 Leer: uno

AT3.1 **AT4.1** **1 Lee las frases y escribe el nombre de la ciudad en el espacio correcto.**

Students look at the weather map and write the correct city for each sentence.

Answers: 1 Soria; 2 Soria; 3 La Coruña; 4 La Coruña; 5 Cádiz; 6 Oviedo

Mark scheme: 1 mark for each correct answer = 5 marks

Assessment criteria: Students who write four or five cities correctly show evidence of performance at AT 3.1.

AT3.2 **2 Une las preguntas con las respuestas.**

Students match the questions and the answers.

Answers: 1 b; 2 a; 3 d; 4 e; 5 c

Mark scheme: 2 marks for each correct answer = 10 marks

Assessment criteria: Students who match four or five correctly show evidence of performance at AT 3.2.

AT3.2 **3 Lee la descripción. ¿Verdad o mentira?**

Students read the description and decide whether the statements are true or false.

Answers: 1 V; 2 M; 3 V; 4 M; 5 M

Mark scheme: 2 marks for each correct answer = 10 marks

Assessment criteria: Students who mark four or five sentences correctly show evidence of performance at AT 3.2.

Hoja 56 Leer: dos

AT3.3 **1** Lee los mensajes. ¿Qué ciudad es?

Students read the emails and identify the cities.

Answers: 1 Madrid; 2 Toledo; 3 Badalona; 4 Madrid; 5 Alicante

Mark scheme: 3 marks for questions 1–3; 2 marks for questions 4–5 = 13 marks

Assessment criteria: Students who name four or five cities correctly show evidence of performance at AT 3.3.

AT3.4 **2** Lee el texto. ¿Verdad, mentira o no se menciona?

Students read the text and mark whether the sentences are true or false or whether the information is not given in the text.

Answers: 1 ?; 2 M; 3 V; 4 M; 5 M; 6 ?; 7 ?; 8 M

Mark scheme: $1^1/_2$ marks for each correct answer = 12 marks

Assessment criteria: Students who mark six or more sentences correctly show evidence of performance at AT 3.4.

Hoja 57 Escribir: uno

AT4.1 **1** Rellena los espacios.

Students complete the text with words given.

Answers: norte; calor; llueve; histórica; turistas; monumentos

Mark scheme: 2 marks for each correct answer = 12 marks

Assessment criteria: Students who complete four or more gaps correctly show evidence of performance at AT 4.1.

AT4.3 **2** Escribe unas frases sobre tu ciudad.

Students write sentences about where they live in answer to the questions given. They can use the text in exercise 1 to help them.

Mark scheme: 8 marks for communicating appropriate answers to the questions; 5 marks for accuracy and variety = 13 marks

Assessment criteria: Students who score 9 or more show evidence of performance at AT 4.3.

Hoja 58 Escribir: dos

AT3.3
AT4.3 **1** Responde a las preguntas.

Students read the letter and answer the questions.

Answers: 1 a la playa; 2 hace mucho calor; 3 bares, restaurantes, parques, playas (y muchos turistas); 4 con sus amigos; 5 al restaurante

Mark scheme: 2 marks for each correct answer = 10 marks

Assessment criteria: Students who score 7 or more show evidence of performance at AT 4.3.

AT4.3 **2** Escribe una postal a un amigo hablando de tus vacaciones en una ciudad. Cambia las palabras subrayadas del ejercicio 1.

Students use the model in exercise 1 to write a postcard to a friend. They change the underlined words and use different information.

Mark scheme: 10 marks for communicating information that is different from the model; 5 marks for accuracy and variety = 15 marks

Assessment criteria: Students who score 10–12 show evidence of performance at AT 4.3. Students scoring 13 or more are performing at 4.4.

Uno Workbook

Página 24 (3.1)

This page can be used with pages 40–41 of the Students' Book.

AT3.1 **1** Empareja los dibujos con su nombre.

Students label the pictures a–j.

Answers: 2 f; 3 e; 4 g; 5 j; 6 a; 7 i; 8 c; 9 h; 10 b

AT3.2 **2** Escoge la frase correcta.

Students read and tick the correct sentence for each picture.

Answers: 2 a; 3 b; 4 a; 5 b; 6 b

AT4.2 **3** En la página 33, escribe frases parecidas a las del ejercicio 2.

Students look at the picture and write sentences similar to those in exercise 2 on page 33, the spare page for writing at the end of the unit.

Answers:
a Voy a la plaza de toros.
b Voy al supermercado.
c Voy a la estación de RENFE.
d Voy a la estación de autobuses.
e Voy al centro comercial.
f Voy al colegio.

Página 25 (3.2)

This page can be used with pages 42–43 of the Students' Book.

AT3.2 **1 Escribe la palabra o las palabras adecuadas.**

Students label the diagrams with the correct phrases from the box.

Answers: bastante cerca; bastante lejos; muy lejos

AT3.2 **2 Escribe la letra correcta en cada casilla.**

Students read the sentences and write the appropriate letter in each box.

Answers: The letters should be arranged:

```
          d       a
c                 b
```

AT3.2 **3 Escoge una frase para cada dibujo.**

Students match a phrase with each diagram.

Answers: 2 f; 3 a; 4 e; 5 b; 6 c

AT3.3 **4 Completa las preguntas y las respuestas. Sigue el**
AT4.3 **ejemplo.**

Students write sentences about the pictures, following the example.

Answers: b ¿Dónde está el polideportivo? Sigue todo recto y toma la primera a la izquierda. c ¿Dónde está el estadio? Toma la segunda a la derecha y la segunda a la izquierda.

Página 26 (3.3)

This page can be used with pages 44–45 of the Students' Book.

AT3.3 **1 Tacha las palabras incorrectas.**

Students cross out the incorrect words.

Answers: The correct words are: a sube; b baja; c cruza; d dobla; e tuerce; f delante; g enfrente; h al lado

AT3.3 **2 ¿Verdad o mentira?**

Students look at the pictures and mark each sentence true or false.

Answers: b ✓; c ✗; d ✓

AT3.4 **3 Pon estos lugares en el mapa.**

Students read the directions and label six of the boxes on the map with the correct letters.

Answers: Reading from left to right
Calle del Carmen: f; e; (blank); a;
Calle Calamanda: b; d; c; Bottom row (blank)

Página 27 (3.4)

This page can be used with pages 46–47 of the Students' Book.

AT3.2 **1 Completa el crucigrama en español.**

Students complete the crossword.

Answers:

AT3.2 **2a Mira el mapa y lee las frases. Hay tres correctas. Subráyalas.**

Students look at the weather map and read the sentences. They underline the three that are correct.

Answers: The correct ones are: a; c; f

AT4.2 **2b** Corrige las frases falsas del ejercicio 2a en la página 33.

Students correct the three false sentences from exercise 2a by writing them correctly on page 33.

Answers:
b En Madrid hace calor y llueve.
d En Valencia hace viento pero/y hace calor.
e En Bilbao hace sol.

AT3.3 **3** Lee la previsión meteorológica e ilustra el mapa.

Students read the forecast and complete the map with weather symbols.

Answers: Glasgow – bad weather; Edinburgh – sunny, cold; Liverpool – rain; Southampton – hot, sunny; London – good weather, windy

Página 28 (3.5)

This page can be used with pages 48–49 of the Students' Book.

AT3.4 **1** Escoge la palabra correcta de la caja para completar el párrafo.

Students complete the text with the words from the box.

Answers: ciudad; España; turistas; playas; buen tiempo; submarino; Las Fallas

AT3.4 **2** ¿Verdad o mentira?

Students read and mark the sentences true or false.

Answers: b ✓; c ✓; d ✗; e ✗; f ✓

AT3.4 **3** Contesta a las siguientes preguntas en inglés.

Students answer the questions in English.

Answers:
a on the Costa Blanca
b antigua = ancient/old or moderna = modern
3 because there are very interesting museums and beautiful beaches
4 good weather all year round
5 L'Oceanogràfic, the aquarium
6 statues of politicians or famous people (made for the occasion)

Página 29 Gramática

This page can be used with page 40 of the Students' Book. The aim of this page is to consolidate the forms of ir that the students have met and to revise prepositional forms.

AT3.2 **1** Verbo *ir*: Escoge la forma apropiada para cada dibujo.

Students look carefully at the pictures to see who is 'speaking' and write the appropriate verb form underneath.

Answers: b voy; c vas; d va

AT3.2 **2** Preposiciones: Escoge la forma correcta.

Students circle the correct prepositional form for each phrase.

Answers: c a la biblioteca; d al cine; e a la playa; f al estadio; g al parque; h al hotel

AT3.3 **3** Traduce las frases al inglés.

Students translate the sentences into English.
Answers:
b I go to the sports centre.
c He goes to the cinema.
d She goes to the supermarket.
e I go to the bus station.
f You go to the park.

AT4.3 **4** Traduce las frases al español.

Students translate the sentences into Spanish.

Answers:
a Voy al restaurante.
b Ella va a la plaza de toros.
c Vas al hospital.
d Él va al parque.
e Voy a la estación de RENFE.

Página 30 Reto

This page can be used with page 50 of the Students' Book.

AT3.5 **1** Completa el párrafo. Escribe las palabras que faltan según los dibujos.

Students complete the text with the words from the box.

Answers: un cine; estación de tren; enfrente; al lado; supermercado; Baja; cruza; derecha; sol; hace frío; nieva

| AT3.3 | |
| AT4.3 | |

2 Las vocales de estas respuestas han desaparecido. Escríbelas de nuevo.

Students complete the missing vowels in the answers.

Answers:
b Hace bastante frío.
c El hospital está al lado del polideportivo.
d No, está bastante cerca.
e Tuerce la segunda a la derecha.

AT3.3 **3 Escribe los contrarios.**

Students find the opposite for each word or phrase.

Answers: 2 a la izquierda; 3 baja; 4 hace mal tiempo; 5 lejos; 6 tranquilo

Dos Workbook

Página 24 (3.1)

This page can be used with pages 40–41 of the Students' Book.

AT3.1 **1 ¿Cuáles de estos lugares aparecen en la ilustración?**

Students look at the picture and tick the places that appear in it.

Answers: d; e; f; g; h; i; j; l; m; n

AT3.2 **2 ¿Dicen la verdad? Escribe Verdad o Mentira.**

Students decide if the people in the pictures are telling the truth and mark the sentences true or false.

Answers: 2 V; 3 M; 4 V; 5 V; 6 M

| AT3.2 | |
| AT4.2 | |

3 Mira los dibujos en el ejercicio 2 y contesta a las siguientes preguntas.

Students look back at the pictures in exercise 2 and answer the questions.

Answers:
b Bombón va al parque.
c Enrique va al polideportivo.
d Catalina va a la playa.

Página 25 (3.2)

This page can be used with pages 42–43 of the Students' Book.

AT3.2 **1 Completa los espacios con las palabras de la caja.**

Students look at the map and complete sentences a–f.

Answers: b muy; c en coche; d cerca; e andando; f bastante

AT3.3 **2 ¿Adónde vas?**

Students read the directions and use the map to find which places they are describing.

Answers: 2 el café internet; 3 la estación de trenes/RENFE; 4 el restaurante

AT4.4 **3 Escribe cuatro frases en la página 33 para explicar a un amigo cómo ir de ... a ...**

Students work out directions for how to get from and to the places mentioned in a–d. They write directions on page 33, the spare page for writing at the end of the unit.

Answers:
a Sigue todo recto y toma la segunda a la derecha. Está a la izquierda.
b Sigue todo recto y toma la segunda a la izquierda. Está a la izquierda.
c Sigue todo recto, toma la segunda a la izquierda y sigue todo recto. Ésta al final de la calle, a la izquierda.
d Sigue todo recto, toma la segunda a la derecha y sigue todo recto. Está a la izquierda.

Página 26 (3.3)

This page can be used with pages 44–45 of the Students' Book.

AT3.1 **1 Empareja las palabras con los dibujos.**

Students match the words with the pictures.

Answers: Reading across the rows: c; f; d; g/h; g/h; (b); a; e

AT3.3 **2 Pon estos lugares en el mapa.**

Students label the boxes with the correct numbers.

Answers:
top row: e, d
middle row: b, c, f
bottom row: blank, a

AT4.4 **3 Escribe unas líneas en la página 33. Cuéntale a un amigo cómo ir del colegio a tu casa.**

Students work out directions for how to get from school to their house and write them on page 33. If it is too far to explain, they write about the nearest shop instead. Answers will vary but check for the correct use of the feminine forms *primera* / *segunda* where relevant. This activity is also suitable for peer correction.

Página 27 (3.4)

This page can be used with pages 46–47 of the Students' Book.

AT3.1 **1** Completa el crucigrama en español.

Students complete the crossword..

Answers:

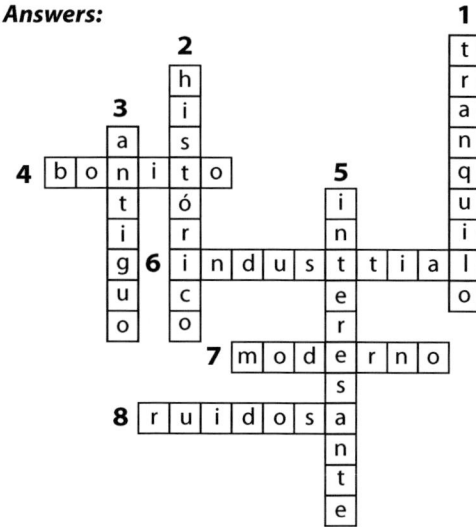

AT3.4 **2** Lee el texto y escribe los nombres que faltan.

Students read the weather forecast and fill in the city names in the correct spaces on the map, using the pictures as clues to help them.

Answers:

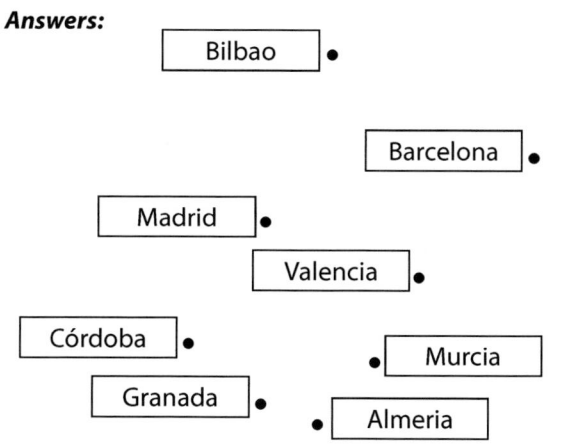

AT4.4 **3** Ahora escribe en la página 33 el parte meteorológico para Gran Bretaña según los dibujos.

Students write out the forecast for Great Britain on page 33, following the picture prompts.

Answers:

1 En Southampton hace calor y hace sol.
1 En Cardiff hay niebla.
1 En Londres hace buentiempo y hace viento.
1 En Liverpool llueve y hay tormenta.
1 En Glasgow hay mal tiempo y hace frío.
1 En Edimburgo hace sol y hace frío.

Página 28 (3.5)

This page can be used with pages 48–49 of the Students' Book.

AT3.4 **1** Escoge la palabra correcta de la caja para completar el párrafo.

Students complete the text with the words from the box.

Answers: este; España; turistas; playas; buen tiempo; llueve; sol; Oceanogràfic; submarino; Las Fallas

AT3.4 **2** Contesta a las siguientes preguntas en inglés.

Students answer the questions in English.

Answers:

1 in the east of Spain
2 antigua = ancient/old or moderna = modern
3 because there are very interesting museums and beautiful beaches
4 it is generally good weather all year but it sometimes rains
5 L'Oceanogràfic, the aquarium
6 statues of politicians and famous people (made for the occasion)

Página 29 Gramática

This page can be used with page 40 of the Students' Book. The aim of this page is to revise all the forms of the verb *ir*, and the use of *al* or *a la*.

AT4.3 **1** Verbo *ir*: Escoge la forma apropiada para cada dibujo.

Students choose the correct form of the verb *ir* to match with each picture.

Answers: voy; van; vais; vas; va; vamos

AT3.4 **2a** Verbo *ir*: Hay cinco errors en el texto. Subráyalos.

Students underline the incorrect forms of *ir*.

Answers: yo vas; mis abuelos vamos; mi hermano voy; mis amigos voy

AT4.4 **2b** Escribe el texto de nuevo en la página 33 corrigiendo los errores.

Students correct the text on page 33.

Answers:

Yo **voy** al polideportivo por la mañana. Después yo **voy** al colegio y por la tarde voy al centro comercial. Mis amigos van a la playa y mis abuelos **van** a la plaza de toros. Por la tarde, mi hermano **va** a la discoteca pero mis padres y yo vamos al cine. Mis amigos **van** al restaurante y mis tíos van al café internet.

| AT4.3 | **3 Preposiciones: Escribe la frase utilizando *al* o *a la*.** |

Students write sentences to practise the correct use of *al* and *a la*.

Answers:

b   Voy al colegio.
c   Voy a la biblioteca.
d   Voy al cine.
e   Voy a la estación de RENFE/trenes.
f   Voy a la estación de autobuses.
g   Voy a la playa.
h   Voy al café internet.
i   Voy al estadio.
j   Voy a la plaza de toros.

Página 30 Reto

This page can be used with page 52 of the Students' Book.

| AT3.4 | |
| AT4.4 | **1 Completa el párrafo. Escribe las palabras que faltan según los dibujos.** |

Students complete the text.

Answers: un cine; estación de treues/RENFE; estación de autobuses; una discoteca; enfrente; al lado; polideportivo; coche; final; ruidosa; histórica; sol; llueve; hace frío; nieva.

| AT3.3 | **2 Empareja las preguntas con las respuestas.** |

Students match the questions and the answers.

Answers: 2 f; 3 a; 4 e; 5 c; 6 b

| AT3.3 | |
| AT4.3 | **3 Escribe los contrarios.** |

Students write the opposite of the words and phrases.

Answers: 2 a la izquierda; 3 baja; 4 hace mal tiempo; 5 lejos; 6 tranquilo

Unit 4   Overview grid

Pages/Contexts/Cultural focus	Objectives	Grammar	Skills and Pronunciation	Key language	Framework	National Curriculum PoS	AT level
54–55 **4.1 Mi casa es…** Different houses	Describe your house Say where your house is	es and está	–	Mi casa es grande, pequeña, no muy grande, enorme y es antigua, moderna, histórica, nueva. Mi piso es grande, pequeño, no muy grande, enorme y es antiguo, moderno, histórico, nuevo Está en el centro de la ciudad, las afueras de la ciudad, el campo, las montañas, la costa, en un barrio Mi casa es adosada.	(L) 7S6 (R) 7W1, 7S9	1a, 1b, 1c, 2a, 2c, 2g, 3b, 3c, 3e, 4a, 5a, 5c, 5d, 5e, 5f, 5g, 5i	1.2–3, 2.2–3, 3.2–3, 4.2–4
56–57 **4.2 En mi dormitorio** Bedrooms	Describe your bedroom Say what there is in your bedroom Say where things are	de + el = del	Spanish pronunciation rules Small but useful words	un ordenador, una silla, unos pósters, un televisor, una alfombra, una lámpara, un espejo, una radio, un teléfono, unas estanterías delante, detrás, al lado, enfrente, en medio, a la izquierda, a la derecha, de, en	(R) 7W2, 7W6, 7S3, 7S4, 7L1	1a, 1c, 2a, 2b, 2c, 2d, 2f, 2g, 2h, 3c, 3e, 4a, 4c, 4d, 5a, 5c, 5d, 5e, 5f, 5g, 5i	1.3, 2.1–2, 3.2–3, 4.1–4
58–59 **4.3 Las habitaciones** Rooms	Say what rooms there are in your house Write a paragraph describing your house	'the' and 'a/an'	g, j and stress	la cocina, el dormitorio, el salón, el comedor, el cuarto de baño, el aseo, el despacho, las escaleras, el garaje, el jardín	(R) 7W4, 7L6	1a, 1b, 1c, 2a, 2b, 2f, 2g, 2h, 3a, 3c, 3e, 4a, 5a, 5c, 5d, 5e, 5f, 5g, 5i	1.1–2, 2.1–2, 3.2–3, 4.1–4
60–61 **Mi rutina diaria** Daily routine	Talk about your daily routine Say at what time you do something Understand reflexive verbs	Reflexive verbs Telling the time	–	Me despierto, me levanto, me ducho, me visto, me peino, desayuno, me lavo los dientes, salgo de casa. ¿A qué hora (te levantas)?	(R) 7S7, 7T1	1a, 1b, 1c, 2a, 2b, 2f, 2g, 2h, 3a, 3c, 3e, 4a, 5a, 5c, 5d, 5e, 5f, 5g, 5i	1.1, 2.2, 3.2–3, 4.3–4
62–63 **4.5 Entre amigos** Cave-houses in Huapoca and Guadix	–	–	–	–	(R) 7C3	1c, 2a, 2c, 2d, 2f, 2i, 3b, 3c, 3e, 4a, 4c, 4d 5d, 5e, 5g, 5h, 5i	1.4, 2.4, 3.4, 4.3–4

AMIGOS 1 UNIT 4 MEDIUM TERM PLAN

About this unit: In this unit students learn when to use *ser* and *estar* and learn about reflexive verbs in the present tense. They learn to talk about types of houses, rooms in a house and daily routine activities. Learning strategies are emphasised, in particular how to avoid repetition of 'there is…', and promoting awareness of Spanish words that are spelt the same as in English, but are pronounced differently.

Framework objectives (launch)	Teaching and learning	Week-by-week overview (assuming 6 weeks' work or approx. 10–12.5 hours)
7S6: compound sentences	Students learn to link two descriptions together, using *y*, e.g. *Mi casa es grande y es antigua.*	**Week 1**
7T4: use basic resources	Use *frases clave* to translate sentences into English	Describe your house and say where your house is; learn how to use *es* and *está*
7C2: aspects of everyday culture	Spanish estate agents	**Week 2**
Framework objectives (reinforce)	**Teaching and learning (additional)**	Describe a bedroom; say what there is in the bedroom and where things are in it; learn some high-frequency words and concentrate on correct pronunciation
7W1: everyday words	When to use *es* and *está*	**Week 3**
7W2: high-frequency words	*Hay, tengo, es, está, tiene, tenemos, mi/mis, un/una, el/la, los/las*	Say what rooms there are in the house and write a paragraph describing your house
7W4: gender and plural	*el/la* and *un/una*	**Week 4**
7W6: letters and sounds	Pronunciation traps with words that look the same as in English, but are pronounced differently (e.g. *radio*)	Talk about your daily routine; say at what time you do something; learn to use reflexive verbs; learn how to say what time it is
7S3: adapting sentences	Students write about Adam's bedroom, using the model on the page and the *Técnica* phrases	**Week 5**
7S4: simple questions	Ask questions with partner on what is in your room	Students apply the language and structures learnt in this unit to reading and answering questions on longer texts which focus on an aspect of Spanish or Latin American culture
7S7: time phrases and past and future events	Present tense reflexive verbs	**Week 6**
7S9: simple sentences for routine communication	Write a description of a dream house	Recycle language of the unit via *Uno, Dos* and *Lectura* pages; students check their progress via the *Ya sé…* self-assessment checklist in the Students' Book and on Hoja 60.
7T1: simple texts	Write a short text on a daily routine for yourself	
7L1: engage with sound patterns	Pronunciation of accented vowels; *j, ll* and vowels in words such as *radio*	
7L3: gist and some detail	Listen to the farmyard song and indicate when you hear a masculine or feminine word	
7L6: improve quality/fluency	Improve the quality of what you say: add more detail when describing your house to your partner	
7C3: authentic materials	Learn about unusual housing in Spain and Latin America	
	Teaching and learning (additional)	
	Spanish and Latin American housing	
	Daily routine	

En mi casa

Unit objectives

Contexts: types of house, rooms in a house, daily routine activities
Grammar: prepositions, reflexive verbs, *ser* and *estar*
Language learning: avoiding repetition of 'there is ...'
Pronunciation: avoiding traps with words that look as if they are pronounced the same as English words
Cultural focus: the Spanish day

Assessment opportunities

Speaking : SB, page 58, activity 4
Reading: SB, page 54, activity 4
Listening: SB, page 58, activity 3
Writing: SB, page 53, activity 2

AT3.1 | **1** Copia y rellena el cuadro.

Students copy the grid and decide where they would put each item. They complete the grid with the appropriate letters as in the example. Their answers may vary.

Answers: En mi dormitorio: a, c, d, e, f, g
En mi salón: a, b, e, f
En mi jardín: d

AT4.2 | **2** Escoge un lugar y escribe una lista de los artículos.

Students write a sentence about one of the places in exercise 1, as in the example.

AT2.2 | **3** Con tu compañero/a, haz un diálogo.

In pairs, students ask and answer about their bedrooms.

Planner

● ●

4.1 **Mi casa es ...** páginas 54–55

Objectives

▶ Describe your house

▶ Say where it is

Resources

Students' Book, pages 54–55
CD 2, tracks 1–2
Uno/Dos Workbooks, page 34

Key language

*Mi casa es grande, pequeña, no muy grande, enorme y es
antigua, moderna, histórica, nueva.*
*Mi piso es grande, pequeño, no muy grande, enorme y es
antiguo, moderno, histórico, nuevo.*
*Está en el centro de la ciudad, las afueras de la ciudad, el
campo, las montañas, la costa, en un barrio.*
Mi casa es adosada.

Programme of Study reference

1a, 1b, 1c, 2a, 2c, 2g, 3b, 3c, 3e, 4a, 5a, 5c, 5d, 5e, 5f, 5g, 5i

Framework reference

(L) 7S6, 7T4
(R) 7W1, 7S9, 7L3

● ●

¡A sus marcas!

Empareja las palabras opuestas.

Students use the pictures to help them find pairs of
opposites.

Answers: En la playa – En la ciudad; Grande – Pequeño;
Antiguo – Moderno; En la montaña – En el campo

AT3.2 | **1 Mira los dibujos y escoge las palabras apropiadas.**

Students choose the correct words to describe the houses
they see in the pictures.

Answers: See exercise 2.

AT1.2 | **2** Escucha y comprueba tus respuestas.

Students listen and check their answers.

Answers: a moderna, grande; b pequeña, antigua;
c moderno, grande

 CD 2, track 1 página 54, actividad 2

a – Mi casa es moderna, pero no está en la ciudad, está en
las montañas. Es una casa grande, entonces podemos ir
a esquiar con la familia.
b – Mi casa está en la costa. Es pequeña y antigua.
c – No vivo en una casa. Vivo en un piso. Es moderno, es
grande, y está en el centro de la ciudad.

AT2.2 | **3 Con tu compañero/a. Describe tu casa o tu piso.**

Ask students round the class to make a complete sentence
about their house or flat using the words in the table. Use
the opportunity to remind about gender agreement, asking
students why 'house' and 'flat' are in separate parts of the
table. Students then continue in pairs.

Zoom gramática

This section contrasts certain uses of *ser* and *estar* for the
first time. When you have discussed the box with the class,
ask students if they remember which was used most in
Unit 3, and why. See if they can remember any of the
direction language using *está*.

AT1.3 | **4 Look carefully at this page. Write a list of words that
go with *es* and those which go with *está*.**

Students make two lists of words.

Answers:
Words with *es*: *grande, pequeño/a, enorme, antiguo/a,
moderno/a, histórico/a, nuevo/a*
Words with *está*: *en (el centro/las afueras de la ciudad,
el campo, las montañas, la costa)*

AT3.3 | **5 Escucha la canción.**

Before playing the CD, divide the students into two groups.
One group puts their hand up when they hear masculine
words and the other group when they hear feminine words.

CD 2, track 2   página 55, actividad 5

A A A Vivo en una casa.
O O O Vivo en un piso.
A A A Vivo en una granja.
O O O Vivo en el zoo.

O O O Vivo en un piso.
O O O Vivo en un castillo.
O O O Vivo con mi primo.
O O O Vivo en el zoo.

El piso es moderno.
El castillo es antiguo.
Mi primo es un cocodrilo.
Vive en el zoo.

A A A Vivo en una casa,
A A A Una casa adosada.
A A A Vivo con mi prima.
A A A Vivo en una granja.

La casa es moderna.
La casa es antigua.
Mi prima es una vaca.
Vive en la granja.

 AT3.3

6 Empareja las descripciones de las casas con los dibujos.

Students read the descriptions a–e and match them with the pictures 1–5.

Answers: a 3; b 2; c 4; d 5; e 1

Reto

AT 4.3/4

Diseña una casa incorporando los deseos de toda la familia. Escribe una descripción.

Ask students to look back at descriptions c, d and e in exercise 6. Make a class list on the board: what type of house is important for each family member? Students plan a house that matches as many of the family's views as possible. They describe it using language from this double-page spread.

Planner

●●●●●●●●●●●●●●●●●●●●●●●●

4.2 **En mi dormitorio**   páginas 56–57

Objectives

▶ Describe your bedroom

▶ Say what there is in your bedroom

▶ Say where things are

Resources

Students' Book, pages 56–57
CD 2, tracks 3–5
Uno/Dos Workbooks, page 35

Key language

un ordenador, una silla, unos pósters, un televisor, una alfombra, una lámpara, un espejo, una radio, un teléfono, unas estanterías
delante (de), detrás (de), al lado (de), enfrente (de), en medio (de)
a la izquierda, a la derecha
en

Programme of Study reference

1a, 1c, 2a, 2b, 2c, 2d, 2f, 2g, 2h, 3c, 3e, 4a, 4c, 4d, 5a, 5c, 5d, 5e, 5f, 5g, 5i

Framework reference

(R) 7W2, 7W6, 7S3, 7S4, 7L1

●●●●●●●●●●●●●●●●●●●●●●●●

¡A sus marcas!

Lee en voz alta. Escucha y compara tu pronunciación.

Students practise reading the words and then compare with the CD.

 CD 2, track 3   página 56, ¡A sus marcas!

un ordenador
una silla
unos pósters
un televisor
una alfombra
una lámpara
un espejo
una radio
un teléfono
unas estanterías

AT1.1 **1 Copia y rellena el cuadro con las palabras.**

Students copy and complete the table with the words given underneath. They work out or find the meaning and then tick the appropriate column.

Answers: Answers will vary but the following word should be in the *Vocabulario en el libro* column: *una mesa.*

The translations are: a table, a wardrobe, some curtains, a collection of plastic dinosaurs, a window, a door, a wall, dirty clothes, some books.

Se pronuncia así

This section reminds students to use Spanish pronunciation even when a word looks very like English. In particular, it covers stressed syllables which may be different, Spanish vowel sounds and the consonants *j* and *ll*.

AT2.1 **2 Practise saying these words. Then listen and check your pronunciation.**

Students practise saying the words bearing in mind the advice in the box. They then listen and check with the CD.

 CD 2, track 4   página 56, actividad 2

lámpara ... lámpara
teléfono ... teléfono
radio ... radio
espejo ... espejo
silla ... silla

AT1.3 **3 Escucha y mira el dibujo. Descubre los dos errores.**

Students listen to Raquel describing her bedroom and look at the picture. They note down two mistakes.

Answers: No hay una foto.
Hay ropa sucia.

 CD 2, track 5   página 56, actividad 3

– Hay una puerta, y una ventana. Hay unas cortinas. Hay unos libros y una cama. Hay una mesa. Hay un espejo y una foto. Hay un televisor. Hay una alfombra. No hay ropa sucia.

AT2.2 **4 Con tu compañero/a. ¿Qué hay? ¿Qué no hay?**

Use the model dialogue to remind the students about forming the negative in Spanish. In pairs, students then continue describing what is and isn't in Raquel's room. After a few minutes, tell them to swap roles so that everyone practises both the positive and the negative.

Zoom gramática

This reminds students that 'de' means 'of' and that when you want to say 'of the', 'de + el' changes to 'del'.

AT3.3 **5 Use the *frases clave* to translate these sentences into English.**

Students translate sentences a–c into English and sentences d–e into Spanish.
The students met a number of these prepositions in Unit 3. With a higher level group, you could ask the students to try doing this with their books closed, building up the translations on the board.

Answers:

a In front of the computer there is a photo.
b Next to the photo there is a phone.
c In the middle of the bed there are some books.
d Enfrente de la cama hay una puerta.
e Detrás del ordenador hay una radio.

AT2.2 **6 Con tu compañero/a, describe una de estas habitaciones.**

In pairs, students choose one of the bedrooms and build up a description of it. If there is time, put pairs of students working on the same bedroom together in groups of 4 to compare their ideas.

AT3.2 **7 Lee. ¿Cuál dormitorio es?**

Students read Adam's description and identify which of the rooms in exercise 6 is his bedroom in England.

Answers: The bedroom on the left (a).

Técnica

This section reminds students of the everyday words they have learnt so far and relates to Framework objective 7W2. Discuss the list with the class and make sure that everyone understands how the words are used. Remind them in particular about the use of *hay* for both singular and plural.

Reto

AT 4.3/4 Describe el otro dormitorio de Adam.

Students describe Adam's bedroom in Spain. They can use the words in the *Técnica* box to help them. They will also find ideas in the model in exercise 7, but remind them to be careful about verb forms, using *tiene* not *tengo* as they are describing Adam's room, not their own.

Answers: Hay una ventana y un armario blanco. Tiene una mesa y una collección de revistas de coches. Hay ropa sucia. A la izquierda de la cama hay una alfombra roja. A la derecha del armario hay una mesa con una lampara y un telvisor.

Planner

● ● ● ● ● ● ● ● ● ● ● ● ● ● ● ● ● ● ● ●

4.3   **Las habitaciones**   páginas 58–59

Objectives

▶ Say what rooms there are in your house

▶ Write a paragraph describing your house

Resources

Students' Book, pages 58–59
CD 2, tracks 6–8
Uno/Dos Workbooks, page 36

Key language

*la cocina, el dormitorio, el salón, el comedor, el cuarto de baño,
el aseo, el despacho, las escaleras, el garaje, el jardín
la planta baja, el primer/segundo/tercer piso*

Programme of Study reference

1a, 1b, 1c, 2a, 2b, 2f, 2g, 2h, 3a, 3c, 3e, 4a, 5a, 5c, 5d, 5e,
5f, 5g, 5i

Framework reference

(R) 7W4, 7L6

● ● ● ● ● ● ● ● ● ● ● ● ● ● ● ● ● ● ● ●

¡A sus marcas!

**Escucha y pon un dedo sobre cada habitación
mencionada.**

Students play finger twister. They listen and put a finger on
each room as they hear it on the CD, but they mustn't
move their fingers off a picture once they have touched it.

 CD 2, track 6   página 58, ¡A sus marcas!

– ¿Listos? Empezamos:
  el dormitorio
  el garaje
  el cuarto de baño
  ¡No muevas los dedos!
  el aseo
  el despacho
  Ahora con dos manos:
  la cocina
  el salón
  el comedor
  las escaleras
  Y el último dedo:
  el jardín

AT2.1   **1** Con tu compañero/a, haz el mismo juego.

In pairs, students play finger twister. You may like to check
the pronunciation of the new vocabulary before they start.

Se pronuncia así

This section reminds students of some of the sound and
spelling rules in Spanish, in particular the pronunciation of
g and *j*. These letters work in the same way as c and *z* in
that g is used where it can be and *j* where it must be.

AT1.1   **2 Try to pronounce this sentence, then check with the
recording.**

Students practise saying the sentence, then listen and
check with the CD.

 CD 2, track 7   página 58, actividad 2

El garaje está en el jardín, pero el baño no está en la cocina.

Zoom gramática

This section reminds students about article use and relates
to Framework objective 7W4. Point out that, in this
particular context, Spanish uses 'a' and 'the' in the same
way as we do in English, but that as the students learn
more Spanish, they will come across some differences.

AT1.2   **3 Escucha (1–4). Identifica la casa.**

Students listen and match the descriptions 1–4 with the
pictures a–d.

Answers: 1 b; 2a; 3d; 4c

 CD 2, track 8   página 58, actividad 3

1 – En la casa hay un cuarto de baño, dos dormitorios, un
     salón, una cocina y un despacho.
2 – En la casa hay un dormitorio grande con un área para la
     cocina. No hay salón. Hay un cuarto de baño pequeño.
3 – La casa tiene un jardín, tres dormitorios, un salón, un
     comedor, la cocina y un cuarto de baño. También hay un
     aseo.
4 – Hay un jardín, dos dormitorios, una cocina, un cuarto de
     baño, y un salón.

AT2.2   **4** Con tu compañero/a, describe e identifica una de las
casas.

In pairs, students take it in turns to describe one of the
houses in the pictures for their partner to identify.

AT3.3 | **5** Mira el dibujo y organiza el texto.

Ask students to look at the picture while you read the first sentence of the description aloud. Students identify the mistakes. Ask them to rewrite the paragraph correctly. You may find it helpful to prepare the corrected version of the text as an overhead or on a projector for students to check.

Answers:

En la planta baja hay una cocina y un comedor. En el primer piso hay un cuarto de baño y un salón. En el segundo piso hay dos dormitorios. En el tercer piso hay un dormitorio grande y un aseo.

AT3.2 | **6** Busca las seis diferencias en los textos a y b.

Ask students to find the six differences between the two texts. In a less confident class, you may need to point out that the differences are in the way things are described, not that the houses are different. When the students have found the differences, they make a list of alternatives to repeating *hay*. You may like to point out that *donde* does not need an accent here because it is not asking a question.

Answers:

En mi casa hay – Vivo en una casa con
Hay un comedor – Tiene un comedor
Hay un salón grande – El salón es grande
Hay un jardín – Tengo un jardín
y hay una piscina – donde hay una piscina
Hay un cuarto de baño – Tenemos un cuarto de baño

AT 4.3/4 | **7** Describe tu propia casa. Evita la repetición.

Students write a description of their house. They use the list of phrases that they made in exercise 6. Students who need more support could follow the model of text b in exercise 6; stronger students can be encouraged to construct their own paragraph.

Reto

AT4.3 | Subraya o haz resaltar los aspectos mejores de tu descripción.

Students underline the phrases in the description that make their text more sophisticated.

Planner

••••••••••••••••••••••••••••

4.4 **Mi rutina diaria**   páginas 60–61

Objectives

▶ Talk about your daily routine

▶ Say at what time you do something

▶ Understand reflexive verbs

Resources

Students' Book, pages 60–61
CD 2, tracks 9–10
Uno/Dos Workbooks, page 37

Key language

¿A qué hora…? A las…
Me levanto, Me ducho, Me visto, Me despierto, Me lavo los dientes, Me peino
Desayuno, Salgo de casa, Voy al instituto, Estudio, Hablo con, Como, Nado

Programme of Study reference

1a, 1b, 1c, 2a, 2b, 2f, 2g, 2h, 3a, 3c, 3e, 4a, 5a, 5c, 5d, 5e, 5f, 5g, 5i

Framework reference

(R) 7S7, 7T1

•••••••••••••••••••••••••••

¡A sus marcas!

Escucha (1–5). Escribe las letras en el orden de los ruidos.

Students listen to the sound effects and look at the pictures a–j. They note down the correct letters according to the actions they hear.

Answers: a; f; g; c; h

CD 2, track 9   página 60, ¡A sus marcas!

1 FX of alarm clock and someone yawning
2 FX of someone eating breakfast
3 FX of someone cleaning their teeth
4 FX of shower
5 FX of closing front door and leaving the house

AT1.1 **1 Escucha el día y nota el error.**

Students listen to the sequence of daily routine activities and identify what is wrong. You may need to play the CD twice so that the students become more familiar with the new verbs.

Answer: *Me ducho* comes too late in the sequence – you get dressed before you have a shower.

CD 2, track 10   página 60, actividad 1

– Me despierto. Me levanto. Me peino. Me visto. Desayuno. Me lavo los dientes. Me ducho. Salgo de casa.

AT3.2 **2 Lee estos anagramas.**

Students work out the anagrams. Once they have solved them, they put them in the correct order to make a possible morning routine.

Answers: Me despierto; Desayuno; Me lavo los dientes; Me ducho; Me visto; Salgo de casa

Zoom gramática

This section introduces reflexive verbs. If students have studied some French, the concept may be familiar to them. If not, discuss with the class that these are actions that you do to yourself. Students have already met *Me llamo*, but the new verbs presented here are probably easier to explain the concept: washing yourself, brushing your teeth, etc.

AT3.2 **3 Copy and complete this table.**

Students copy and complete the table with the Spanish phrases, the literal meaning and the normal English expression.

Answers:

		I get up
me visto	I dress myself	
me peino		I brush/comb my hair
me ducho	I shower myself	

AT3.2 **4 Translate these into English.**

Look at the note about *me llamo* etc. with the students to remind them of the other reflexive forms that they have met. Students then translate the verb forms.

Answers: a you have a wash; b you wake up; c you have a shower; d he/she gets dressed or you (usted) get dressed; e he/she gets up or you (usted) get up; f he/she brushes/combs his/her hair or you (usted) brush/comb your hair

Zoom gramática

This section introduces simple clock times (*a las* / *a la* = 'o'clock'). Students meet all the clock times in 6.3. You could play clock bingo to revise the numbers and practise the new language. Students draw six clock faces showing different 'o'clock' times and cross them out as you call out routine verbs and times in a random order e.g. *Me despierto a las siete*.

AT4.3 **5 Find all the times on this page. Say what each time means in English.**

Students make a list of all the times in exercises 6–Reto and note the English equivalent.

Answers:
a las siete – at seven o'clock
a las ocho – at eight o'clock
a las once – at eleven o'clock
a las nueve – at nine o'clock
a las diez – at ten o'clock
a las doce – at twelve o'clock
a la una – at one o'clock

AT3.2 **6 Con tu compañero/a, lee la entrevista.**

Model the dialogue first with a confident student reading the answers to your questions. Remind students that *h* is silent (*¿A qué hora?*). In pairs, students then practise reading the interview. Tell them to swap roles once they have read it once.

AT2.2 **7 Lee y compara con la entrevista. Hay un error.**

Students read the text and compare it with the interview in exercise 6. They call out the mistake.

Answer: Fátima gets dressed at eight o'clock (after her shower), not at nine o'clock.

AT3.2 **8 Con tu compañero/a, lee las frases. ¿Qué significan en inglés?**

In pairs, students take it in turns to read out the sentences for their partner to give the meaning. As class feedback, you may like to discuss that we can't always translate word-for-word, and that for *hablo con*, we would usually say 'speak to' rather than 'speak with'.

Answers:
I have cereal for breakfast at seven o'clock.
I go to school on the bus at eight o'clock.
I study Spanish at nine o'clock.
I speak to the teacher at ten o'clock.
I eat sandwiches at twelve o'clock.
I swim in the swimming pool at one o'clock.

Reto

AT 4.3/4 **Escribe una rutina diaria imposible de hacer. Mezcla las frases de arriba. Haz dibujos.**

Students make up nonsense sentences as in the example and draw a picture to illustrate the meaning.

Planner

● ●

4.5 ## Entre amigos: Casa normales, casas extraordinarias *páginas 62–63*

Resources
Students' Book, pages 62–63
CD 2, track 11
Uno/Dos Workbooks, page 38

Programme of Study reference
1c, 2a, 2c, 2d, 2f, 2i, 3b, 3c, 3e, 4a, 4c, 4d, 5d, 5e, 5g, 5h, 5i

Framework reference
(L) 7C2
(R) 7C3

● ●

AT1.4 | **1** Escucha y lee el artículo sobre las casas-cueva.

Students listen to and read the article about cave dwellings.

 CD 2, track 11 *página 62, actividad 1*

Vivir en una cueva. ¿Una casa prehistórica, o una casa moderna?
Huapoca
En el Cañón de Huapoca en el norte de Méjico están las casas-cueva de 'Cuarenta Casas' y 'Cueva Grande'. Tienen 800 años. Hoy están en ruinas. Es un importante sitio arqueológico, pero no es una atracción turística. Es una región muy remota y no hay transporte.
Las casas están cerca de un río, en una cueva detrás de una cascada de agua. Hay paredes grandes con puertas y ventanas. En el río hay una piscina natural. Es un sitio mágico para vivir.
Guadix
En Guadix, en las montañas cerca de la ciudad de Granada en el sur de España, hay casas-cueva. La diferencia es que hay familias que viven en las casas-cueva de Guadix.
Típicamente al exterior es una casa normal, con ventanas y puerta. Pero las habitaciones de la casa están dentro de la cueva. Son casas modernas, con cuarto de baño, dormitorios, cocina, salón y tienen televisión, teléfono, como una casa normal.
Son un atractivo para los turistas. Una de las casas es un hotel: ¡una cueva con jacuzzi, piscina, sala de conferencias y acceso para discapacitados!
Las casas tienen 500 años. Son tradicionales, pero prácticas porque tienen una temperatura constante de 19 grados: perfecto durante el calor de agosto y aceptable durante el frío de diciembre.

AT3.4 | **2** Answer the questions. Is it Huapoca (H), Guadix (G) or both?

Students answer the questions using H, G or 'both'.

Answers: a H; b G; c G; d H; e G; f H; g H; h G; i G; j H; k G; l H; m both; n H

AT3.4 | **3** Which cave houses would you like to live in and why? Explain in English, using information from page **64**.

Students decide which of the cave houses they prefer and give their reasons.

Answers: Students' own answers

AT4.3 | **4** Copia esta descripción. Cambia las palabras en negrita por dibujos.

Students write out the description replacing the words in bold with a drawing or symbol.

AT2.4 | **5** Mira tu versión con palabras y dibujos. Lee a tu compañero/a.

In pairs, students read the description to their partner from their word and picture version. If time is short, they could take in turns to read sentences.

AT4.4 | **6** Escribe una descripción similar de tu casa.

Students write a description of where they live, similar to the description in exercise 4.

Repaso *página 64*

Resources
Students' Book, page 64

Programme of Study reference
1c, 2a, 2c, 2f, 3b, 3c, 3e, 4a, 4c, 5d, 5e, 5f, 5g, 5h, 5i

AT2.2 | **1** Con tu compañero/a, haz un diálogo. Utiliza el diagrama.

Model the dialogue with a confident student. In pairs, students then take it in turns to interview their partner. They use the model questions and follow the flowchart.

AT4.3 | **2** Utiliza el diagrama y escribe una descripción de una casa.

Students write a description of the house they chose using the words in the flowchart.

Answers: Students' own answers

AT4.3 | **3** Haz un diagrama para encontrar el dormitorio ideal de tu compañero/a.

You may want to pool a class list of ideas about bedrooms on the board before students plan their own flowchart. Make sure that they understand that they need to have two options at each point.

Vocabulario
página 65

This page provides a theme-based Spanish–English summary of the key language of this unit. It can be used for reference throughout the unit or as an aid to learning vocabulary.

C59 | Copymaster 59 contains a summary of the key language of the unit and can be given to the students at this point to help with revision.

W41 | Page 41 of the *Uno/Dos* Workbooks also provides a summary of the key language of the unit.

Ya sé
página 66

The *Ya sé* page provides an end-of-unit checklist of learning objectives. At the foot of the page are activities at three levels of difficulty to extend the work of the unit. Encourage students to select an activity at the most appropriate level.

C60 | Copymaster 60 contains a checklist and activities to keep track of the students' progress.

W42 | Page 42 of the *Uno/Dos* Workbooks gives an end-of-unit checklist in Spanish and English, together with activities to keep track of the students' progress.

Unidad 4 Uno
página 102

Objectives
This reinforcement page is intended for those students who need further practice of core language of the unit. It can be used by students who finish other activities early or as alternative class or homework material.

Resources
Students' Book, page 102
CD 2, track 12

Programme of Study reference
1c, 2a, 2c, 2h, 2i, 3b, 3c, 3e, 4a, 4c, 5a, 5c, 5d, 5e, 5f, 5g, 5i

AT1.2 | **1** ¡A contrarreloj! Una persona dice el inglés. La otra dice el español.

Students work in pairs. They test each other against the clock by one saying the word in English, and the other replying with the Spanish word.

AT3.2 | **2** Pon las palabras en orden.

Students re-order the words to make sentences.

Answers: b Es una casa grande. c Está en el centro de la ciudad. d En mi casa hay dos dormitorios. e Hay un salón y una cocina. f Me gusta mi dormitorio. g Tengo un ordenador en mi dormitorio.

AT2.2 | **3** Escoge adjetivos para describir una casa. Tu compañero/a tiene que adivinar qué dibujo es.

Students work in pairs. One says different adjectives in Spanish until the other guesses which picture they are describing.

AT1.2 | **4** Escucha y apunta la hora para cada actividad.

Students listen and write down the correct time for activities a–g.

Answers: b 8.00; c 9.00; d 10.00; e 2.00; f 4.00; g 10.00

 CD 2, track 12   página 102, actividad 4

a – Me levanto a las siete.
b – Desayuno a las ocho.
c – Veo el fútbol en la televisión a las nueve.
d – Voy al parque a las diez.
e – Como a las dos.
f – Voy al cine a las cuatro.
g – Me acuesto a las diez.

Unidad 4 Dos
página 103

Objectives
This extension page is intended for more able students who are confident with the core language of the unit. It can be used by students who finish other activities quickly or as alternative class or homework material.

Resources
Students' Book, page 103
CD 2, track 13

Programme of Study reference
1c, 2a, 2c, 2f, 3b, 3c, 3e, 4a, 5a, 5d, 5e, 5g, 5i

AT1.3 **1** Escucha y contesta a las preguntas.

Students listen and note down the answers to questions a–f.

Answers: a un piso; b antiguo; c en la costa; d ocho; e sí; f porque está cerca de la costa

CD 2, track 13   página 103, actividad 1

- ¿Vives en una casa o en un piso?
- Vivo en un piso.
- ¿Es moderno o antiguo?
- Es un piso bastante antiguo.
- ¿Dónde está?
- Está en la costa.
- ¿Cuántas habitaciones tiene?
- Tiene ocho habitaciones: la cocina, el salón, dos cuartos de baño, el comedor, y tres dormitorios.
- ¿Te gusta vivir en tu piso?
- Sí, porque está cerca de la costa, y me gusta mucho ir a la playa.

AT4.4 **2** Prepara seis preguntas para tu compañero/a. ¿Cuales son las preguntas que tienes que modificar?

Students prepare six questions like the ones in exercise 1 to ask their partner. They will have to modify some from third to second person.

Answers: a ¿Vives en una casa o en un piso? e ¿Te gusta vivir allí?

AT2.4 **3** Entrevista a tu compañero/a sobre su casa o piso.

Students work in pairs. They use their prepared questions to interview their partner about where they live.

AT3.4 **4** ¿Quién vive en esta casa?

Students read the three texts to decide which person lives in the house described in the list in English.
Answer: Rafa

Unidad 4 Lectura: uno   página 114

Objectives

This page is to encourage independent reading. Students should attempt it once they are confident with the core language of the unit. It can be used by students who finish other activities early or as alternative class or homework material.

Resources

Students' Book, page 114
CD 2, track 14

Programme of Study reference

1c, 2a, 2c, 2d, 2i, 3b, 3c, 3e, 4a, 5a, 5e, 5f, 5g, 5i

AT3.2 **1** Completa las frases con la palabra correcta. Copia y completa el crucigrama.

Students complete the sentences with the correct word from the choice at the end of the exercise. They then copy out and fill in the crossword using the words from the completed sentences.

Answers: a casa; b familia; c dormitorios; d jardín; e ciudad

AT3.3 **2** Decide cuál es el artículo que no debe de estar en la habitación.

Students read the statements about the contents of the different rooms and decide which item does not belong in each one.

Answers: a cama; b armario; c mi ropa sucia; d bicicleta; e ordenador

AT1.2 **3** Escucha y lee. Sigue las líneas. ¿Cuáles de las descripciones son falsas?

Students listen to and read the descriptions. They follow the lines to the pictures and decide which descriptions are incorrect.

Answers: 1 M; 2 M; 3 V; 4 M

CD 2, track 14   página 114, actividad 3

1 – Una casa cerca de la costa, con jardín. No tiene garaje.
2 – Un piso en el centro de la ciudad con balcón.
3 – Una casa pequeña en el campo, con una piscina y un jardín grande.
4 – Una casa antigua y grande. No tiene jardín. Está en las montañas.

Unidad 4 Lectura: dos   página 115

Objectives

This page is to encourage independent reading. Students should attempt it once they are confident with the core language of the unit. It can be used by students who finish other activities early or as alternative class or homework material.

Resources

Students' Book, page 115

Programme of Study reference

1c, 2a, 2c, 2d, 2i, 3b, 3c, 3e, 4a, 5a, 5e, 5f, 5g, 5i

AT3.3 **1 Contesta al sondeo.**

Students read and complete the survey for themselves.

AT3.4 **2 Lee y contesta al sondeo para Mateo y Deepa.**

Students read the texts about Mateo and Deepa and complete the survey again for each of these two people.

Answers: Mateo 1 c; 2 a; 3 a; 4 c; 5 b / c; 6 b; Deepa 1 a; 2 c; 3 d; 4 a; 5 c; 6 a

Copymasters

Hoja 61 ¡A sus marcas!

This can be used after pages 54–55 in the Students' Book.

AT2.1 **1 El profesor o una pareja lee las palabras de la lista. Tienes que tocar rápidamente la zona correcta. ¿Cuántos puedes hacer sin errors en un minuto?**

You may want to play the game first as a whole class, with you reading out the words for the students to hit the correct shape according to the number and gender of the words. If there is time, students can then continue in pairs, timing themselves for a minute each.

Answers:
el: piso; salón; dormitorio; jardín; televisor; comedor; ordenador; hamster; sofá; teléfono
la: casa; cocina; lámpara; mesa; radio; alfombra; cama; ducha; foto
los: posters
las: escaleras; flores; sillas; estanterías; cortinas

AT3.2 **2 Conecta las palabras para formar una frase y hacer un dibujo.**

Students join the words to make a sentence using grammatically logical word order.

Answers: Vivo en una casa antigua cerca de la costa. (The shape revealed is a house.)

Hoja 62 Reto

This can be used after pages 54–55 in the Students' Book.

AT 3.2/3 **1 Haz corresponder las respuestas con las preguntas.**

Students match the questions and the answers.

Answers: 2 b; 3 d; 4 a; 5 c; 6 g; 7 e

2 Lee y señala los puntos que ya entiendes. Escoge los tres más importantes.

Students tick the points that they understand and complete the Olympic podium with the three that they feel are most important. (There is no correct answer for this activity, but you could invite class discussion about which points students feel are most useful to them.)

Hoja 63 Escuchar: uno

This can be used after pages 54–55 in the Students' Book.

AT 1.2/3 **1 Escucha sin tomar notas. Completa la canción con las palabras de los cuadros. Escucha y verifica tus respuestas.**

Students listen again to the song, but with pens down. They then complete it using the words in the boxes.

Answers:
casa; piso; granja; zoo
piso; castillo; zoo
moderno; antiguo
moderna; antigua

 CD 3, track 34   Hoja 63, actividad 1

A A A Vivo en una casa.
O O O Vivo en un piso.
A A A Vivo en una granja.
O O O Vivo en el zoo.

O O O Vivo en un piso.
O O O Vivo en un castillo.
O O O Vivo con mi primo.
O O O Vivo en el zoo.

El piso es moderno.
El castillo es antiguo.
Mi primo es un cocodrilo.
Vive en el zoo.

A A A Vivo en una casa,
A A A Una casa adosada.
A A A Vivo con mi prima.
A A A Vivo en una granja.

La casa es moderna.
La granja es antigua.
Mi prima es una vaca.
Vive en la granja.

Hoja 63 Escuchar: dos

AT1.3 **2 Escucha y pon una señal junto a los muebles que hay en el dormitorio.**

Students listen and tick the items round the side of the main picture if the recording mentions that they are in the bedroom.

Answers: table; computer; bookcase; television; posters; window; carpet; dirty washing

 CD 3, track 35　　　　　　　Hoja 63, actividad 2

– Esa es mi habitación. Al lado de mi cama, a la derecha, tengo una mesa. En la mesa está mi ordenador. A la izquierda, al otro lado de mi cama, tengo mis libros en una estantería. Enfrente de mi cama tengo mi televisor, así que puedo ver la televisión desde mi cama. En la pared detrás del televisor tengo dos pósteres de Madonna. La ventana en mi dormitorio está enfrente de la puerta. Hay una alfombra en medio de la habitación. La ropa sucia está debajo de la ventana.

Hoja 64 Hablar: uno

This can be used after pages 54–55 in the Students' Book.

AT 2.2/3 **1** Haz preguntas a tu compañero/a.

2 Responde a las preguntas de tu compañero/a.

In pairs, students ask and answer the questions about where they live.

Hoja 64 Hablar: dos

AT 2.3/4 **3a** Explica la rutina diaria a tu compañero/a.

3b Haz preguntas a tu compañero/a.

Students working at a higher level describe the daily routines shown in the pictures.

Hoja 65 Leer y escribir: uno

This can be used after pages 58–59 in the Students' Book.

AT4.1 **1** Mira los dibujos y escribe la palabra correcta para descubrir un mensaje secreto.

Students complete the puzzle with the correct words according to the pictures and read down the highlighted boxes to find the secret message.

Answers:

d	o	r	m	i	t	o	r	i	o		
c	o	c	i	n	a						
		c	u	a	r	t	o	d	e	b	a	ñ	o
		s	a	l	ó	n					
d	e	s	p	a	c	h	o				
		a	s	e	o						

The secret message is: mi casa.

AT3.3 **2** Utiliza las palabras para completar esas frases.

Students complete the sentences using the words from exercise 1.

Answers: a dormitorio; b cuarto de baño; c salón; d despacho; e cocina

AT 3.3/4 **3a** Mira el dibujo. Lee y subraya donde hay errors en la descripción.

Students look at the picture and underline the mistakes in the description.

Answers: See 3b.

AT4.3 **3b** Ahora escribe una descripción correcta.

Students write a corrected description of the house in 3a.

Answers:
Vivo en una casa **grande** en la costa. **Hay un** jardín pero **no** hay (un) garaje. Es una casa **moderna**.

Hoja 66 Leer y escribir: dos

This can be used after pages 56–57 in the Students' Book.

AT3.4 **1** Mira el plano del dormitorio. Corrige la puntuación de la descripción.

Students correct the punctuation in the description, using the picture to help them follow the sense.

Answers: Mi dormitorio tiene una cama en medio. Hay una mesa a la derecha. Hay una lámpara a la izquierda. Tengo una alfombra. En la alfombra hay unos libros. En la cama está mi gato.

AT3.3 **2** Completa las frases para describir tu casa ideal.

Students circle the words they prefer to make up a description of their ideal house. Ask volunteers to read their descriptions out for the class. If there is time, you could work out as a class if anyone has chosen exactly the same type of house.

AT 4.3/4 **3** Imagine y describe la casa de los Beckham o de Penélope Cruz.

Students write an imaginary piece about the Beckhams' house or Penélope Cruz's house. Depending on the students' interests, you may want to allow them to choose a different celebrity and the class could then be asked to guess whose house it is.

Hoja 67 Gramática

This can be used after pages 56–57 in the Students' Book.

AT3.3

1 Decide if it is normal or ridiculous.

Discuss the first ¡Recuerda! box with the class. Students then read and decide whether the sentences are normal or ridiculous.

Answers: 1 ✓; 2 ✓; 3 !; 4 !; 5 !; 6 ✓; 7 !; 8 ✓

AT4.2

2 Complete the answers to the questions.

Look at the ¡Recuerda! box with the students. They then complete the answers with the correct reflexive pronoun.

Answers: a me despierto; b me levanto; c me ducho; d me visto; e me lavo los dientes; f me acuesto

Hoja 68 Técnica

This can be used after pages 58–59 in the Students' Book.

AT3.1

1 Underline the word hay every time it appears.

Read the note with the class and then ask them to underline every instance of hay.

Answers: <u>Hay</u> una cocina. En la cocina <u>hay</u> una mesa. <u>Hay</u> un salón. En el salón <u>hay</u> un televisor.

AT3.3

2 Read the sentences and put them in the right category in the table.

Discuss the second ¡Recuerda! box with the class. The students then think about the function of each sentence and complete the table with the letters in the correct columns.

Answers:
Describe it: a, e
Say where: c, h
Say what: b
Use *with*: d
Use *have*: f, g

AT 4.3/4

3 Describe this house without repeating hay.

Students write a description of the house in the picture using the various ways of avoiding repetition that they have studied. Answers will vary, but you may want to prepare the sample answer, or your own, as an overhead or on the projector.

Answers: Vivo en una casa grande con un jardín. El garaje está a la izquierda de la casa. Hay una cocina, un comedor y un salón donde veo la televisión. La casa tiene tres dormitorios y el cuarto de baño está al lado de mi dormitorio.

AT4.4

4 Read the description, then write a better one; avoid repeating hay.

Students write a more sophisticated paragraph avoiding repetition. Again, answers will vary, but you may want to prepare the sample answer, or your own, as an overhead or on the projector.

Answers:
Mi pueblo es bastante grande, con muchas casas y tiendas, y tiene tres supermercados también. Hay dos colegios. Mi colegio está cerca del parque, y el parque está al lado del río. Puedo ir al cine con mis amigos pero mi pueblo no tiene (un) teatro.

Hoja 69 Cultura

This can be used after pages 62–63 in the Students' Book.

AT 3.2/3

1 Read the English and the Spanish texts. Find the Spanish for the words below.

Students use the parallel texts to find the meanings of the new words.

Answers: open-air = al aire libre; typical houses = casas típicas; palaces = palacios; towers = torres; streets = calles; in the South of Spain = en el sur de España; a white front = la fachada blanca; small windows = ventanas pequeñas; narrow = estrecho/a; shade = sombra
Note: If students ask about *la fachada*, you can explain that it is similar to personal description: 'tienen <u>la</u> piel blanca'. The Spanish text says literally 'the houses have <u>the</u> front white' but in English we would say 'a white front'. Use any discussion to remind students that we cannot always translate word-for-word.

Hoja 70 Se pronuncia así

This can be used after pages 56–57 in the Students' Book.

AT3.1

1 Underline the parts of these Spanish words that may contain traps. If you have colours, use red for very dangerous, orange for medium danger, and yellow for warning.

Students think about the possible pronunciation problems in each word and mark them, following the colour scheme suggested.
In going over the exercise, remember to stress the correct pronunciation, not what the students might be getting wrong. The answers below give the pronunciation reminders that are specific to each word, but it is always useful to remind students about the short vowels of Spanish and that a single written vowel never sounds like an English diphthong, (e.g. the o in *hotel* is not the same as in English).

Answers:

parque: sounding the 'r', -que

hospital: silent 'h', stress on the final syllable

hotel: silent 'h'

televisión: 'v' like a 'b', 's' not as in the English equivalent, stress on the final syllable

lámpara: no real problem, but remind about stress and short vowels

piano: no real problem, but remind about short final 'o'

violín: 'v' like a 'b', short 'i' sound at the beginning not as in the English equivalent

garaje: stress on the middle syllable, sound of 'j'

jardín: sound of 'j', stress on the final syllable

radio: short 'a' sound, not as in the English equivalent

teléfono: stress on the second syllable where the 'e' sound is stronger than in the English equivalent, short 'o' sounds

profesor: stress on the final syllable, all vowel sounds short and strong (not weak as is the last syllable of English *professor*)

baño: sound of 'ñ', short final 'o'

salón: stress on the final syllable

 2 Listen and decide if the words in exercise 1 are being said in Spanish or in English. Tick the ones that are pronounced correctly in Spanish.

Students listen and tick the Spanish words.

Answers: See transcript.

> 🎧 **CD 3, track 36** Hoja 70, actividad 2
>
> parque (Sp) ... hospital ... hotel (Sp) ... television ... lámpara (Sp) ... piano ... violín (Sp) ... garaje (Sp) ... jardín (Sp) ... radio ... teléfono (Sp) ... professor ... baño (Sp) ... salon

 3 Practise pronouncing the words below correctly with a partner. Then listen and compare your pronunciation with the recording.

Students practise saying the Spanish words correctly and then listen and check.

> 🎧 **CD 3, track 37** Hoja 70, actividad 3
>
> parque ... hospital ... hotel ... televisión ... lámpara ... piano ... violín ... garaje ... jardín ... radio ... teléfono ... profesor ... baño ... salón

Control Unidad 4

Resources

Copymasters 71–76
CD 3, tracks 38–41

Hoja 71 Escuchar: uno

 1 Escucha y pon en el orden correcto.

Students listen and number the pictures 1–5

Answers: a 4; b 3; c 5; d 1; e 2

Mark scheme:
Students who attempt *uno* only: 3 marks for each correct answer = 15 marks
Students who attempt *uno* and *dos*: 1 mark for each correct answer = 5 marks

Assessment criteria: Students who number four or five correctly show evidence of performance at AT 1.2.

> 🎧 **CD 3, track 38** Hoja 71, actividad 1
>
> 1 – Este es mi piso. Vivo en la ciudad.
> 2 – Este es mi dormitorio. Vivo con mi familia.
> 3 – Tengo una casa moderna en el campo.
> 4 – Vivo cerca del mar en una casa antigua.
> 5 – Tengo una casa grande con un jardín.

 2 Escucha y completa las frases.

Students listen and complete the sentences.

Answers: a pequeña; b tres; c jardín; d grande; 5 salón

Mark scheme: Students who attempt *uno* only: 2 marks for each correct answer = 10 marks
Students who attempt *uno* and *dos*: 1 mark for each correct answer = 5 marks

Assessment criteria: Students who complete four or five sentences correctly show evidence of performance at AT 1.2.

> 🎧 **CD 3, track 39** Hoja 71, actividad 2
>
> a – Vivo en una casa pequeña con mi familia.
> b – Hay tres dormitorios.
> c – No hay jardín, pero hay un parque enfrente de la casa.
> d – Mi dormitorio es grande.
> e – Hay un televisor en el salón.

Hoja 71 Escuchar: dos

AT1.3 | **3** Escucha y rellena los espacios.

Students listen and complete the text.

Answers: grande; estantería; amigos; ordenador; ventana; balcón

Mark scheme: 1 mark for each correct answer = 6 marks

Assessment criteria: Students who complete five or more gaps correctly show evidence of performance at AT 1.3.

 CD 3, track 40　　　　　Hoja 71, actividad 3

- Mi dormitorio es bastante grande.
  Tengo mi colección de discos compactos en una estantería y mis fotos de mis amigos en la mesa al lado de mi ordenador.
  No tengo televisor en mi dormitorio.
  Hay una ventana enfrente de la cama con un balcón con vista al mar. Es mi habitación favorita.

AT1.4 | **4** Escucha e indica si es verdad or mentira.

Students listen and mark the sentences true or false.

Answers: a V; b M; c V; d M; e V; f V; g V; h M

Mark scheme: 1 mark for each correct answer = 8 marks

Assessment criteria: Students who mark six or more sentences correctly show evidence of performance at AT 1.4.

 CD 3, track 41　　　　　Hoja 71, actividad 4

- Me levanto a las siete y voy a la cocina donde desayuno. Luego me lavo los dientes y me visto. Salgo de casa a las ocho y voy al colegio. A las dos vuelvo a la casa. Como en la cocina. Estudio en mi dormitorio con mi ordenador. Hablo por teléfono con mis amigos. A las nueve ceno con mi familia en el comedor. A las diez me ducho y me acuesto.

Hoja 72 Hablar: uno

AT2.3 | **1** Prepara una presentación sobre tu casa. Sigue los dibujos.

Students prepare and then give a presentation using the picture prompts. You or a partner can evaluate them using the scheme shown on the sheet.

Mark scheme: 5 marks each for: use of vocabulary, pronunciation, correct gender, variety of structures, use of reflexive verbs = 25 marks

Assessment criteria: Students who score 15 or more show evidence of performance at AT 2.3.

Hoja 72 Hablar: dos

AT2.4 | **2** Prepara una presentación sobre tu casa.

Students prepare and then give a presentation covering all the aspects listed on the sheet. You or a partner can evaluate them using the scheme shown.

Mark scheme: 5 marks each for: use of vocabulary, pronunciation, correct gender, variety of structures, use of reflexive verbs = 25 marks

Assessment criteria: Students who score 15 or more show evidence of performance at AT 2.3. Students who score 18 or more are performing at AT 2.4.

Hoja 73 Leer: uno

AT3.2 | **1** ¿Verdad or mentira?

Students mark the boxes according to whether the caption matches the pictures.

Answers: 1 V; 2 V; 3 M; 4 V; 5 M

Mark scheme: 1 mark for each correct answer = 5 marks

Assessment criteria: Students who mark four or five correctly show evidence of performance at AT 3.2.

AT3.3 | **2** Lee y subraya los nombres de las habitaciones. Haz una lista en inglés.

Students read the text, underlining the rooms. They then translate them into English.

Answers: living room; dining room; kitchen; bedroom; bathroom; office

Mark scheme: 1 mark for each correct answer = 6 marks

Assessment criteria: Students who translate five or six correctly show evidence of performance at AT 3.3.

AT3.4 | **3** Lee las descripciones de las casas. Contesta a las preguntas escribiendo el nombre correcto.

Students read the three descriptions and write the correct name for each sentence.

Answers: a José; b Isa; c Rafa; d Rafa; e Rafa; f José; g José

Mark scheme: 2 marks for each correct answer = 14 marks

Assessment criteria: Students who answer five or more correctly show evidence of performance at AT 3.4.

Hoja 74 Leer: dos

AT3.3 **1 Haz corresponder las respuestas con las preguntas.**

Students match the questions and the answers.

Answers: 1 e; 2 c; 3 d; 4 b; 5 a; 6 f; 7 g

Mark scheme: 1 mark for each correct answer = 7 marks

Assessment criteria: Students who match five or more correctly show evidence of performance at AT 3.3.

AT3.3 **2 Escoge la palabra correcta.**

Students choose the correct word for each sentence.

Answers: a es; b está; c moderna; d cuartos de baño; e Como; f mi

Mark scheme: 1 mark for each correct answer = 6 marks

Assessment criteria: Students who choose five or six correct words show evidence of performance at AT 3.3.

AT3.4 **3 Lee y contesta en inglés.**

Students read the text and answer the questions in English.

Answers: a four; b five; c one; d 6 o'clock; e he has a shower; f because his brother takes an hour to have a bath and comb his hair

Mark scheme: 2 marks for each correct answer = 12 marks

Assessment criteria: Students who answer four or more correctly show evidence of performance at AT 3.4.

Hoja 75 Escribir: uno

AT4.1 **1 Completa las palabras con las letras que faltan.**

Students complete the words.

Answers: a ordenador; b televisor; c cama; d sofá; e mesa

Mark scheme: 1 mark for each correct answer = 5 marks

Assessment criteria: Students who compelte four or five words correctly show evidence of performance at AT 4.1.

AT 4.2/3 **2 Completa la descripción.**

Students complete the list of places in the house.

Answers: En mi casa hay dos dormitorios, un cuarto de baño, un salón, un comedor, una cocina y un jardín. / ... Hay también un jardín.

Mark scheme: 1 mark for each correct place = 5 marks

Assessment criteria: Students who name all five places with some spelling errors show evidence of performance at AT 4.2. Students who spell everything correctly are performing at AT 4.3.

AT4.3 **3 Contesta en español con una frase correcta.**

Students answer the questions about themselves and where they live. They should use full sentences.

Mark scheme: 5 marks for information; 10 marks for correct sentences with verbs = 15 marks

Assessment criteria: Students who score 12 or more show evidence of performance at AT 4.3.

Hoja 76 Escribir: dos

AT4.2 **1 Completa las frases con una palabra lógica.**

Students complete the sentences with a word that makes sense and fits the grammatical context. As long as their sentence makes sense, students may draw on any known vocabulary.

Answers: a (masculine noun); b (feminine noun); c (plural noun); d ducho, baño, peino, lavo los dientes; e (a verb form: students may use two or more words if necessary here); f (feminine adjective): (masculine adjective)

Mark scheme: 1 mark for each correct answer = 7 marks

Assessment criteria: Students who complete five or more sentences correctly show evidence of performance at AT 4.2.

AT 4.3/4 **2 Lee la carta y escribe a Emilia mencionando 4 aspectos de tu casa.**

Students write a reply to Emilia's letter answering four of her questions. They describe their house, the place where they live, their bedroom, and say how many rooms there are in the house.

Mark scheme: 4 marks

Assessment criteria: Students who communicate all the ideas but with a number of language errors show evidence of performance at AT 4.3. Students with very few errors are performing at AT 4.4.

AT 4.3/4 **3 Escribe una frase con cada una de esas palabras.**

Students write a sentence with each of the words in the box. They can use any known vocabulary.

Mark scheme: 2 marks for each sentence (1 mark for sense; 1 mark for correct language) = 14 marks

Assessment criteria: Students who score 9–11 show evidence of performance at AT 4.3. Students scoring 12 or more are performing at AT 4.4.

Uno Workbook

Página 34 (4.1)
This page can be used with pages 54–55 of the Students' Book.

AT3.3 **1a** Lee la descripción. ¿Qué casa es: A, B o C? Pon una señal en la casilla correcta.

Students read the speech bubble and tick the correct picture.

Answer: Picture C

AT4.2 **1b** Completa la descripción.

Students choose either house A or house B and then complete the description accordingly using the words in the box. Tell them to circle A or B in the first sentence to make it clear.

Answers:
La casa A está en la montaña. Es una casa moderna y es bastante pequeña. Tiene un jardín con árboles de frutas. La casa B está en la ciudad. Es una casa antigua y es bastante grande. Tiene unos arboles.

AT3.3 **2** Lee el email de Susana. ¿Verdad o mentira?

Students read the email and mark the sentences true or false.

Answers: a M; b M; c M; 4 V; 5 V

AT4.3 **3** Habla con un compañero/a. ¿Cómo es su casa ideal? Escribe unas frases en la página 43.

In pairs, students talk in Spanish about their ideal house. Using the language supplied, they then write sentences about their partner's ideal house on page 43, the spare page for writing at the end of the unit

Página 35 (4.2)
This page can be used with pages 56–57 of the Students' Book.

AT4.1 **1** Escribe los nombres.

Students label the pictures. Remind them first to use the correct form of the indefinite article.

Answers: 2 un espejo; 3 una cama; 4 unas fotos; 5 unos pósters; 6 un armario; 7 un ordenador; 8 una radio

AT3.3 **2** Mira el dibujo y escoge las palabras correctas.

Students look at the picture and circle the correct words.

Answers: a al lado de; b detrás de; c a la derecha de; d en medio del; e en; f a la izquierda de

AT3.3 **3** Lee y dibuja el dormitorio en la página 43.

Students read the description and draw a plan of the bedroom on page 43.

Answers: a small bed beside a window; bookshelves with lots of books and CDs behind the door; opposite the bookshelves, a table with a computer and a big chair; a wardrobe to the left of the bed

Página 36 (4.3)
This page can be used with pages 58–59 of the Students' Book.

AT4.1 **1** Completa el crucigrama. ¿Qué palabra encuentras?

Students complete the crossword with parts of the house and find the word in the shaded squares.

Answers: The word is: *jardín.*

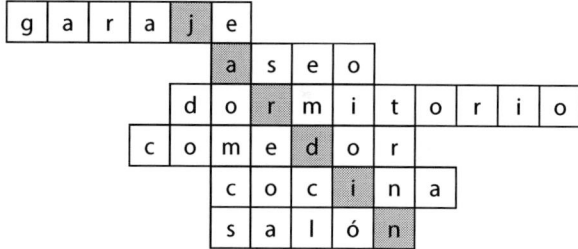

AT3.3 **2a** Lee el texto. Subraya los verbos.

Students read the text and underline the verbs.

Answers: hay; tiene; está; hay; está; Es; hay; tiene

AT3.1 **2b** ¿Cuándo se usan los verbos?

Students match the verbs with their uses.

Answers: 1 b; 2 d; 3 a; 4 c

AT4.3 **3 Eres una de estas personas. Describe tu casa en la página 43.**

Students choose one of the people shown in the pictures. Using the support language given, they invent and write a description of this person's house on page 43. Their ideas will vary.

When students have finished, remind them to check through their work for the correct use of verbs and adjective agreement.

Página 37 (4.4)

This page can be used with pages 60–61 of the Students' Book.

AT3.3 **1a Lee los textos. ¿Cuál es la rutina de Roberto: a, b o c?**

Students look at the pictures and the clocks. They then read the three texts and choose the routine that matches the sequence shown.

Answers: Routine b

AT4.3 **1b Completa el texto sobre la rutina diaria de Rachida.**

Students use the pictures to help them complete Rachida's routine.

Answers: Me despierto a las ocho y desayuno. Me peino y me lavo los dientes. Salgo de casa a las nueve.

AT3.3 **2 Empareja las frases españolas con las inglesas.**

Students match the Spanish sentences with the correct English translation.

Answers: 1 a; 2 b; 3 b; 4 a; 5 b; 6 b

Página 38 (4.5)

This page can be used with pages 62–63 of the Students' Book.

AT3.4 **1 Lee el texto. Subraya todas las palabras que tienen que ver con casas.**

Students read the text and underline all the words to do with houses. Some students may not include *televisión* or *teléfono*; others may include *modernas*, *jacuzzi* and *piscina*.

Answers: ventanas; puerta; habitaciones; cuarto de baño; dormitories; cocina; salón; televisión; teléfono

AT4.3 **2 Diseña un póster para el hotel-cueva de Guadix.**

Students make a poster advertising the Guadix cave hotel and surrounding area. They work in English, as if advertising to British tourists. They draw a picture as in the Students' Book and use the information in the text to help them. They can imagine other details about the inside of the hotel if they wish.

Página 39 Gramática

This page can be used with page 54 of the Students' Book. The aim of this page is to revise the use of *ser* and *estar* to talk about houses and to consolidate the reflexive verbs for daily routine.

AT4.1 **1a Completa las preguntas.**

Look at the Flashback box with the class. Students then complete the questions with the correct verb.

Answers: 1 es; 2 Es; 3 Está, está; 4 es; 5 está

AT3.3 **1b Lee las respuestas de Felipe Fanfarrón. Emparéjalas con las preguntas de 1a.**

Students read Felipe Show Off's answers and match them with the questions in exercise 1a.

Answers: a 4; b 1; c 3; d 5; e 2

AT4.3 **2 Escribe las frases en inglés.**

First use the *Flashback* box to remind the students of the different reflexive pronouns. They then translate the sentences into English.

Answers:
a I go to bed at eleven o'clock.
b He/She combs his/her hair and gets dressed.
c Do you get up at eight o'clock?
d Does he/she have a shower at seven o'clock?

AT4.3 **3 Eres Lechoso. Mira los dibujos y describe tu rutina en la página 43.**

Students look at the pictures and write a description on page 43 of their daily routine as if they were Lechoso the dog.

Answers:
a Me despierto a las nueve.
b Desayuno (en la cama) a las nueve.
c Me levanto a las once.
d Me peino a las doce.
e Me visto a la una.
f Salgo de casa a la tres.
g Ceno a las cinco.
h Me acuesto a las seis.

Página 40 Reto

This page can be used with page 64 of the Students' Book.

AT4.3 | **1 Las casas no se venden: ¿por qué? ¿Qué no tienen/no hay?**

Students look at the pictures and decide what is missing from each house. They then complete the sentences.

Answers:
La casa A no tiene (un) cuarto de baño.
En la casa B no hay (una) cocina.
La casa C no tiene aseo ni dormitorio.

AT4.2 | **2 Completa las frases sobre tu dormitorio.**

Students complete the sentences about their bedroom. Answers will vary but this activity would work well for peer correction as the answers will be quite similar.

AT3.3 | **3 Lee las frases. ¿Es la Señorita Perfecta o la Señorita Dormilona? Escribe P o D.**

Students look at the pictures to identify the characters and then read the sentences. They mark them P or D.

Answers: a D; b D; c P; d P; e P; f P; g D; h D

Dos Workbook

Página 34 (4.1)

This page can be used with pages 54–55 of the Students' Book.

AT3.3 | **1a Lee la descripción. ¿Qué casa es: A, B, o C? Pon una señal en la casilla correcta.**

Students read the speech bubble and tick the correct picture.

Answers: Picture C

AT4.3 | **1b Escribe una descripción de una de las otras casas.**

Students choose one of the other house pictures in exercise 1a and write a description of it.

Answers:
La casa A está en la montaña. Es una casa moderna y es bastante pequeña. Tiene un jardín con muchos árboles de frutas.
La casa B está en la ciudad. Es una casa antigua y es bastante grande. Tiene un árbol en el jardín.

AT3.3 | **2 Lee y completa el email.**

Students complete the email with the words in the word box.

Answers: muy; centro; grande; es; Está; campo; pequeña; playa; dormitorios

AT2.3
AT4.3 | **3 Habla con un/una compañero/a. ¿Cómo es su casa ideal? Descríbela en la página 43.**

In pairs, students talk in Spanish about their ideal house. Using the language supplied, they then write sentences about their partner's ideal house on page 43, the spare page for writing at the end of the unit

Página 35 (4.2)

This page can be used with pages 56–57 of the Students' Book.

AT4.1 | **1 Escribe los nombres.**

Students label the pictures. Remind them first to use the correct form of the indefinite article.

Answers: 2 un espejo; 3 una cama; 4 unas fotos; 5 unos pósters; 6 un armario; 7 un ordenador; 8 una radio

AT4.3 | **2 Escribe las frases en español.**

Students translate the sentences into Spanish.

Answers:
1 Hay unos pósters en la pared.
2 Tengo un armario detrás de la puerta.
3 Mi dormitorio no tiene cortinas.
4 No hay (un) televisor en mi dormitorio.
5 Tengo una silla delante de la ventana.
6 La cama está en medio del cuarto/dormitorio.
7 Hay un teléfono encima de la estantería.
8 Tengo mi radio enfrente.

AT3.3 | **3 Lee y dibuja el dormitorio en la página 43.**

Students read the description and draw a plan of the bedroom on page 43.

Answers: a small bed beside a window; bookshelves with lots of books and CDs behind the door; opposite the bookshelves, a table with a computer and a big chair; a wardrobe to the left of the bed

Página 36 (4.3)

This page can be used with pages 58–59 of the Students' Book.

AT4.1 **1 Completa el crucigrama. ¿Qué palabra encuentras?**

Students complete the crossword with parts of the house and find the word in the shaded squares.

Answers: The word is: *jardín*.

g	a	r	a	j	e				
				a	s	e	o		
		d	o	r	m	i	t	o	r	i	o
c	o	m	e	d	o	r			
			c	o	c	i	n	a	
			s	a	l	ó	n		

AT3.3 **2 Lee y escoge la palabra correcta.**

Students complete the text with the words in the word box.

Answers: hay; tiene; está; hay; está; es; hay; tiene

AT4.4 **3 Describe la casa de una de estas personas/familias en la página 43.**

Students choose one of the people shown in the pictures. They invent and write a description of this person's house on page 43. Their ideas will vary.
When students have finished, remind them to check through their work for the correct use of verbs and adjective agreement.

Página 37 (4.4)

This page can be used with pages 60–61 of the Students' Book.

AT3.3 **1a Lee los textos. ¿Cuál es la rutina de Roberto: a, b o c?**

Students look at the pictures and the clocks. They then read the three texts and choose the routine that matches the sequence shown.

Answer: Routine b

AT4.4 **1b Escribe un texto sobre la rutina de Rachida.**

Using the prompts in the picture and the models in exercise 1a, students write about Rachida's daily routine.

Answers: Me despierto a las ocho y desayuno. Me peino y me lavo los dientes. Salgo de casa a las ocho y media.

AT3.2 **2 Pon las palabras en el orden correcto.**

Students put the words in order to make correct sentences or questions.

Answers:
1 ¿A qué hora te levantas?
2 Me lavo los dientes y me acuesto a las once.
3 ¿Te duchas a las ocho?
4 ¿Julia se viste a qué hora? / ¿A qué hora se viste Julia?
5 Se peina y desayuna cereales.

AT4.3 **3 Escribe frases sobre la rutina de Penélope Perezosa (lazy Penelope) en la página 43.**

Students read the start of the model and imagine a routine for a character called lazy Penelope. They write about it on page 43. (They can change the start of the text as they wish.)

Página 38 (4.5)

This page can be used with pages 62–63 of the Students' Book.

AT3.4 **1 Lee el texto sobre Huapoca. Rellena los espacios con *hay, es, están* o *tienen*. ¡No mires tu libro!**

Students complete the text using the four words given, without referring back to the Students' Book.

Answers: están; Tienen; Es; es; Es; hay; están; Tienen; hay; Es

AT3.4 **2a Lee el texto sobre Guadix. Subraya todas las palabras que tienen que ver con casas.**

Students read the text and underline all the words to do with houses. Some students may not include *televisión* or *teléfono*; others may include *modernas, jacuzzi* and *piscina*.

Answers: ventanas; puerta; habitaciones; cuarto de baño; dormitorios; cocina; salón; televisión; teléfono

AT3.4 **2b Escribe los adjetivos.**

Students write out all the adjectives from the text about Guadix.

Answers: normal; modernas; tradicionales; prácticas; constante; perfecto; aceptable

AT4.4 | **3** Escribe unas frases sobre una casa extraordinaria.

Students write a few sentences about an unusual house starting with the words given.

Página 39 Gramática

This page can be used with pages 54–55 of the Students' Book.
The aim of this page is to revise the use of *ser* and *estar* to talk about houses and to consolidate the reflexive verbs for daily routine.

AT4.2 | **1a** Completa las preguntas.

Look at the *Flashback* box with the class. Students then complete the questions using *es* or *está*.

Answers: 1 es; 2 es; 3 Está, está; 4 es; 6 está

AT4.3 | **1b** Eres una persona famosa. Contesta a las preguntas de 1a.

Students answer the questions in exercise 1a as if they were a famous person. Answers will vary, but remind the students to check for the correct use or *ser* or *estar*. This activity is suitable for peer correction.

AT3.2 | **2** Escribe las frases en inglés.

First use the *Flashback* box to remind the students of the different reflexive pronouns. They then translate the sentences into English.

Answers:
1 I go to bed at eleven o'clock.
2 He/She brushes his/her hair and gets dressed.
3 Do you get up at eight o'clock?
4 No, I always get up at nine o'clock.
5 You have a shower at seven o'clock, don't you?
6 He/She doesn't brush his/her teeth.

AT4.4 | **3** Eres Lechoso. Mira a los dibujos y describe tu rutina en la página 43.

Students look at the pictures and write a description on page 43 of their daily routine as if they were Lechoso the dog.

Answers:
a Me despierto a las nueve.
b Desayuno (en la cama) a las nueve.
c Me levanto a las diez.
d Me peino a las once.
e Me visto a las doce.
f Salgo de casa a la una.
g Como a las dos.
h Me acuesto a las tres.

Página 40 Reto

This page can be used with page 66 of the Students' Book.

AT4.3 | **1** Las casas no se venden: ¿por qué? ¿Qué no tienen/no hay?

Students look at the pictures and decide what is missing from each house. They then write sentences.

Answers:
La casa A no tiene (un) cuarto de baño.
En la casa B no hay (una) cocina.
La casa C no tiene aseo y no tiene dormitorio.

AT4.3 | **2** Contesta a las preguntas sobre tu dormitorio.

Students answer the questions about their own bedroom. Answers will vary but encourage the students to check their work for gender and number agreement and for the correct use of *ser* or *estar*.

AT4.3 | **3** Describe tu rutina. Primero eres la Señorita Perfecta, después la Señorita Dormilona.

Students write about their routine as if they were the characters in the pictures.

Possible Answers:
Me despierto, me levanto, me lavo los dientes, me visto, me peino, y desayuno a las ocho.
Me despierto, me levanto, no me lavo los dientes, no me visto, no me peino, no desayuno y salgo de casa a las nueve.

Unit 5   Overview grid

Pages/Contexts/Cultural focus	Objectives	Grammar	Skills and Pronunciation	Key language	Framework	National Curriculum PoS	AT level
68–69 **5.1 En mis ratos libres** Free-time activities	Say what activities you like to do; Give opinions; Recognize infinitives and look up verbs in the dictionary	Infinitives	Stressing accented letters	*nadar, escuchar música, ver la televisión, leer, tocar la trompeta, hablar por teléfono, ir a la playa, navegar por Internet, bailar* *Me gusta, no me gusta, prefiero, odio, me chifla, me encanta, jugar con videojuegos, navegar por Internet, hablar por teléfono, ver la televisión con mi padre/madre* *pero, y, porque* *Si hace sol, calor, frío, si hay tormenta, si llueve, si hace viento*	(R) 7C2, 7T4 (unit opener page), 7W7, 7S5	1a, 1b, 1c, 2a, 2c, 2d, 2f, 2h, 2i, 3b, 3c, 3e, 4a, 4c, 5a, 5b, 5d, 5e, 5f, 5g, 5h, 5i	1.3, 2.2, 3.2–4, 4.3–4
70–71 **5.2 ¿Qué deportes practicas?** Sports	Say what sports you play; Say what sports you like and why; Ask other people what sports they play and like	*practicar* and *jugar*	–	*Juego al baloncesto. Juego al voleibol. Juego al rugby. Juego al fútbol.* *Practico el atletismo. Practico el esquí. Practico el ciclismo. Practico la equitación. Practico la natación. Practico la vela. Practico la gimnasia.* *Es violento/a, es lento/a, es rápido/a, es divertido/a, es aburrido/a, es fácil, es difícil, es relajante*	(R) 7W1, 7W5, 7S6	1a, 1b, 1c, 2a, 2b, 2c, 2d, 2e, 2f, 2g, 2h, 2i, 3a, 3b, 3c, 3e, 4a, 4c, 5a, 5b, 5c, 5d, 5e, 5h, 5i	1.2, 2.2–3, 3.1–4, 4.3–4
72–73 **5.3 Ayudar en casa** Jobs in the house	Say what jobs you do at home; Say what jobs other people do	-ar verb endings (present tense)	–	*lavar los platos, ayudar en el jardín, lavar el coche, arreglar mi dormitorio, pasear al perro, lavar la ropa, cambiar la arena del gato* *el lunes, el martes, el miércoles, el jueves, el viernes, el sábado, el domingo* *No hago nada.*	(R) 7L2, 7L5, 7T3	1a, 1b, 1c, 2a, 2b, 2c, 2d, 2f, 3b, 3c, 3d, 3e, 4a, 4c, 4d, 5a, 5d, 5e, 5f, 5g, 5i	1.2–3, 2.2–4, 3.3–4, 4.3–4
74–75 **5.4 Hacer planes** Arrangements	Invite someone out; Arrange a meeting; Accept an invitation	*a + el = al*; The immediate future	–	*¿Diga? ¿Quieres ir a ...? ¿Cuándo?* *¿Dónde nos encontramos? ¿A qué hora? A la una, A las siete.* *¿Qué vas a hacer? el fin de semana, durante la semana*	(R) 7W5	1a, 1b, 1c, 2a, 2b, 2c, 2d, 2f, 2i, 3b, 3c, 3e, 4a, 4c, 4d, 5a, 5c, 5d, 5e, 5f, 5g, 5i	1.2–3, 2.2–4, 3.2–3, 4.3
76–77 **5.5 Entre amigos** Questionnaire about free time	–	–	–	–	(R) 7C3	1c, 2a, 2c, 2d, 2f, 2g, 2h, 2i, 3a, 3b, 3c, 3e, 4a, 4c, 4d, 5a, 5d, 5e, 5f, 5g, 5h, 5i	1.4, 2.3, 3.2–6, 4.3

AMIGOS 1 UNIT 5 MEDIUM TERM PLAN

About this unit: In this unit students learn how to form compound sentences when talking about their hobbies and giving opinions about them. They understand increasingly complex spoken and written texts containing some unfamiliar language and show mastery of a few familiar verbs in the singular forms. They are introduced to the immediate future, using *ir + a +* infinitive. They take part in simple dialogues to talk about what sports and activities they do, and which they like and why.

Framework objectives (reinforce)	Teaching and learning (additional)	Week-by-week overview (assuming 6 weeks' work or approx. 10–12.5 hours)
7W1: everyday words	*Me gusta, no me gusta, prefiero, odio, me chifla, me encanta*	**Week 1** Say what activities you like to do; give opinions about them; recognize infinitives and look up verbs in the dictionary
	pero, y, porque	**Week 2** Say what sports you play; say what sports you like and why; ask other people what sports they play and like
7W5: verbs present (+ past)	Present tense of *practicar* and *jugar,* learning the immediate future (*voy a* + infinitive)	
7W7: learning about words	Learning that the accent over a letter shows which vowel is to be stressed	**Week 3** Say what jobs you do at home; say what jobs other people do
7S5: simple negatives	*No me gusta*	**Week 4** Invite someone out; arrange a meeting and accept an invitation; learn about the immediate future
7S6: compound sentences	Using connectives (*pero, y* and *porque*) to make compound sentences, e.g. *Me gusta nadar en la piscina pero no me gusta si hace frío.*	**Week 5** Students apply the language and structures learnt in this unit to reading and answering questions on longer texts which focus on an aspect of Spanish or Latin American culture
7T3: appraise texts	Scan text for certain vocabulary items	
7T4: use basic resources	Research sports	
7L2: improve capacity to follow speech	Listening to what jobs Fátima does, and then listening again to see which jobs she likes doing	
7L5: spontaneous talk	Take it in turns with your partner to ask what jobs they do about the house	**Week 6** Recycle language of the unit via *Uno, Dos* and *Lectura* pages; students check their progress via the *Ya sé…* self-assessment checklist in the Students' Book and on Hoja 78.
7C2: aspects of everyday culture	Find out about Spanish sports personalities and teams, or a popular Spanish sport, such as *pelota*	
7C3: authentic materials	Teenagers' free time in Spain, Argentina and the UK	
	Teaching and learning (additional)	
	Free time for Spanish teenagers	

5 Los pasatiempos

Unit objectives

Contexts: free-time activities, household chores, going out, days of the week
Grammar: infinitives, opinions, *-ar* verbs, *voy a*
Cultural focus: some Spanish sports

Assessment opportunities

Speaking: SB, page 71, Reto
Reading: SB, page 69, activity 7
Listening: SB, page 70, activity 1
Writing: SB, page 73, Reto

AT1.1 | **1** Escucha. ¿Qué deporte es?

Students listen to the sound effects and give the number of the picture. They can try to say the sport in Spanish if they are confident.

Answers: 1 c el tenis; 2 a el baloncesto; 3 b la equitación; 4 f el fútbol; 5 e la natación; 6 d la gimnasia

 CD 2, track 15   página 67, actividad 1

1 FX of tennis ball
2 FX of basketball
3 FX of a horse running
4 FX of crowd noise and 'Go-o-o-l' as in a Spanish football match
5 FX of swimming
6 FX of music for gym floor routine

AT3.1 | **2** Empareja los deportes con los balones.

Students use their world knowledge to match the sports 1–8 with the balls a–h.

Answers: 1 b; 2 f; 3 e; 4 c; 5 g; 6 d; 7 h; 8 a

AT4.1 | **3** Investigate one of the following.

Students use the Internet or books to research a Spanish star or sport. They can prepare posters to display in the classroom. If they write about a star, they can use the language they know for personal description. If they research a sport, they could use a dictionary to label the equipment.

Planner

● ●

 5.1 ## En mis ratos libres   páginas 68–69

Objectives

► Say what activities you like to do

► Give opinions

► Recognize infinitives and look up verbs in the dictionary

Resources

Students' Book, pages 68–69
CD 2, tracks 16–18
Uno/Dos Workbooks, page 44

Key language

nadar, escuchar música, ver la televisión, leer, tocar la trompeta, hablar por teléfono, ir a la playa, navegar por Internet, bailar
Me gusta, no me gusta, prefiero, odio, me chifla, me encanta, jugar con videojuegos, navegar por Internet, hablar por teléfono, ver la televisión con mi padre/madre
pero, y, porque
Si hace sol, calor, frío, si hay tormenta, si llueve, si hace viento

Programme of Study reference

1a, 1b, 1c, 2a, 2c, 2d, 2f, 2h, 2i, 3b, 3c, 3e, 4a, 4c, 5a, 5b, 5d, 5e, 5f, 5g, 5h, 5i

Framework reference

(R) 7C2, 7T4 (Unit opener page), 7W7, 7S5

● ●

¡A sus marcas!

Copia y rellena el cuadro. ¿Cuáles actividades te gustan y no te gustan? Escribe la letra.

Students copy and complete the table putting the letters in the correct column according to whether or not they like the activity.

Answers: Students' own answers

AT1.3 **1 ¿Les gusta o no les gusta? Escucha y rellena el cuadro.**

Students copy the table adding in the names shown underneath. You may want to suggest that they simply listen the first time. Then play the CD again. This time students draw hearts for the activities that the characters like and crossed-out hearts (as in *¡A sus marcas!*) for the activities that they don't like.

Answers:
Carlos: ✓✗✗✓✓
Jorge: ✗✓✓✓✗
Fátima: ✓✗✓✗✗
Raquel: ✗✓✗✗✗

 CD 2, track 16   página 70, actividad 1

– Me gusta nadar. No me gusta bailar. No me gusta leer. Me gusta hablar por teléfono. Me gusta ver la televisión.
– Me gusta bailar y leer. No me gusta ver la televisión y no me gusta nadar. Me gusta hablar por teléfono.
– No me gusta bailar. Me gusta leer y nadar. No me gusta ver la televisión y no me gusta hablar por teléfono.
– Sólo me gusta bailar. No me gusta nada más.

AT2.2 **2 Con tu compañero/a, pregunta y contesta.**

Ask two confident students to model the dialogue and ensure that everyone understands the game. In pairs, students then play the game using the model dialogue.

Se pronuncia así

This section highlights the use of the written accent, reinforcing Framework objective 7W7. If the students are not yet familiar with the rules for regular stress in Spanish, you may like to introduce those first:

Words ending in vowels, *n* or *s* are naturally stressed on the penultimate syllable (*ca̱sa, ha̱blan, o̱jos*).

Words ending in all other consonants are naturally stressed on the last syllable (*comedo̱r*).

Explain that the written accent is used where the stress falls on a **different** syllable. If the students have studied any French, make sure that they understand that the written accent in Spanish does not affect the pronunciation in any way apart from the stress.

You may want to explain that a few words in Spanish have accents to distinguish them from words that are the same, for example:

sí (yes) and *si* (if)

tú (you) and *tu* (your)

 CD 2, track 17   página 68, se pronuncia así

Música	Teléfono	Televisión
Música	Teléfono	Televisión
Música	Teléfono	Televisión

AT2.2 **3 Now practise these sentences and compare your pronunciation with the recording.**

Students practise saying the sentences and then listen and compare with the CD.

CD 2, track 18   página 68, actividad 3

La música en la televisión: ¡Sí!
La música en el teléfono: ¡No!

Zoom gramática

This section introduces the infinitive and explains that knowing the infinitive of a verb helps students to use a dictionary more effectively. This reinforces Framework objective 7W7.

AT3.2

4 Find these verbs in your dictionary.

Students find the Spanish translations of the English infinitives.

Answers: a cantar; b comer; c pintar; d estudiar; e cocinar; f escribir

---

AT3.3

5 Busca las ocho diferencias entre a y b.

Students compare the two texts and find eight differences. If necessary, remind them that they are looking for differences in style, not content.

Answers:
me gusta jugar – me gusta <u>mucho</u> jugar
videojuegos. Me gusta – videojuegos <u>pero prefiero</u>
bailar. No me gusta – bailar <u>y odio</u>
Me gusta ir – Me <u>chifla</u> ir
playa. Me gusta – <u>porque</u> me <u>encanta</u>

AT3.4

6 Traduce el texto b al inglés.

Students translate text b, the more sophisticated version, into English.

Answer:
In my free time I like playing computer games a lot but I prefer to surf the net. I don't like dancing and I hate singing. I'm crazy about going to the beach because I love swimming.

AT2.2

7 ¡A contrarreloj! ¿Cuántas frases lógicas puedes hacer en dos minutos? Reta a tu compañero/a.

In pairs, students time each other for two minutes while they make up as many logical sentences as they can. Each sentence must use a phrase from each box. If students disagree about whether a sentence is logical, they can put it to a class vote at the end of the activity.

Reto

AT4.4 **Escribe una versión sofisticada de este texto. Utiliza opiniones diferentes y conjunciones.**

Students write a more sophisticated version of the text. Make sure they understand that they can give different opinions and encourage them to use as many of the *Frases clave* as possible.

Answer: Answers will vary, but there should be limited use of *Me gusta / No me gusta*.

Planner

 5.2 ¿Qué deportes practicas? páginas 70–71

Objectives

▶ Say what sports you play

▶ Say what sports you like and why

▶ Ask other people what sports they play and like

Resources

Students' Book, pages 70–71
CD 2, tracks 19–21
Uno/Dos Workbooks, page 45

Key language

Juego al baloncesto, al voleibol, al tenis, al rugby, al fútbol.
Practico el atletismo, el esquí, el ciclismo, la equitación, la natación, la vela, la gimnasia.
Es violento/a, es rápido/a, es lento/a, es divertido/a, es aburrido/a, es fácil, es difícil, es relajante

Programme of Study reference

1a, 1b, 1c, 2a, 2b, 2c, 2d, 2e, 2f, 2g, 2h, 2i, 3a, 3b, 3c, 3e, 4a, 4c, 5a, 5b, 5c, 5d, 5e, 5h, 5i

Framework reference

(R) 7W1, 7W5, 7S6

¡A sus marcas!

Escucha y lee. ¿Qué deportes se mencionan dos veces?

Students listen and note down the sports that are mentioned twice.

Answers: tenis; esquí

 CD 2, track 19   página 70, ¡A sus marcas!

– juego al baloncesto
– juego al voleibol
– juego al tenis
– juego al rugby
– juego al tenis
– juego al fútbol
– practico el atletismo
– practico el esquí
– practico el ciclismo
– practico la equitación
– practico la natación
– practico la vela
– practico la gimnasia
– practico el esquí

AT1.2 **1 Escucha (1–4). ¿Qué deportes practican?**

Students listen and note down the letters of the sports that each character does. To give feedback, they add the Spanish word as in the example.

Answers: Fátima: b (voleibol), I (gimnasia); Carlos: d (rugby), h (ciclismo); Jorge: a (baloncesto), g (esquí)

 CD 2, track 20   página 70, actividad 1

– Hola, me llamo Adam y juego al fútbol, ¡Me gusta mucho! También practico la vela.
– Juego al voleibol, y practico la gimnasia en mi tiempo libre. No juego al tenis.
– Hola, me llamo Carlos. Juego al rugby en mi colegio. Practico también el ciclismo.
– Hola, soy Jorge. Me gustan mucho los deportes. Juego al baloncesto y practico el esquí.

AT2.2 **2 En grupos, pregunta y contesta. ¿Qué deportes juegas y qué deportes practicas?**

Focus attention on the verbs with each activity in *¡A sus marcas!* Ask several students the two questions, varying your use of *juegas* and *practicas*. Then divide the class into small groups to ask and answer, following the model.

Zoom gramática

This section introduces the singular verb endings for *-ar* verbs and the *o* to *ue* radical change in *jugar*. Students will study more radical-changing verbs in 6.2.

AT3.2 **3 Find examples of these verbs used in expressions on this page and say what they mean.**

Ask students to call out examples of the different forms of *practicar* and *jugar* used on the page. Make a list on the board and ask the students to translate them.

Answers: *Juego* – I play; *Practico* – I do; *¿Qué deportes practican?* – What sports do they do?; *¿Qué deportes juegas?* – What sports do you play? *¿Qué deportes practicas?* – What sports do you do?

AT 3.3/4 **4 Escucha y rellena el cuadro. ¿Qué deporte les gusta y por qué?**

Read the *Frases clave* box with the class. Ask students to guess the meaning of as many words as they can and remind them that they can use the glossary on page 79 to check the others. When students are familiar with the adjectives, ask them to copy and complete the chart, adding the names underneath. They then listen and complete it with the correct sports and letters according to the opinions given.

Answers: Rosa: rugby, a; Julio: ciclismo, i; Luis: equitación, d

CD 2, track 21 página 71, actividad 4

– Hola, Ignacio. ¿Qué deporte te gusta?
– Me gusta el fútbol porque es rápido.

– Hola, Rosa. ¿Qué deporte te gusta?
– Me gusta mucho el rugby porque es violento.

– Hola, Julio. ¿Qué deporte te gusta?
– Me gusta el ciclismo porque es relajante.

– Hola, Luis. ¿Qué deporte te gusta?
– Me gusta muchísimo la equitación porque es divertida.

AT 2.2/3

5 Con tu compañero/a. ¿Qué piensas de los deportes?

In pairs, students ask each other their opinions on sport, following the model dialogue.

Reto

AT3.2

Which bubble in exercise 5 could you remove?

Ask students to look carefully at the bubbles and to find the one that can be removed without changing the meaning of the dialogue.

Answer: *¿Por qué?* could be removed so that instead of A asking 'Why?', B gives their reason when they answer the first question. Students need to remember the rule that *¿Por qué?* asks the question 'Why?' and *porque* gives the reason 'because'.

Planner

● ●

 5.3 **Ayudar en casa** páginas 72–73

Objectives

▶ Say what jobs you do at home

▶ Say what jobs other people do

Resources

Students' Book, pages 72–73
CD 2, tracks 22–23
Uno/Dos Workbooks, page 46

Key language

lavar los platos, ayudar en el jardín, lavar el coche, arreglar mi dormitorio, pasear al perro, lavar la ropa, cambiar la arena del gato
el lunes, el martes, el miércoles, el jueves, el viernes, el sábado, el domingo
No hago nada

Programme of Study reference

1a, 1b, 1c, 2a, 2b, 2c, 2d, 2f, 3b, 3c, 3d, 3e, 4a, 4c, 4d, 5a, 5d, 5e, 5f, 5g, 5i

Framework reference

(R) 7L2, 7L5, 7T3

● ●

¡A sus marcas!

Mira los dibujos. Escucha y levanta la mano si tú tienes que hacer esa tarea en casa.

Give students a couple of minute to familiarize themselves with the phrases under each picture. Students then listen to the list of chores and put up their hands for the ones that they are asked to do.

 CD 2, track 22 página 72, ¡A sus marcas!

a lavar los platos
b ayudar en el jardín
c lavar el coche
d arreglar el dormitorio
e pasear al perro
f lavar la ropa
g sacar la basura
h cambiar la arena del gato

 AT 1.2/3 **1 Lee ¿Qué trabajos hace Fátima? Escucha y apunta: ¿qué trabajos le gusta hacer?**

Students read the short dialogue between Carlos and Fátima. They note which chores Fátima does. Then explain that the students are going to hear a longer version of the dialogue. Students listen and this time they note which chores Fátima likes doing.

Answers: She walks the dog and helps in the garden. She likes both these chores, but she prefers walking the dog.

 CD 2, track 23 página 72, actividad 1

– ¿Paseas al perro?
– Sí, paseo al perro.
– ¿Te gusta?
– Sí, me encanta pasear al perro.
– ¿Ayudas en el jardín?
– Sí, ayudo en el jardín.
– ¿Te gusta?
– Sí me gusta, pero prefiero pasear al perro.
– ¿Sacas la basura?
– No, no saco la basura.

AT 2.3/4 **2 Con tu compañero/a, cambia la conversación para Raquel y Jorge.**

In pairs, students change the details in the dialogue in exercise 1 to talk about the chores that Raquel and Jorge do. One student answers in the role of Raquel then the other student answers in the role of Jorge.

Answers:
Raquel's chores:
¿Lavas el coche?
Sí, lavo el coche.
¿Arreglas tu dormitorio?
Sí, arreglo mi dormitorio.
¿Lavas la ropa?
No, no lavo la ropa.
Jorge's chores:
¿Cambias la arena del gato?
Sí, cambio la arena del gato.
¿Sacas la basura?
Sí, saco la basura.
¿Lavas los platos?
No, no lavo los platos.

 AT 2.2/3 **3 Con tu compañero/a, pregunta y contesta.**

In pairs, students ask and answer about what chores they do at home.

Zoom gramática

This section gives students the full paradigm for *-ar* verbs to help them talk about all the members of their family. It is useful to model and practise the correct pronunciation of the verb forms so that students are not tempted to stress the endings of *-o*, *-as*, *-a* and *-an*.

AT4.3

4 Write a sentence for each of Raquel and Jorge, saying what they do.

Students practise the third person singular form of *-ar* verbs by writing sentences about the chores that Raquel and Jorge do.

Answers: Raquel lava el coche y cambia la arena del gato. Jorge arregla su dormitorio y saca la basura.

AT 3.3/4

5 Copia y rellena el cuadro. ¿Quién hace las tareas en la familia de Adam?

(You may wish to focus on the *Frases clave* box so that students are familiar with the days of the week and the phrase *No hago nada* for when they read Adam's text.) Students copy the table headings. They then read Adam's text and make notes in the table about what chores each person does.

Answers:
Adam: tidies his room, changes the cat litter, takes the rubbish out, helps in the garden
His Mum: washes the clothes, washes the car, walks the dog
His Dad: washes the car

Reto

AT 4.3/4

Escribe. ¿Qué tareas hacen los miembros de tu familia normalmente cada semana?

Students use Adam's text as a model to help them write about the jobs that members of their family do on different days of the week.

Planner

●●●●●●●●●●●●●●●●●●●●●●●●●

5.4 **Hacer planes** páginas 74–75

Objectives

▶ Invite someone out

▶ Arrange a meeting

▶ Accept an invitation

Resources

Students' Book, pages 74–75
CD 2, tracks 24–27
Uno/Dos Workbooks, page 47

Key language

¿Diga?
¿Quieres ir a…?
¿Cuándo? ¿A qué hora? A la una/las siete
¿Dónde nos encontramos?
¿Qué vas a hacer?
El fin de semana, durante la semana

Programme of Study reference

1a, 1b, 1c, 2a, 2b, 2c, 2d, 2f, 2i, 3b, 3c, 3e, 4a, 4c, 4d, 5a, 5c, 5d, 5e, 5f, 5g, 5i

Framework reference

(R) 7W5

●●●●●●●●●●●●●●●●●●●●●●●●●

¡A sus marcas!

Lee y escucha. ¿Qué pasa? ¿Qué información entiendes?

Students listen to and read the dialogue. As a class, discuss what is happening and how much everyone has understood.

Answer: Raquel is inviting Adam to the cinema on Saturday. They agree to meet at the park at seven o'clock.

 CD 2, track 24 página 74, ¡A sus marcas!

– ¿Diga?
– Hola, soy Raquel. ¿Quieres ir al cine?
– Sí. ¿Cuándo?
– El sábado.
– ¿Dónde nos encontramos?
– En el parque.
– ¿A qué hora?
– A las siete.
– ¡Perfecto! A las siete en el parque. ¡Adiós!
– Adiós.

Zoom gramática

This section reinforces *a + el = al*.

AT 3.2/3 **1 Find examples of 'to the' on this page.**

Students look for examples on the page. (For further practice, you could ask students around the class to change Raquel's question *¿Quieres ir…?* using all the places in exercise 2 below.)

Answers: al cine, al restaurante

AT1.2 **2 Escucha. ¿Cuántos lugares menciona Jorge? ¿Adónde quiere ir Fátima?**

Students listen to the dialogue. They count all the places that Jorge mentions and note down where Fátima really wants to go.

Answers: Jorge mentions six places: *la playa, el café, el cine, el polideportivo, el parque* and *la discoteca.* Fátima wants to go to the bathroom.

 CD 2, track 25 página 74, actividad 2

– ¿Quieres ir a la playa?
– No.
– ¿Quieres ir al café?
– No.
– ¿Quieres ir al cine?
– No.
– ¿Al polideportivo?
– ¡NO!
– Pues, ¿quieres ir al parque?
– ¡No!
– ¿Quieres ir a la discoteca?
– ¡No! Quiero ir al cuarto de baño. ¡Adiós!

AT2.2 **3 Con tu compañero/a, juega.**

In pairs, students play the same guessing game, taking it in turns to choose a place and answer or to ask the questions. You may want to set a rule that they must choose a place illustrated in exercise 2. Monitor the students' pronunciation as they play, making sure that they are pronouncing *No* in Spanish.

AT1.3 **4 Escucha y apunta para Teresa, Mario y Jorge.**

Make sure that students understand the three questions. Students then listen to the three dialogues and make notes in Spanish.

Answers:
Teresa: al cine, en la puerta del cine, a las dos
Mario: al café, en la casa de Juan, a las cinco
Jorge: a la playa, en la plaza, a las doce

CD 2, track 26 página 75, actividad 4

1 – ¿ Diga? Hola, Teresa, soy Arturo. ¿Quieres ir al cine?
  – Sí, ¡qué buena idea! ¿Dónde nos encontramos?
  – En la puerta del cine.
  – Muy bien. ¿A qué hora?
  – A las dos.
  – Muy bien, adiós.
2 – Hola, Mario, soy Juan.
  – ¿Qué tal, Juan?
  – Muy bien, gracias. ¿Quieres ir al café?
  – Perfecto. ¿Dónde nos encontramos?
  – En mi casa.
  – ¿A qué hora?
  – A las cinco.
3 – Hola, Jorge, soy Antonio. ¿Quieres ir a la playa?
  – Sí. ¿Dónde nos encontramos?
  – En la plaza a las doce. ¿Está bien?
  – Claro que sí, ¡adiós!

AT 2.3/4 **5** Con tu compañero/a, haz un diálogo como Adam y Raquel. Utiliza la información del ejercicio 4.

Students use Adam and Raquel's dialogue in *¡A sus marcas!* on page 74 as a model to make up their own. They can choose the details of where, when and what time from the notes they took in exercise 4.

Answers:
Teresa:
¿Diga?
Hola, soy Arturo. ¿Quieres ir al cine?
¿Cuándo?
El sábado.
¿Dónde nos encontramos?
En la puerta del cine.
¿A qué hora?
A las dos.
¡Perfecto! A las dos en la puerta del cine. ¡Adiós!
Adiós.

Mario:
¿Diga?
Hola, soy Juan. ¿Quieres ir al café?
¿Cuándo?
El sábado.
¿Dónde quedamos?
En mi casa.
¿A qué hora?
A las cinco.
¡Perfecto! A las cinco en tu casa. ¡Adiós!
Adiós.

Jorge:
¿Diga?
Hola, soy Antonio. ¿Quieres ir a la playa?
¿Cuándo?

El sábado.
¿Dónde nos encontramos?
En la plaza.
¿A qué hora?
A las doce.
¡Perfecto! A las doce en la plaza. ¡Adiós!
Adiós.

Zoom gramática

This section introduces the immediate future *ir + a + infinitive*, reinforcing Framework objective 7W5. Remind the students of the different forms of *ir* that they studied in 3.1 (page 40).

AT4.3 **6** The verb 'to sing' is *cantar*. How would you say 'I'm going to sing'? Now think of two more examples of the immediate future.

Students translate the sentence. They then think of other examples. (They have been concentrating on *-ar* verbs in this unit, but you may want to remind them that other verbs follow the same pattern: *voy a comer.*)

Answers: Voy a cantar. Students find other examples.

AT3.3 **7** Lee. ¿Qué va a hacer Fátima?

To find out what Fátima is going to do, students match 1–5 (the first part of the sentences) with a–e, choosing the most logical place.

Answers: 1 a; 2 d; 3 e; 4 b; 5 e

AT1.3 **8** Escucha y comprueba tus respuestas.

Students listen and check. You may want students to repeat the sentences to practise the new language.

CD 2, track 27 página 75, actividad 8

a Voy a ver la nueva de Harry Potter en el cine.
b Voy a jugar al fútbol en el parque.
c Voy a comer con amigos en un restaurante.
d Voy a nadar a la playa.
e Voy a bailar en la discoteca.

Reto

AT 2.2/3 Con tu compañero/a, pregunta y contesta. ¿Qué vas a hacer esta semana?

In pairs, students ask and answer about what they are going to do this/the following week. They can use the picture cues in any order they want. Encourage more confident students to use other known language, e.g. *El viernes voy a pasear al perro.*

Planner

●●●●●●●●●●●●●●●●●●●●●●●●●

 5.5 **Entre amigos: Los ratos libres en España y en Argentina** páginas 78–79

Resources

Students' Book, pages 76–77
CD 2, track 28
Uno/Dos Workbooks, page 48

Programme of Study reference

1c, 2a, 2c, 2d, 2f, 2g, 2h, 2i, 3a, 3b, 3c, 3e, 4a, 4c, 4d, 5a, 5d, 5e, 5f, 5g, 5h, 5i

Framework reference

(R) 7C3

●●●●●●●●●●●●●●●●●●●●●●●●●

| AT3.4 | **1 Lee el cuestionario.** |

Students read the questionnaire. (Exercise 2 draws out much of the important new vocabulary, so try to discourage students from asking about every new word.)

| AT3.3 | **2 Busca estas palabras en español.** |

Students find the Spanish equivalents in the text for the English words a–l.

Answers: a resultados; b cuestionario; c jóvenes; d chicos; e chicas; f tareas domésticas; g aproximadamente; h pasatiempos; i popular; j películas; k teleserie; l deportes

| AT3.3 | **3 Draw a bar chart to show** |

a How much money Spanish young people have to spend.
b What they watch on TV.

Students use the information to draw two bar charts.

Answers:

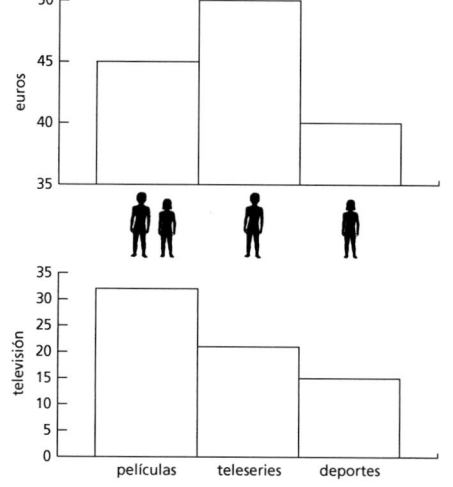

| AT3.4 | **4 ¿Verdad o mentira?** |

Students read the sentences and decide whether they are true or false according to the information given.

Answers: a V; b V; c M; d M; e V; f M

| AT3.4 | **5** How does the survey of Spanish teenagers' free time compare with your own? Write in English, using information from page **76**. |

Students compare how they personally use their free time with the results of the Spanish survey. Encourage them to cover as many points in the text as they can, but be aware that some students may not wish to give details of their pocket money.

| AT1.4 | **6 Escucha. Contesta a las preguntas.** |

Students listen to the information about young people's free time in Argentina and answer the questions.

Answers: a football; b any five from: watching TV, going out with friends, listening to music, dancing, playing computer games, chatting to friends on the phone; c play computer games; d chat to friends on the phone

---

 CD 2, track 28 página 77, actividad 6

En Argentina el fútbol es el deporte más popular. El equipo nacional es uno de los mejores del mundo. El club más famoso es Boca Juniors.
Las actividades típicas en los ratos libres son ver la televisión, salir con amigos, escuchar música, bailar. Los chicos prefieren jugar con videojuegos. Las chicas prefieren hablar con sus amigas por teléfono.

| AT2.3 | **7 Entrevista a tu compañero/a.** |

Students work in pairs. Stdent A asks the questions on the left for Student B to answer. Student B then asks the questions on the right for Student A to answer.

Answers:
A escuchar música; los ordenadores y los videojuegos; leer
B fútbol; jugar con videojuegos; hablar con sus amigas por teléfono

| AT4.3 | **8 Copia y completa estas preguntas.** |

Students copy and complete the sentences with their own views.

Answers: Students' own answers.

Repaso

página 78

Resources

Students' Book, page 78

Programme of Study reference

1c, 2a, 2c, 2f, 3c, 4a, 5d, 5a, 5d, 5f, 5g, 5i

| AT3.2 | **1 Mi familia. Rapea en español utilizando las actividades.** |

Ask if students can tell you why *tenis* matches with *Denis*. Explain the new word *la vela* (sailing). Students then continue to use rhyme to complete the activities rap. You could practise it first as a class and then in pairs with students taking alternate lines.

Answers: Asunción – la natación; Adela – la vela; Anastasia – la gimnasia; Ernesto – baloncesto; Emiliano – el piano; Mariví – el esquí

| AT3.4 | **2 Lee y decide qué animal les conviene mejor.** |

Students read the descriptions of the people and decide which pet would suit them best.

Answers: Jorge – un perro; Ana – un gato; Sofía – un pez de colores

Vocabulario

página 79

This page provides a theme-based Spanish–English summary of the key language of this unit. It can be used for reference throughout the unit or as an aid to learning vocabulary.

| C77 | Copymaster 77 contains a summary of the key language of the unit and can be given to the students at this point to help with revision. |

| W51 | Page 51 of the *Uno/Dos* Workbooks also provides a summary of the key language of the unit. |

Ya sé

página 80

The *Ya sé* page provides an end-of-unit checklist of learning objectives. At the foot of the page are activities at three levels of difficulty to extend the work of the unit. Encourage students to select an activity at the most appropriate level.

| C78 | Copymaster 78 contains a checklist and activities to keep track of the students' progress. |

| W51 | Page 51 of the *Uno/Dos* Workbooks gives an end-of-unit checklist in Spanish and English, together with activities to keep track of the students' progress. |

Unidad 5 Uno

página 104

Objectives

This reinforcement page is intended for those students who need further practice of core language of the unit. It can be used by students who finish other activities early or as alternative class or homework material.

Resources

Students' Book, page 104
CD 2, track 29

Programme of Study reference

1a, 1c, 2a, 3e, 4a, 4d, 5a, 5d, 5e, 5f, 5i

| AT4.1 | **1 Escribe las palabras en el orden correcto.** |

Students complete the days of the week, and then write them out in the correct order.

Answer: lunes; martes; miércoles; jueves; viernes; sábado; domingo

| AT1.2 | **2 Escucha. Copia y rellena el cuadro.** |

Students listen and complete the grid with the people's hobbies and interests.

Answers: Hugo rugby, tocar la trompeta; Itzcoátl nadar, navegar por Internet; Bibi equitación, ver la televisión

---

 CD 2, track 29　　　　　página 104, actividad 2

1 – Me llamo Rachid. En mis ratos libres me gusta jugar al tenis con mis amigos. En la casa me gusta escuchar música en mi mp3.
2 – Soy Hugo. Me gusta jugar al rugby en el club de rugby. También me gusta tocar la trompeta.
3 – Me llamo Itzcoátl. Me gusta nadar en la piscina. Me gusta mucho navegar por Internet en mi ordenador.
4 – Me llamo Bibi. Me gusta practicar la equitación. En mis ratos libres me gusta ver la televisión.

| AT2.3 | **3 Utiliza tus respuestas para hacer tres diálogos.** |

Students work in pairs or small groups. They use the answers they gave to exercise 2 to make up and practise three more dialogues based on the example.

AT3.3 | **4** Lee la entrevista. Contesta a las preguntas en inglés.

Students read the interview with Ana about sports. They answer the questions in English. This could be done as an individual or a group activity.

Answers: a skiing; b to ski; c yes; d basketball; e no; f it's boring

AT4.3 | **5** Escribe tres frases para contestar a las mismas preguntas que Ana.

Students write their own personal answers to the same three questions as Ana in exercise 4. This could be the basis for a piece of display work.

Unidad 5 Dos
página 105

Objectives

This extension page is intended for more able students who are confident with the core language of the unit. It can be used by students who finish other activities quickly or as alternative class or homework material.

Resources

Students' Book, page 105
CD 2, track 30

Programme of Study reference

1c, 2a, 2c, 2d, 2h, 2i, 3e, 4a, 4d, 5a, 5d, 5e, 5f, 5i

AT3.3 | **1** Lee la postal y completa las frases.

Students read the postcard from Héctor and use the information to complete sentences a–i.

Answers: b juega; c habla; d hablan; e visitan; f juegan; g juega; h juega; i bailar

AT1.3 | **2** Escucha a Carmen. ¿Verdad o mentira?

Students listen to Carmen talking about her family and their hobbies and interests and decide if statements a–h are true or false.

CD 2, track 30 página 105, actividad 2

– ¿Qué te gusta hacer con tu familia?
– Pues, a mí me gusta la natación, pero voy a la piscina con mis amigos, no con mi familia. Es porque mi hermano no nada. No le gusta el agua fría.
– Entonces, ¿qué haces con tu hermano?
– Mi hermano prefiere el bádminton, entonces el fin de semana Jorge y yo jugamos al bádminton en el jardín.
– ¿Practicas algún deporte con tu hermana?
– No, mi hermana no practica ningún deporte. Prefiere hablar por teléfono todo el día.

– ¿Y con tus padres?
– Pues mis padres escuchan música clásica y bailan. Yo no bailo, y no me gusta la música clásica.

AT4.4 | **3** Escribe un párrafo sobre esta familia.

Students write a paragraph about the family shown in the picture. They can use the previous two exercises to help them.

Unidad 5 Lectura: uno
página 116

Objectives

This page is to encourage independent reading. Students should attempt it once they are confident with the core language of the unit. It can be used by students who finish other activities early or as alternative class or homework material.

Resources

Students' Book, page 116
CD 2, track 31

Programme of Study reference

1a, 1c, 2b, 2g, 2h, 2i, 3b, 3c, 3d, 3e, 4a, 4d, 5d, 5e, 5f, 5g, 5i

AT3.2 | **1** Lee y empareja las dos mitades de las frases.

Students read statements a–e and match them up with the other halves of the sentences 1–5.

Answers: a 3; b 1; c 5; d 2; e 4

AT3.2 | **2** Completa las frases con la palabra correcta.

Students read sentences a–g and fill in the gasp with the words from the list on the right.

Answers: b nadar; c playa; d salón; e música; f bailar; g hablar

AT1.2 | **3** Escucha y lee. Apunta en inglés los detalles de estas invitaciones.

Students listen and read the invitations. In English, they note down the inportant details – who, where and when.

CD 2, track 31 página 116, actividad 3

a – Claudia te invita a una fiesta en la discoteca "XOX" para celebrar su cumpleaños el día veintiuno de septiembre a las nueve.
b – ¿Quieres ir a la playa? Voy el martes con unos amigos. Juan Carlos
c – El sábado voy a ver 'King Kong' en el cine. ¿Quieres ir? Es a las cuatro o a las ocho. Tu amiga, Elena

Unidad 5 Lectura: dos

página 117

Objectives

This page is to encourage independent reading. Students should attempt it once they are confident with the core language of the unit. It can be used by students who finish other activities early or as alternative class or homework material.

Resources

Students' Book, page 117

Programme of Study reference

1a, 1c, 2b, 2c, 2f, 2h, 3b, 3c, 3d, 3e, 4a, 4c, 4d, 5c, 5d, 5f, 5g, 5i

AT3.4 | **1 Lee y nota quién menciona las actividades en la lista de Jenny y de Michael.**

Students read the texts and decide which of the possible penfriends mention the same activities as Jenny and Michael. (At this stage, encourage the students simply to find words and phrases that match; they will go on to work out whether the people actually enjoy these activities in the following exercise.)

Answers:

Jenny: Virginia mentions the cinema, horse riding and swimming. Sergio mentions reading, watching films, swimming, horse riding and football.
Michael: Ángel mentions skiing, music, dancing and rugby. Ricardo mentions skiing, music and dancing. He also mentions dangerous sports and violent activities (which the students may associate with rugby from Michael's list).

AT3.4 | **2 Busca el/la amigo/a con los intereses más similares a los de Jenny y Michael.**

Students decide which potential penfriend has the closest set of interests to Jenny or Michael.

Answers:

Jenny and Sergio share all the same likes and dislikes.
(Virginia likes going to the cinema and horse riding, but does not like swimming, which Jenny does like, and does like watching football, which Jenny does not like. Sergio likes reading, watching films, swimming, and horse riding and he hates watching football. Jenny does not like bad weather, and Sergio likes to stay at home when it rains.
Michael and Ricardo have two interests in common and dislike the same things.
(Ángel likes skiing and music, but also likes dancing and rugby which Michael does not like. Ricardo likes skiing and music and does not like dancing. He also dislikes violent activities (such as rugby, perhaps)).

AT3.4 | **3 Lee los correos electrónicos de Rafa y Mohammed. ¿Verdad o mentira?**

Students read the two emails from Rafa and Mohammed and decide if statements a–j are true or false.

Answers: a V; b V; c M; d M; e V; f M; g M; h M; i V; j M

Copymasters

Hoja 79 ¡A sus marcas!

This can be used after pages 68–69 in the Students' Book.

AT3.3 | **1 Haz corresponder las partes de las frases.**

You may want to suggest that students work first in pencil on this activity and then finish in pen when they are sure. Students read the parts of the sentences carefully and find four logical sentences.

Answers:

Me gusta jugar al baloncesto el fin de semana en el polideportivo./Me gusta jugar al baloncesto con mi padre en el parque el sábado y el domingo.
No me gusta practicar el deporte pero me gusta ver el fútbol en la televisión.
Mi deporte favorito es el tenis y me gusta jugar en el club el fin de semana.
Me gusta jugar al fútbol con mi padre en el parque el sábado y el domingo.

AT4.2 | **2 Pon esas frases en orden.**

Students write the sentences with the words in the correct order.

Answers:

a Me gusta el rugby.
b Me gusta el deporte y mi favorito es el rugby.
c Es mi deporte favorito porque es violento.
d No me gusta jugar al rugby.
e Prefiero ver el rugby en la televisión.

AT3.1 | **3 Colorea sólo las actividades deportivas.**

Students colour in just the sporting activities, leaving the others blank.

Answers: Students should colour: *practicar el esquí; nadar; jugar al tenis; montar a caballo; practicar el atletismo; jugar al baloncesto.*

Hoja 80 Reto

This can be used after pages 72–73 in the Students' Book.

AT 4.2/3 **1 Completa la tabla con la forma correcta del verbo.**

Students complete the table.

Answers:

	lavo el coche		lava el coche
		paseas el perro	pasea el perro
	arreglo	arreglas	
nadar	nado	nadas	nada

AT3.2 **2 Haz corresponder el lugar con la actividad.**

Students match the activity with the place where they would do it.

Answers: 1 d; 2 b; 3 e; 4 a; 5 c

AT3.1 **3 Encuentra al intruso. Explica la razón.**

Students find the odd one out and explain why.

Answers:
a montar (The rest are all to do with swimming.)
b juego   (The rest are all infinitives.)
c esquí (The rest are all ball games.)
d jugar (The rest have something to do with music / the arts.)
e leer (The rest are -ar verbs.)

Hoja 81 Escuchar: uno

This can be used after pages 68–69 in the Students' Book.

AT1.2 **1 Escucha y pon las cinco actividades en orden.**

Students listen and put the activities in order.

Answers: 1; 3; 5; 4; 2

 CD 3, track 42   Hoja 81, actividad 1

a – Me gusta ir a la playa con mis amigos y jugar al fútbol.
b – No me gusta nadar en el mar, prefiero nadar en la piscina.
c – Pienso que el tenis es aburrido. No me interesa.
d – Me gusta ver la televisión, sobre todo el deporte.
e – Me encanta hablar por teléfono con mis amigos. A mi padre no le gusta.

AT 1.2/3 **2 Escucha otra vez y decide si le gusta o si no le gusta.**

Students listen again (see transcript for activity 1) and draw a happy or sad face according to whether the opinion expressed is positive or negative.

Answers: phoning: le gusta; football: le gusta; swimming: le gusta; 4 TV: le gusta; 5 tennis: no le gusta

Hoja 81 Escuchar: dos

AT1.3 **3 Escucha. ¿Cuál es su actividad preferida?**

Students listen and tick the correct box.

Answers: 1 b – dancing; 2 b – sport on TV; 3 c – basketball; 4 a – football; 5 b – singing

 CD 3, track 43   Hoja 81, actividad 3

1 – Me gusta bailar y cantar, pero prefiero bailar.
2 – No me gusta jugar al fútbol, pero me gusta mucho ver el fútbol en la televisión.
3 – Me gusta nadar, pero mi actividad favorita es el baloncesto.
4 – El fútbol es mi actividad preferida. No me gusta el tenis.
5 – Me gusta la música. Toco la trompeta, pero pienso que prefiero cantar.

AT 1.3/4 **4 Escucha. Completa la tabla.**

Students listen and complete the table.

Answers:
el viernes: (quieres ir) al cine
el sábado: (puedes ir) a la discoteca, no me gusta bailar
el domingo: (nos encontramos en) el parque; estudiar

 CD 3, track 44   Hoja 81, actividad 4

– Hola. ¿Quieres ir al cine el viernes?
– El viernes, ¿al cine? Me gustaría, pero tengo que ayudar a mi padre a lavar el coche.
– Entonces, ¿puedes ir a la discoteca el sábado?
– ¿A la discoteca? No, gracias. No me gusta bailar.
– ¿Nos encontramos en el parque el domingo?
– Lo siento, el domingo no puedo. Tengo que estudiar para un examen el lunes.

Hoja 82 Hablar: uno

This can be used after pages 74–75 in the Students' Book.

AT 2.2/3 **1a Da una opinión según los dibujos.**

In pairs, students take it in turns to make appropriate sentences about the activities and the opinions suggested.

1b Da tu propia opinión.

Students then give their own opinion about the activities shown.

AT 2.3/4

2 Haz frases sólo con palabras en ese cuadro. Puedes repetir.

Students make up sentences using the vocabulary in the box. They can use words more than once. You might like to set a time limit for this part of activity to make it into a competition.

Hoja 82 Hablar: dos

AT 2.3/4

3 Turnaros para sugerir una cita e inventar un pretexto.

Students working at a higher level take it in turns to invite each other to go somewhere or to do something. The other person has to give an excuse not to go.

Hoja 83 Leer y escribir: uno

This can be used after pages 68–69 in the Students' Book.

AT3.2

1 ¿En la casa o no? Utiliza flechas.

Students draw arrows from the words to the house or the park and sports centre, depending on where the activities are usually done.

Answers:

House: *tocar la trompeta; ver la televisión; leer; navegar por Internet*

Park or sports centre: *jugar al tenis; nadar; montar en bicicleta; jugar al golf*

AT3.1

2 Busca cinco actividades y cinco adjetivos en la sopa de letras.

Students find and circle the words.

Answers:

n	u	a	e	l	g	o	l	f	u
r	ó	c	e	r	b	q	z	o	q
á	d	i	v	e	r	t	i	d	o
p	y	s	c	l	i	c	u	i	d
i	b	ú	u	a	c	e	x	r	i
d	g	m	v	j	t	b	f	r	f
o	u	a	c	a	l	a	x	u	í
w	r	l	z	n	y	o	n	b	c
v	l	l	m	t	f	d	z	a	i
u	e	l	t	e	n	i	s	q	l

AT4.2

3 Haz corresponder los adjetivos con las actividades.

Students use the words from exercise 2 to make five logical sentences. Answers will vary but check for the correct agreement of the adjectives ending in -o/-a (masculine with *el golf*, *el tenis* and *el rugby*; feminine with *la música* and *la natación*).

Hoja 84 Leer y escribir: dos

This can be used after pages 68–69 in the Students' Book.

AT 3.3/4

1 Lee la carta y subraya las actividades en rojo y las opiniones en negro.

Students read the letter and underline the activities in red and the opinion language in black.

Answers:

Red: nadar; no practico el esquí; monto en bicicleta; (hablamos); jugamos al tenis; ayudar a mi madre

Black: ¿Te gusta?; Me gusta; (¿Qué te gusta? = asking for an opinion); Prefiero; quiero

AT 3.4/5

2 Contesta en inglés.

Students read the letter again and answer the questions in English.

Answers:

1 swim (in the pool)
2 in the swimming pool
3 because she doesn't live near the coast
4 skiing
5 rides her bike, sees friends, talks/chats, plays tennis
6 practise her English

AT4.4

3 Escribe una carta de Rajan a Celestina. Menciona las siguientes cosas.

Students write a letter from Rajan in reply to Celestina's, covering the points suggested. You might want to encourage stronger groups to use an example of the immediate future. Answers will vary, but it may help to take in the students' work at the end of one lesson, to check what opinions / activities most students have included, and to use that as a basis for preparing a version to discuss in the next lesson.

Hoja 85 Gramática

This can be used after pages 68–69 in the Students' Book.

AT 3.2/3

1 Fill in the missing endings in these verbs. Then write the English underneath.

Students complete the verb forms and translate them.

Answers: bailas = you dance; baila = he/she/Ud dances; we dance; you (plural) dance; they dance
practico = I do; practicas = you do; practica = he / she/Ud does; practicamos = we do; practicáis = you (plural) do; practican = they do

AT4.3 | **2** Translate into Spanish.

Students translate the sentences.

Answers:

1 ¿Bailas? / ¿Bailáis? (Ud: ¿Baila? / Uds: ¿Bailan?)
2 No bailo, pero mi hermana baila.
3 Nadamos en la piscina, pero no nado en la playa.
4 ¡Mi hermana escucha a Coldplay, escucho a Green Day y mis padres escuchan a los / The Beach Boys!
5 Paseo al perro, mi hermana lava los platos, y mis padres bailan en el salón.

Hoja 86 Técnica

This can be used after pages 70–71 in the Students' Book.

AT2.2 | **1** Read this sentence to a partner. They have to follow the arrows from box to box as you speak.

In pairs, students take it in turns to read and follow the sentence.

AT 2.3/5 | **2** Make up your own sentences. See how many times you can go round without contradicting yourself.

Students work on their own making up sentences in the same way. Monitor as they work and remind them that they need to make as many sentences as possible to use in the following activity.

AT 2.3/5 | **3** With a partner, take turns to follow the arrows to build a sentence. It must make a correct sentence. The person who doesn't make sense or who can't carry on loses.

In pairs, students take it in turns to build sentences until one of them is unable to make a logical sentence.

Hoja 87 Cultura

This can be used after pages 76–77 in the Students' Book.

AT3.4 | **1** Look at the programme and find these things.

Students scan the cultural events programme to find items 1–10.

Answers: 1 the orchestral concert, the flamenco concert, the Shakaso concert; 2 the orchestral concert; 3 the film; 4 the Shakaso concert; 5 the flamenco concert; 6 the Plena Luna festival, the Castillo de Arena competition; 7 the Luna Llena festival at 23:00 (Luna Llena = full moon); 8 sandcastle competition at 17:00 (earliest because perhaps children are involved); 9 the Shakaso concert (entrada €30); 10 students' own answers

Hoja 88 Se pronuncia así

This can be used after page 68 in the Students' Book.

AT3.1 | **1** Underline the words in exercise 2a.

Discuss the *¡Recuerda!* box with the class. Students then underline the words in activity 2a using the colour scheme suggested.

Answers:

red: el esquí; la natación; la equitación; rápido; fácil; difícil
blue: el patinaje; el tenis; el baloncesto; el atletismo; el ciclismo; la gimnasia; juego; divertido; aburrido; lento; violento; peligroso; interesante
green: jugar; practicar

AT3.1 | **2a** Colour in the syllable that is stressed.

Students highlight the syllable that is stressed.

Answers:

el pati**na**je; el **te**nis; el balon**ces**to; el atle**tis**mo; el es**quí**; el ci**clis**mo; la gim**na**sia; la nata**ción**; la equita**ción**; ju**gar**; **jue**go; practi**car**; diver**ti**do; abu**rri**do; **rá**pido; **len**to; vio**len**to; peli**gro**so; **fá**cil; di**fí**cil; intere**san**te

AT2.1 | **2b** Say the words from activity 2a aloud, then listen to check your pronunciation.

Students practise saying the words and then listen and check.

 CD 3, track 45   Hoja 88, actividad 2b

el patinaje ... el tenis ... el baloncesto … el atletismo ... el esquí ... el ciclismo … la gimnasia ... la natación ... la equitación … jugar ... juego ... practicar ... divertido ... aburrido ... rápido … lento ... violento ... peligroso … fácil ... difícil ... interesante

AT4.3 | **3** Now make up sentences using these words for your partner to practise.

Students make up sentences using the words. In pairs they then take turns to read each other's sentences. Monitor to make sure that students are stressing the words correctly.

Control Unidad 5

Resources

Copymasters 89–94
CD 3, tracks 46–47

Hoja 89 Escuchar: uno

1a Escucha y haz corresponder las personas con el deporte que mencionan.

Students listen and match the people with the sports a–g.

Answers: Mario d; Virgilio f; Paula e; Eva g; Sergio c; Igor b

Mark scheme: Students who attempt *uno* only: 2 marks for each correct answer = 12 marks. 1 extra mark for accuracy. Students who attempt *uno* and *dos*: 1 mark for each correct answer = 6 marks

Assessment criteria: Students who match 4 correctly show evidence of performance at AT 1.2.

CD 3, track 46   Hoja 89, actividad 1

- Soy Chema. Me gusta el voleibol, sobre todo en la playa.
- Soy Mario. Me gusta la natación. Voy todos los días a la piscina.
- Me llamo Virgilio. No me gusta mucho el deporte, pero me gusta la equitación.
- Aquí Paula. El baloncesto es mi deporte favorito.
- Soy Eva. Me gusta mucho ver el fútbol en la televisión
- Hola. Soy Sergio. No me gusta practicar el esquí.
- Me llamo Igor. Me encanta jugar al tenis.

1b Escucha otra vez y decide si le gusta el deporte o no.

Students listen again and draw a happy or sad face according to the opinions expressed.

Answers: Mario ☺; Virgilio ☺; Paula ☺; Eva ☺; Sergio ☹; Igor ☺

Mark scheme: Students who attempt *uno* only: 2 marks for each correct answer = 12 marks
Students who attempt *uno* and *dos*: 1 mark for each correct answer = 6 marks

Assessment criteria: Students who draw 4 faces correctly show evidence of performance at AT 1.2. Students who draw all the faces correctly are performing at AT 1.3.

Hoja 89 Escuchar: dos

2 Escucha y completa las frases.

Students listen and complete the sentences.

Answers: jugar; tenis; ir; favorito; difícil; prefiero; fútbol

Mark scheme: 2 marks for each correct answer = 12 marks
1 extra mark for accuracy.

Assessment criteria: Students who complete five or more gaps correctly show evidence of performance at AT 1.3.

CD 3, track 47   Hoja 89, actividad 2

- ¿Me gusta el deporte? Sí, claro. Me gusta jugar con mis amigos. Por ejemplo el fin de semana voy a jugar al tenis con Ángel. También me gusta ir al gimnasio o a la piscina. ¿Mi favorito? Es difícil decir, pero pienso que prefiero el baloncesto. No me gusta ver la televisión, excepto el fútbol.

Hoja 90 Hablar: uno

1 Haz preguntas a tu compañero/a.

2 Responde a las preguntas de tu compañero/a.

In pairs, students ask and answer about free time activities and chores at home, using the picture prompts.

Mark scheme:
Students who attempt uno only: 15 marks for communication; 10 marks for accuracy and variety = 25 marks
Students who attempt *uno* and *dos*: 6 marks for communication; 4 marks for accuracy and variety = 10 marks

Assessment criteria: Students who score 60% of the available marks at their level show evidence of performance at AT 2.3. Students who score 80% or more are performing at AT 2.4.

Hoja 90 Hablar: dos

3a Haz preguntas a tu compañero/a.

3b Responde a las preguntas de tu compañero/a.

In pairs, students ask and answer about the use of their own free time.

Mark scheme: 9 marks for communication; 6 marks for accuracy and variety = 15 marks

Assessment criteria: Students who score 9–12 show evidence of performance at AT 2.3. Students who score 13–15 or more are performing at AT 2.4. AT 2.5 can be awarded for students using a particularly wide range of structures and opinion language.

Hoja 91 Leer: uno

1 Haz corresponder las frases con los dibujos.

Students match the sentences with the pictures.

Answers: a 5; b 2; c 3; d 1; e 4

Mark scheme: 2 marks for each correct answer = 10 marks

Assessment criteria: Students who match four or five correctly show evidence of performance at AT 3.2.

AT3.2 | **2 Lee e identifica las personas.**

Students read what the people say about their free time activities and write the correct name next to each set of pictures.

Answers: 1 David; 2 Elena; 3 Juan; 4 Isa; 5 Hammú

Mark scheme: 3 marks for each correct answer = 15 marks

Assessment criteria: Students who match four or five correctly show evidence of performance at AT 3.2.

Hoja 92 Leer: dos

AT3.3 | **1 Lee e identifica las actividades. Separálas en dos listas en inglés.**

Students complete the table with the free time activities and jobs translated into English.

Answers:
Free time: read; play (with the dog), watch television
Jobs: tidy (my books); help (my mother in the garden); prepare food / lunch

Mark scheme: 1 mark for each correct answer = 6 marks

Assessment criteria: Students who list four or more correctly show evidence of performance at AT 3.3.

AT3.4 | **2 Lee y decide si es Verdad o Mentira.**

Students read the text and mark the sentences true or false.

Answers: 1 V; 2 M; 3 M; 4 V; 5 M; 6 M; 7 M

Mark scheme: 1 mark for each correct answer = 7 marks

Assessment criteria: Students who mark five or more sentences correctly show evidence of performance at AT 3.4.

AT 3.3/4 | **3 Haz corresponder las respuestas con las preguntas.**

Students match the questions and the answers.

Answers: 1 b; 2 e; 3 d; 4 f; 5 c; 6 a

Mark scheme: 2 marks for each correct answer = 12 marks

Assessment criteria: Students who match four or five correctly show evidence of performance at AT 3.3. Students who match them all correctly are performing at AT 3.4

Hoja 93 Escribir: uno

AT 4.1/2 | **1 Escribe las palabras.**

Students label the pictures.

Answers: 1 fútbol; b tenis; c baloncesto; d rugby; e esquí

Mark scheme: 1 mark for each correct answer (Half a mark for the correct sport; half a mark for the correct spelling and accents) = 5 marks

Assessment criteria: Students who score 2–3.5 show evidence of performance at AT 4.1. Students who score 4 or more are performing at AT 4.2.

AT4.2 | **2 Rellena los espacios para completar estas frases.**

Students complete the sentences with their own ideas. Answers will vary but should be logical and make grammatical sense.

Mark scheme: 2 marks for each correct answer (1 mark for communication; 1 mark for accuracy) = 12 marks

Assessment criteria: Students who score 9 or more show evidence of performance at AT 4.2.

AT4.3 | **3 Escribe una frase para cada imagen.**

Students write an appropriate sentence for each picture, using the appropriate opinion language.

Answers:
1 Me gusta ver la televisión.
2 No me gusta escuchar música.
3 Me gustar montar en bicicleta / practicar ciclismo.
4 No me gusta nadar / la natación.

Mark scheme: 2 marks for each correct answer (1 mark for the opinion language; 1 mark for the activity = 8 marks

Assessment criteria: Students who score 6 or more show evidence of performance at AT 4.3.

Hoja 94 Escribir: dos

AT4.3 | **1 Escribe una frase para cada día.**

Students use the information in the table to write sentence about each day.

Answers:
El martes juego al fútbol.
El miércoles mi hermano y yo lavamos el coche.
El jueves mi tío practica el boxeo.
El viernes mis padres nadan.
El sábado mi hermana baila.
El domingo toco la trompeta.

Mark scheme: 1 mark for each correct answer (Half a mark for the correct day of the week; half a mark for the correct verb form) = 6 marks

Assessment criteria: Students who score 4.5 or more show evidence of performance at AT 4.3.

AT 4.3/4 | **2 Imagina que eres Urbano. Escribe un párrafo sobre tus ratos libres.**

Students write a paragraph covering all the information given.

Answers:
En mis ratos libres me gusta leer, escuchar música, ver la televisión y jugar al tenis. Me encanta jugar al tenis. / Es mi deporte favorito. No me gusta jugar al fútbol ni la natación, y no me gusta pasear el perro. En casa lavo los platos. El fin de semana juego al tenis.

Mark scheme: 2 marks for each category (1 mark for communication; 1 mark for accuracy) = 10 marks

Assessment criteria: Students who score 6–8 show evidence of performance at AT 4.3. Students who score 9–10 are performing at AT 4.4.

AT 4.3/5 **3 Contesta a esas preguntas.**

Students write about their own free time, answering the three questions.

Mark scheme: 3 marks for each correct answer (2 marks for communication; 1 mark for accuracy) = 9 marks

Assessment criteria: Students who score 5–7 show evidence of performance at AT 4.3. Students who score 8–9 are performing at AT 4.4. AT 4.5 can be awarded to students using a particularly wide range of structures.

Uno Workbook

Página 44 (5.1)
This page can be used with pages 68–69 of the Students' Book.

AT3.2 **1a ¿Qué hace Rocío en su tiempo libre?**

Students circle eight activities in the puzzle.

Answers: bailar; nadar; escuchar música; leer; ver la televisión; tocar la guitarra; hablar por teléfono; ir a la playa

AT4.2 **1b Ahora escribe las actividades.**

Students label the pictures with the words they found in exercise 1a.

Answers: a leer; b hablar por teléfono; c bailar; d tocar la guitarra; e nadar; f ver la televisión; g ir a la playa; h escuchar música

AT3.3 **2 Lee lo que dicen estos chicos. ¿Quién habla?**

Students read the sentences and look at the information in the table. They then write the correct name for each sentence.

Answers: b Sandra; c Carla; d Carla; e Abelardo; f Charo; g Sandra; h Abelardo

AT4.4 **3 ¿Qué te gusta y no te gusta hacer en tu tiempo libre?**

Students write about what they do in their free time, using page 53.

Página 45 (5.2)
This page can be used with pages 70–71 of the Students' Book.

AT3.1 **1 ¿Qué deportes practica Lola? Subráyalos.**

Students look at Lola's sports equipment and underline the sports that she does.

Answers: el baloncesto; el tenis; el fútbol; el esquí; el ciclismo; la natación; la equitación

AT3.2 **2 ¿Qué significa la palabra?**

Students match the Spanish words with the English translations.

Answers: aburrido = boring; difícil = difficult; ruidoso = noisy; divertido = fun; violento = violent; lento = slow; fácil = easy; relajante = relaxing

AT3.3 **3 Completa estas frases.**

Students choose from the adjectives in exercise 2 to complete the sentences. Answers will vary, but check for appropriate sense according to the opinion language in the sentence, and for the feminine agreement of adjectives where necessary with *la gimnasia*.

AT4.4 **4 Ahora inventa otras tres frases.**

Students make up three more sentences using the opinion language and adjectives on the page. Answers will vary, but check for appropriate positive or negative adjectives according to the opinion language that the students have used, and for adjectival agreement with feminine sports and activities.

Página 46 (5.3)
This page can be used with pages 72–73 of the Students' Book.

AT3.3 **1 Escoge una frase para cada dibujo.**

Students write the correct letter in the box to match the phrases with the pictures.

Answers: 2 e; 3 g; 4 h; 5 b; 6 c; 7 f; 8 a

| AT3.3 | **2 Mira la tabla. ¿Verdad o mentira?** |

Students look at the information in the table and mark the sentences true or false.

Answers: b M; c M; d V; e V; f V

| AT2.4 |
| AT4.4 | **3 ¿Y tú? ¿Ayudas en casa?** |

Students think about what they do to help at home and write sentences on page 53, the spare page for writing at the end of the unit. They then talk to a partner and make a note of their answers. As a follow-up, encourage them to write full sentences using the correct third person singular form of the verbs.

Página 47 (5.4)

This page can be used with pages 74–75 of the Students' Book.

| AT2.3 |
| AT3.3 | **1 Rellena las nubes.** |

Students choose the correct language from the word box to complete each speech bubble, making a logical conversation.

Answers:
¿Diga?
Hola, soy Jorge. ¿Quieres ir a la playa?
Sí, ¿cuándo?
El fin de semana, el sábado.
¿A qué hora?
A las once.
¿Dónde nos encontramos?
En tu casa.
Estupendo. A las once en mi casa. ¡Adiós!
Adiós.

| AT4.3 | **2 ¿Qué vas a hacer? Escribe cinco frases.** |

Students write five sentences choosing a day of the week and then a phrase from each column in the table. Answers will vary. You may want to allow them to make up nonsense sentences as long as they can tell you and the class what they mean, but note that they then use the sentences for the following activity as well.

| AT2.4 | **3 Haz preguntas con tu compañero/a.** |

In pairs, students take it in turns to ask about their partner's plans for each day of the week. They use the model question given and the sentences that they wrote in exercise 2.

Página 48 (5.5)

This page can be used with pages 76–77 of the Students' Book.

| AT3.4 | **1 Une las frases con los dibujos.** |

Students match the sentences with the pictures.

Answers: 1 b; 2 e; 3 f; 4 c; 5 a; 6 d

| AT3.2 | **2 Escoge la frase correcta.** |

Students circle the correct sentence for each picture.

Answers: 2 a; 3 b; 4 b; 5 b; 6 a

| AT4.3 | **3 ¿Cuántos euros tienes para tus ratos libres cada semana?** |

Students calculate their pocket money in euros and complete the sentence in Spanish.

| AT 3.5/6 | **4 Proyecto de información: ¿Quién es Diego Maradona? Encuentra la siguiente información.** |

Students carry out Internet research to find the facts and answer the questions about Diego Maradona. Students with a particular interest in football may want to take this further.

Página 49 Gramática

This page can be used with pages 68–69 of the Students' Book. This page revises the structure of verb infinitives, highlighting the endings and the root, and also consolidates the endings of regular -ar verbs.

| AT3.2 | **1a Verbos: escribe el verbo correcto.** |

Students write the correct verb for each picture.

Answers:
Reading down the left-hand column: ir; leer
Reading down the right-hand column: nadar; tocar; ver

| AT3.2 | **1b ¿En qué letra acaban todos estos verbos?** |

Students check how each verb ends in its infinitive form.

Answers: the letter -r

| AT3.2 | **1c Ahora marca la raíz de todos los verbos.** |

Students highlight the root of the verbs in exercise 1a.

Answers: le-; nad-; bail-; v-; (*ir* es irregular); toca-;

| AT4.2 | **2 Verbos regulares, present de indicative: completa la tabla.** |

Students complete the table with the singular forms of *nadar* and *escuchar*.

Answers:
nado; nadas; nada
escucho; escuchas; escucha

AT 3.4/5 **3 Verbos, future inmediato: completa esta tabla.**
Students complete the table.

AT 4.4/5 **Answers:**
Voy a navegar por internet.
Voy a practicar la natación.
I go swimming.
Voy a lavar los platos
I am going to wash the dishes.
Voy a sacar la basura.
I put out the rubbish.

Página 50 Reto
This page can be used with page 78 of the Students' Book.

AT3.4 **1 Escribe las palabras apropiadas en los espacios.**
Students write the correct phrase from the word box for each picture.

Answers: la equitación; me chifla; voy a la playa; toco la guitarra; Me gusta; no me gusta; paseo al perro; arreglo mi dormitorio

AT3.4 **2 ¿Cuántas frases puedes encontrar en cinco minutos?**
Read the English instructions with the class and make sure that everyone understands the rules. Students then make as many sentences as they can and write them on page 53. You will probably need to extend the time limit with some **AT4.4** groups.

Dos Workbook

Página 44 (5.1)
This page can be used with pages 68–69 of the Students' Book.

AT3.2 **1 Mira los dibujos de las actividades que Rocío hace en su tiempo libre.**
Students look at the pictures of Rocío's hobbies and then find the words in the word snake. They work out which activity is missing from the snake.

Answers: The missing activity is: *navegar por internet*

AT3.4 **2 Lee lo que dicen estos chicos y mira la tabla. ¿Es verdad o mentira?**
Students read the sentences and look at the information in the table. They then mark the sentences true or false.

Answers: b V; c M; d M; e M; f M

AT4.4 **3 Corrige las frases incorrectas del ejercicio 2. Hay más de una respuesta correcta.**
Students correct the statements from exercise 2. There is more than one possible answer.

Answers:
a Me encanta escuchar música.
b Odio leer y no me gusta hablar por teléfono.
c Si llueve, me chifla escuchar música pero odio ver la televisión.
e Odio leer pero me gusta nadar.
f Me gusta ir a la playa, pero odio navegar por internet.

Página 45 (5.2)
This page can be used with pages 70–71 of the Students' Book.

AT3.3 **1a Completa la tabla de contrarios.**
AT4.3 Students complete the table of opposites in Spanish and English as shown in the example.

Answers:

divertido	fun	**aburrido**	**boring**
peligroso	**dangerous**	relajante	**relaxing**
difícil	**difficult**	**fácil**	**easy**

AT4.4 **1b Ahora escribe cuatro frases utilizando algunos de estos adjetivos.**
Remind the students about the sports that they have been working on in the Students' Book. They then write four sentences using some of the adjectives in exercise 1a. (If they wish, students may use other language, not just sports.) Answers will vary, but check for correct adjectival agreement.

AT3.4 **2 Lee esta entrevista de radio imaginaria. El sonido no es muy bueno y faltan palabras o trozos.**
AT4.4 Students complete the radio interview with appropriate words.

Answers: buenos; deporte practicas; natación; juego; fútbol; baloncesto; me; baloncesto; aburrido; ciclismo; practico; ciclismo; relajante; violento; juegas; porque; peligroso; adios

AT4.4 | **3 Ahora contesta a las preguntas para ti mismo.**

Students answer the questions in the radio interview about themselves on page 53, the spare page for writing at the end of the unit.

Página 46 (5.3)

This page can be used with pages 72–73 of the Students' Book.

AT4.3 | **1 Completa el crucigrama.**

Students complete the crossword.

Answers:

```
                           8
  1 | L | A | V | A | R | L | O | S | P | L | A | T | O | S |
                                    | A |
  2 | S | A | C | A | R | L | A | B | A | S | U | R | A |
                                    | E |
  3 | C | A | M | B | I | A | R | L | A | A | R | E | N | A | D | E | L | G | A | T | O |
                                    | R |
  4 | A | Y | U | D | A | R | E | N | E | L | J | A | R | D | I | N |
                                    | L |
  5 | L | A | V | A | R | L | A | R | O | P | A |
                                    | E |
              6 | L | A | V | A | R | E | L | C | O | C | H | E |
                                    | R |
  7 | A | R | R | E | G | L | A | R | M | I | D | O | R | M | I | T | O | R | I | O |
```

AT3.4 | **2a Mira la tabla. ¿Quién habla?**

Students look at the information in the table and write the correct name or family member for each sentence.

Answers:
a mi hermana; b mi madre; c Carlos; d mi hermana; e mi padre; f mi padre

Página 47 (5.4)

This page can be used with pages 74–75 of the Students' Book.

AT3.4 | **1 Pon las frases en orden para recrear la conversación.**

AT4.4 | Students write the sentences in the correct order to make a logical conversation.

Answers:
¿Diga?
Hola, soy Jorge. ¿Quieres ir a la playa?
Sí, ¿cuándo?
El fin de semana, el sábado.
¿A qué hora?
A las once.
¿Dónde nos encontramos?
En mi casa.
Estupendo. A las once en tu casa. ¡Adiós!
Adiós.

AT4.3 | **2 ¿Qué vas a hacer? Escribe cinco frases en la página 53 utilizando la tabla.**

Students write five sentences on page 53 choosing a day of the week and then a phrase from each column in the table. Answers will vary. You may want to allow them to make up nonsense sentences as long as they can tell you and the class what they mean.

Página 48 (5.5)

This page can be used with pages 76–77 of the Students' Book.

AT3.4 | **1 Une las frases con los dibujos apropiados.**

Students match the sentences with the pictures.

Answers: 1 b; 2 e; 3 f; 4 c; 6 d

AT3.3 | **2 ¿Verdad o mentira?**

Students mark the sentences true or false.

Answers: b V; c V; d M; e M; f M

AT4.3 | **3 Corrige las frases incorrectas del ejercicio 2.**

Students correct the false sentences from exercise 2..

Answers:
a Tengo cincuenta euros.
d Tengo diecinueve euros.
e Tengo veinte euros.
f Tengo ocho euros.

AT4.3 | **4 ¿Cuántos euros tienes para tus ratos libres cada semana?**

Students calculate their pocket money in euros and write the number in Spanish.

AT 3.5/6 | **5 Proyecto de información: ¿Quién es Diego Maradona? Encuentra la siguiente información.**

Students carry out Internet research to find the facts and answer the questions about Diego Maradona. Students with a particular interest in football may want to take this further.

Página 49 Gramática

This page can be used with pages 68–69 of the Students' Book.
This page revises the structure of verb infinitives, highlighting the endings and the root, and also consolidates the endings of regular -ar verbs.

AT3.2 | **1a** Verbos: une los dibujos con el verbo correcto.

Students match the pictures with the verbs in the boxes.

Answers: Reading across the rows:
bailar; escuchar; hablar; ir; leer;
nadar; navegar; jugar; tocar; ver

AT3.2 | **1b** Marca la raíz de todos los verbos.

Students highlight the root of the verbs in exercise 1a.

Answers: bail-; escuch- habl-; (*ir* es irregular); le-; nad-;
naveg-; jug-; toc-; v-

AT4.3 | **2** Verbos regulares, presente de indicativo: completa la tabla.

Students complete the table with the present simple forms of regular -*ar* verbs.

Answers:
hablo; hablas; habla; hablamos; habláis; hablan
navego; navegas; navega; navegamos; navegáis; navegan
nado; nadas; nada; nadamos; nadáis; nadan
escucho; escuchas; escucha; escuchamos; escucháis; escuchan

AT3.4 | **AT4.4** | **3** Verbos, futuro inmediato: cambia estas frases del presente al futuro inmediato.

Students change the sentences into the immediate future.

Answers:
Voy a navegar por internet.
Voy a leer Harry Potter.
Voy a jugar al fútbol.
Voy a practicar la natación.
Voy a lavar los platos.
Voy a ir a la playa.
Voy a pasear al perro.
Voy a arreglar mi dormitorio.
Voy a sacar la basura.

Página 50 Reto

This page can be used with page 80 of the Students' Book.

AT3.4 | **1** Escoge el adjetivo correcto.

Students choose the correct form of the adjective for each sentence. As a follow-up, you could ask students to identify which of the incorrect forms are the wrong gender (a, b, d) and which do not exist at all (c, f).

Answers: b violento; c relajante; d peligroso; e aburrida;
f difícil

AT3.4 | **2** ¿Cuántas frases puedes encontrar en cinco minutos?

AT4.4 | Read the English instructions with the class and make sure that everyone understands the rules. Students then make as many sentences as they can and write them on page 53. You will probably need to extend the time limit with some groups.

Unit 6 Overview grid						National Curriculum	
Pages/Contexts/ Cultural focus	Objectives	Grammar	Skills and Pronunciation	Key language	Framework	PoS	AT level
82–83 **6.1 Las asignaturas** School subjects	Say the school subjects in Spanish Say what subjects you like Describe the subjects	*gustar*	–	*¿Qué asignaturas te gustan? ¿Cuál es tu asignatura favorita? el inglés, el español, el francés, el alemán, el dibujo, la historia, la música, la geografía, la tecnología, la informática, la educación física, la religión, los idiomas, las ciencias, las matemáticas Me gusta/me gustan divertido/a, aburrido/a, difícil, fácil, útil, estresante, relajante, interesante No me gusta nada.*	(R) 7W2	1a, 1b, 1c, 2a, 2b, 2c, 2d, 2f, 2i, 3b, 3c, 3e, 4a, 4c, 4d, 5a, 5c, 5d, 5e, 5f, 5g	1.1, 1.3, 1.4, 2.1, 2.2/3, 2.3/4, 3.3, 3.2/3, 4.1–4
84–85 **6.2 Opiniones sobre el instituto** Opinions about subjects at school	Say what other people think of subjects Talk about what you can do in lessons	Radical-changing verbs	Verb + infinitive	*Pienso que, piensa que, digo, dice, dicen, tengo que, tiene que, tienen que porque tengo que..., pero Puedo*	(R) 7S8	1a, 1b, 1c, 2a, 2b, 2c, 2f, 2i, 3b, 3c, 3e, 4a, 4c, 4d, 5a, 5d, 5e, 5f, 5g, 5i	1.3, 2.3–4, 3.1–4, 4.1–4
86–87 **6.3 El horario** School timetables	Talk about the times of day Talk about your favourite day	Telling the time	–	*empezar, terminar, el recreo, la hora de comer A las..., Son las..., ¿Qué hora es?, Voy a casa a las..., Las clases terminan a las..., ¿Cuál es tu día favorito?, Prefiero el ...*		1a, 1b, 1c, 2a, 2c, 2d, 2f, 2g, 2h, 2i, 3b, 3c, 3d, 3e, 4a, 4c, 4d, 5a, 5c, 5d, 5e, 5f, 5g, 5i	1.1–2, 2.2–4, 3.1–4, 4.3–4
88–89 **6.4 El transporte** Transport	Say how you get to school Describe different forms of transport Talk about how long it takes to get there	–	–	*Es..., no es..., práctico, rápido, lento, cómodo, conveniente, necesario en coche, en autobús, en autocar, a pie, en avión, en tren, en barco, a caballo, en bicicleta, en patines, en monopatín diez, veinte, treinta, cuarenta, cincuenta, sesenta, setenta, ochenta, noventa, cien, treinta y tres, cuarenta y cuatro*		1a, 1b, 1c, 2a, 2b, 2c, 2d, 2f, 3b, 3c, 3e, 4c, 4d, 5a, 5c, 5d, 5e, 5f, 5g, 5i	1.3, 2.2, 3.3–4, 4.1–4
90–91 **6.5 Entre amigos** Unusual schools in Mexico and Spain	–	–	–	–	(R) 7C3	1c, 2a, 2c, 2f, 2h, 2i, 3b, 3c, 3e, 4a, 4c, 4d, 5d, 5e, 5g, 5h, 5i	1.4, 2.3, 3.1–4, 4.4

AMIGOS 1 UNIT 6 MEDIUM TERM PLAN

About this unit: In this unit students learn and use a range of new language in the context of school and transport. Students are encouraged to form compound sentences with *porque* to say which school subjects they like or dislike and why. Students build upon what they already know about using a verb + infinitive, and apply this to *puedo* and *tengo que*. Students are encouraged to think about the differences and similarities between Spanish and English schools.

Framework objectives (launch)	Teaching and learning	Week-by-week overview (assuming 6 weeks' work or approx. 10–12.5 hours)
7W2: high-frequency words	*gustar* (*me gusta/me gustan*) and radical-changing verbs *pensar, tener* and *decir*	**Week 1** Students learn to say school subjects in Spanish; to say what subjects they like and describe the subjects
7S8: punctuation and orthographic features	Separating the word snake so that it makes a sentence.	**Week 2** Say what other people think of subjects and talk about what you do in lessons
7C3: authentic materials	Students learn about different types of schools in Spain and Latin America	**Week 3** Talk about the times of day; telling the time and talk about your favourite day
Framework objectives (reinforce)	**Teaching and learning (additional)**	**Week 4** Say how you get to school; describe different forms of transport and talk about how long it takes to get there
	Spanish, Latin American and English schools: their differences	**Week 5** Students apply the language and structures learnt in this unit to reading and answering questions on longer texts which focus on an aspect of Spanish or Latin American culture
		Week 6 Recycle language of the unit via *Uno, Dos* and *Lectura* pages; students check their progress via the *Ya sé…* self-assessment checklist in the Students' Book and on Hoja 96.

En el cole

Unit objectives

Contexts: school subjects, opinions, times, transport, numbers 10–100
Grammar: *me gusta(n)*, radical changing verbs
Language learning: building on your understanding of verb + infinitive
Cultural focus: differences between Spanish and English schools

Assessment opportunities

Speaking: SB, page 83, activity 8
Reading: SB, page 83, activity 6
Listening: SB, page 83, activity 7
Writing: SB, page 85, activity 5

AT3.1 | **1** Decide cuál de las fotos es un instituto español.

Students look at the two photos and decide which of the two schools shown is a Spanish one.

Answer: b

AT3.3 | **2** Decide which are aspects of a typical English school, and which are more Spanish.

Students read the five pairs of statements and decide which ones fit each type of school. This could be done as a whole class or small group activity.

Answers: 1 a English, b Spanish; 2 a Spanish, b English; 3 a Spanish; b English; 4 a Spanish; b English; 5 a Spanish, b English

AT3.2 | **3** Lee y comprueba tus respuestas.

Students read the short text about a Spanish school to check their answers to exercise 2.

Planner

●●●●●●●●●●●●●●●●●●●●●●●●●●●●

6.1 Las asignaturas páginas 82–83

Objectives

▶ Say the school subjects in Spanish

▶ Say what subjects you like

▶ Describe the subjects

Resources

Students' Book, pages 82–83
CD 2, tracks 32–35
Uno/Dos Workbooks, page 54

Key language

¿Qué asignaturas te gustan?
¿Cuál es tu asignatura favorita?
el inglés, el español, el francés, el alemán, el dibujo, la historia,
la música, la geografía, la tecnología, la informática,
la educación física, la religión, los idiomas, las ciencias,
las matemáticas
Me gusta/me gustan
divertido/a, aburrido/a, difícil, fácil, útil, estresante, relajante,
interesante
No me gusta nada.

Programme of Study reference

1a, 1b, 1c, 2a, 2b, 2c, 2d, 2f, 2i, 3b, 3c, 3e, 4a, 4c, 4d, 5a,
5c, 5d, 5e, 5f, 5g, 5i

Framework reference

(R) 7W2

●●●●●●●●●●●●●●●●●●●●●●●●●●●●

¡A sus marcas!

Escucha. Levanta la mano si la palabra está en español.

Students listen and raise their hand if they hear a word in Spanish.

Answers: English, Spanish, Spanish, Spanish, English, Spanish, English, Spanish, English, Spanish, English, Spanish, English, English, Spanish, Spanish, English, English, Spanish, Spanish

 CD 2, track 32 página 82, ¡A sus marcas!

mathematics ... inglés ... matemáticas ... música ... technology ... ciencias ... religious studies ... educación física ... science ... religión ... English ... español ... Religious Studies ... ICT ... tecnología ... geografía ... geography ... history ... historia ... informática

---

AT2.1 **1** Mira los dibujos. Una persona dice la asignatura en inglés. La otra persona lee la palabra en español.

Students work in pairs. One says a subject in English, and the other finds the word and reads it in Spanish.

AT1.1 **2** Escucha y comprueba tu pronunciación.

Students listen and check to see if they were pronouncing the words correctly.

 CD 2, track 33 página 82, actividad 2

a – el inglés
b – el español
c – el francés
d – el alemán
e – el dibujo
f – la historia
g – la música
h – la geografía
i – la tecnología
j – la informática
k – la educación física
l – la religión
m – los idiomas
n – las ciencias
o – las matemáticas

AT1.4 **3** Escucha y apunta cuáles son las cinco asignaturas que le gustan a Fátima.

Students listen to Fátima talking about school subjects and note down which five she likes.

Answers: historia, educación física, tecnología, ciencias, inglés

 CD 2, track 34 página 82, actividad 3

– Fátima, ¿Cuál es tu asignatura favorita?
– Prefiero la historia. Me gusta mucho.
– ¿Qué otras asignaturas te gustan?
– Me gustan la educación física y la tecnología. También me gustan las ciencias.
– ¿Te gustan los idiomas?
– Me gusta el inglés, no me gusta el francés.
– ¿Qué asignaturas no te gustan?
– No me gusta el dibujo.

AT 2.2/3 **4** Explica a tu compañero/a cuáles son las asignaturas que te gustan y no te gustan.

In pairs, students use the table to tell their partner in Spanish which subjects they like and which ones they dislike.

Zoom gramática

This section explains the use of the verb *gustar* when referring to singular and plural items. It also highlights the use of the definite article in Spanish when talking about school subjects.

AT4.2

5 How would you say 'I like history'? And how would you say 'I like science'?

Answers: Me gusta la historia; me gustan las ciencias.

AT3.3

6 Lee y mira el cuadro. Identifica a las tres personas.

Students look at the grid and read the three short texts to decide which person is speaking in each one.

Answers: Raquel c; Adam a; Carlos b

AT 1.3/4

7 Escucha a Raúl. ¿Cuántas asignaturas le gustan? ¿Cuántas no?

Students listen to Raúl talking about school subjects and count how many he likes and how many he dislikes.

Answers: He likes six subjects and dislikes one.

CD 2, track 35   página 83, actividad 7

– Listo … ¡Empieza!
– Me gusta el francés porque es útil.
– Uno.
– Me gusta el inglés porque es fácil.
– Dos.
– Me gustan las matemáticas porque son divertidas.
  Me gusta la historia porque es interesante.
  Me encanta la educación física porque es fácil.
  Odio la informática porque es aburrida.
  Me gusta el dibujo porque es relajante.
– ¡Un minuto!

AT 2.3/4

8 ¡A contrarreloj! ¿Cuántas opiniones puedes dar en dos minutos?

Students work in pairs or small groups. They use the table to help them, and see how many opinions about school subjects, both positive and negative, they can give in two minutes.

Reto

AT 4.3/4

Escribe tus propias opiniones. Utiliza la tabla.

Students use the table in exercise 8 to help them write down what they think about school subjects, giving their reasons and opinions.

Planner

●●●●●●●●●●●●●●●●●●●●●●●●

6.2 **Opiniones sobre el instituto** páginas 84–85

Objectives

▶ Say what other people think of subjects

▶ Talk about what you can do in lessons

Resources

Students' Book, pages 84–85
CD 2, track 36
Uno/Dos Workbooks, page 55

Key language

pienso que / piensa que / piensan que
digo / dice / dicen
tengo que / tiene que / tienen que
porque tengo que…
pero
puedo

Programme of Study reference

1a, 1b, 1c, 2a, 2b, 2c, 2f, 2i, 3b, 3c, 3e, 4a, 4c, 4d, 5a, 5d, 5e, 5f, 5g, 5i

Framework reference

(R) 7S8

●●●●●●●●●●●●●●●●●●●●●●●●

¡A sus marcas!

¿Puedes leer esta frase?

Students see if they can separate out the words to make a sentence.

Answer: Me gusta el español porque es divertido y es útil y me gusta el profesor.

AT3.4 **1** Lee el texto y las frases. **Verdad o mentira?**

Students read the text about what Adam thinks about studying languages and decide if statements a–f are true or false.

Answers: a M; b V; c M; d M; e M; f V

Zoom gramática

This section explains about radical-changing verbs, using the example of an *-ar* verb. Ask if students can remember other forms of *tener* and *decir* that they have met so far (*tienes*, *tiene*, *dice*, etc). Point out that a radical-changing verb may have two vowels (*pienso*, *tienes*) but that some have only one (*dices*).

 2 Match each sentence to the correct picture.

Students match sentences a–d with the pictures.

Answers: a 2; b 3; c 4; d 1

AT3.3 **3** Empareja las actividades con las asignaturas.

Students match subjects 1–5 with the descriptions a–e.

Answers: 1 b; 2 d; 3 c; 4 e, 5 a

AT1.3 **4** Escucha y comprueba tus respuestas.

Students listen and check their answers.

🎧 **CD 2, track 36** página 85, actividad 4

1 – Me gusta la geografía porque puedo estudiar los volcanes y los ríos.
2 – Me gusta la música porque puedo tocar instrumentos como el piano y la guitarra.
3 – No me gusta el español porque tengo que leer poemas, pero me gusta escribirlos.
4 – No me gusta la educación física porque tengo que jugar al fútbol. Me gustaría jugar al baloncesto con mis amigos.
5 – Me gusta la historia, pero tengo que estudiar los vikingos.

AT 4.3/4 **6** Copia y completa este texto, cambiando las imágenes por palabras.

Students write out the text replacing the pictures with the words and phrases in the box at the end.

Answer: Me gusta *la geografía* porque puedo *estudiar volcanes*, pero *no me gusta la historia* porque tengo que *estudiar los vikingos*. Pienso que *la educación física* es divertida, porque *me gusta jugar al fútbol*. Mi amigo *piensa* que *la música* es aburrida, porque tiene que *tocar la trompeta*.

Técnica

This section builds on the use of the verb + infinitive.

 6 Find where *puedo* and *tengo* are used on this page. Say what each sentence means in English. Explain the rule for using *puedo* or *tengo que* in a sentence.

Students find examples of the constructions on the page.

Answers:
Puedo estudiar volcanes. – I can study volcanoes.
Tengo que estudiar los vikingos. – I have to study the Vikings.
We use *puedo* if something is possible and *tengo que* for something that we have to do and we use the infinitive after both forms.

Reto

Da tu opinión sobre tres asignaturas y explica por qué te gustan / no te gustan.

Students give their opinions about three school subjects and their reasons for them. This could be done as pair work or as a whole class survey.

Planner

● ●

6.3 **El horario** páginas 86–87

Objectives

▶ Talk about the times of the day

▶ Talk about your favourite day

Resources

Students' Book, pages 88–89
CD 2, track 37
Uno/Dos Workbooks, page 56

Key language

empezar, terminar, el recreo, la hora de comer
A las…, Son las…, ¿Qué hora es?, Voy a casa a las…, Las
clases terminan a las…, ¿Cuál es tu día favorito?, Prefiero el
…

Programme of Study reference

1a, 1b, 1c, 2a, 2c, 2d, 2f, 2g, 2h, 2i, 3b, 3c, 3d, 3e, 4a, 4c,
4d, 5a, 5c, 5d, 5e, 5f, 5g, 5i

¡A sus marcas!

Empareja los relojes con las horas.

Students match the clocks and the times.

Answers: a 3 Las ocho y media; b 1 Las nueve y cuarto; c 2
Las once menos cuarto

Zoom gramática

This section explains how to tell the time in Spanish.

AT 3.1/2 **1 Mira los dibujos y escoge la hora correcta.**

Students look at the pictures and choose the correct time
to complete the sentence from the choices at the end of
the exercise.

Answers: a ocho y media; b nueve y cuarto; c once menos
cuarto; d once y cuarto; e dos; f cuatro; g cinco; h cinco y
veinte

AT 1.1/2 **2 Escucha y comprueba tus respuestas.**
Students listen and check their answers.

 CD 2, track 37 página 86, actividad 2

> a – Las clases empiezan a las ocho y media.
> b – Tengo español a las nueve y cuarto.
> c – Es el recreo a las once menos cuarto.
> d – Tengo historia a las once y cuarto.
> e – Es la hora de comer a las dos.
> f – Tengo matemáticas a las cuatro.
> g – Las clases terminan a las cinco.
> h – Voy a casa a las cinco y veinte.

AT2.2 **3 Con tu compañero/a, lee este diálogo.**

Students work in pairs to read the dialogue between Raquel
and Jorge.

AT 2.3/4 **4 Prepara otro diálogo similar con la información de los dibujos.**

Students use exercise 3 as a template to prepare another
dialogue, this time choosing information from the cues in
exercise 4.

Answers:
¿Cuál es tu día favorito?
Prefiero el jueves/el lunes.
¿Por qué?
Porque tengo clase de geografía/música.
¿A qué hora?
Tengo geografía/música a las 11.00/12.00.
¿Te gusta la geografía/la música?
Sí, me gusta. Es interesante/divertida.

AT3.4 **5 Lee y contesta en inglés.**

Students read the text about Fátima's favourite day and
answer questions a–f in English.

Answers: a Tuesday; b 9.00; c (She likes it because) it's
interesting; d 20 minutes; e science; f PE

Reto

AT4.4 Escribe un párrafo sobre tu día favorito en el colegio.

Students use the text in exercise 5 as a model to help them
write a paragraph about their favourite school day.

Planner

●●●●●●●●●●●●●●●●●●●●●●●●●

6.4 **El transporte** páginas 88–89

Objectives

► Say how you get to school

► Describe different forms of transport

► Talk about how long it takes to get there

Resources

Students' Book, pages 88–89
CD 2, tracks 38–39
Uno/Dos Workbooks, page 57

Key language

Es… / No es…
práctico, rápido, lento, cómodo, conveniente, necesario
en coche, en autobús, en autocar, a pie, en avión, en tren, en
barco, a caballo, en bicicleta, en patines, en monopatín
diez, veinte, treinta, cuarenta, cincuenta, sesenta, setenta,
ochenta, noventa, cien, treinta y tres, cuarenta y cuatro

Programme of Study reference

1a, 1b, 1c, 2a, 2b, 2c, 2d, 2f, 3b, 3c, 3e, 4c, 4d, 5a, 5c, 5d,
5e, 5f, 5g, 5i

¡A sus marcas!

**Pronuncia estas palabras, poniendo atención. Luego
escucha y compara.**

Students try to say the words, remembering Spanish
pronunciation rules. They then listen and check their
pronunciation.

 CD 2, track 38 página 88, ¡A sus marcas!

a en coche
b en autobús
c en autocar
d a pie
e en avión
f en tren
g en barco
h a caballo
i en bicicleta
j en patines
k en monopatín

AT 3.3/4 **1 Lee y decide de qué forma de transporte se trata.**

Discuss the *Frases clave* with the class and check
comprehension. Students then read statements a–f and
decide which form of transport each is describing.

Answers: a a pie; b en avión; c en coche; d en barco, e a
caballo; en autobús

AT1.3 **2 Escucha y comprueba tus respuestas.**

Students listen and check their answers.

 CD 2, track 39 página 88, actividad 2

a – Ir a pie es lento pero práctico para ir al instituto si es una
distancia corta.

b – Ir en avión es muy rápido para ir de vacaciones, por
ejemplo a España, pero no para ir al instituto.

c – Ir en coche es cómodo, pero tienes que ir con tus padres.

d – Ir en barco no es necesario normalmente para ir al
instituto, si no vives en una isla.

e – Ir a caballo no es muy práctico porque no se permiten
animales en el instituto.

f – Ir en autobús es muy común para ir al instituto, pero no
muy conveniente porque tienes que esperar.

AT2.2 **3 Haz un sondeo sobre el transporte al instituto.**

Students carry out a survey to find out how other people
get to school. Divide the class into groups of 5 or 6. In
their groups, students ask and take notes of the answers.
Compile the results of each group on the board to create a
class survey about how everyone gets to school.

AT3.3 **4 Busca los números en el texto.**

Before students read the text, focus on the *Frases clave*
box. Students then read the text and identify the different
numbers. You could ask them to make two lists: numbers
and clock times.

Answers: 10, 30, 20, 10, 50, 60; 8.00, 8.30, 8.40, 5.00, 5.30

AT3.4 **5 Lee y rellena los espacios.**

Students read the statements and fill in the gaps with the
words at the end of the exercise.

Answers: a a pie; b media; c mi madre; d rápido; e a las cinco;
f cinco y media

AT 4.3/4 **6 Escribe unas frases sobre cómo vas al instituto.**

Students write about how they go to school. They can use
the phrases given to help them.

Reto

AT3.4 Calcula a qué hora llega a casa esta persona.

Students read the text and work out what time the person
gets home.

Answer: A las seis menos diez.

Planner

6.5 **Entre amigos:**   páginas 90–91
Dos institutos ...

Resources

Students' Book, pages 90–91
CD 2, tracks 40–41
Uno/Dos Workbooks, page 58

Programme of Study reference

1c, 2a, 2c, 2f, 2h, 2i, 3b, 3c, 3e, 4a, 4c, 4d, 5d, 5e, 5g,
5h, 5i

Framework reference

(R) 7C3

AT1.4 | **1** Escucha y lee sobre las dos escuelas especiales.

Students listen and read the two texts about two different
schools in two very different places.

CD 2, track 40   página 90, actividad 1

– Mi escuela es la Telesecundaria de Otloquizingo. Es similar
a un instituto normal, pero ¡en las clases vemos la
televisión!
No vivo en una ciudad. En mi comunidad hay 800
habitantes, y sólo hay un profesor. Se llama Señor Ochoa, y
es buen profesor. Pero no es experto en todas las
asignaturas. Entonces en las clases vemos la televisión, en
el canal de la Telesecundaria. Ofrece programas basados en
el Sistema Educativo Nacional.
Estudiamos español, matemáticas, historia y cultura de
México, geografía y otras asignaturas. Pero también
podemos estudiar tecnología para la agricultura o para la
pesca.
Las clases son de las siete de la mañana a las doce y media.
Los programas de televisión empiezan a las ocho. No sólo
vemos la televisión. En las clases tenemos que trabajar:
hablar y resolver problemas, leer y escribir.
En mi instituto sólo hay treinta estudiantes. En México, más
de un millón de alumnos estudian la Telesecundaria.
– Mi escuela es el Colegio de San Ildelfonso en Madrid.
Durante 364 días del año es una escuela normal. Pero un
día muy especial cada año los alumnos del colegio salen
en la televisión. Y todos los españoles prestan atención.
Es una tradición (desde 1771) en la que los niños del
colegio cantan los números de la lotería nacional de
Navidad.

Los otros 364 días es un colegio normal. Estudiamos
matemáticas, inglés, historia, geografía, música, etc. como
todo los otros colegios en España. Las clases empiezan a
las nueve. La hora de comer es a la una y media. Por la
tarde las clases terminan a las cinco menos cuarto.
También tenemos una hora de deberes.
En el colegio hay 300 alumnos, 100 son internos y viven en
el colegio de lunes a viernes.

AT3.4 | **2** ¿Verdad o mentira?

Students read statements a–j about the two texts and
decide if they are True or False.

Answers: a M; b V; c V; d M; e V; f M; g V; h M; i V; j M

AT4.4 | **3** Escoge el instituto de Lety o de Valdemar. Contesta a
estas preguntas en español.

Students answer questions a–f in Spanish about either Lety
or Valdemar's school. They can refer back to page 92 to
help them with their answers.

Answers:
Lety
a Se llama la Telesecundaria de Otloquizingo.
b No es un instituto normal. En las clases ven la televisión.
c Estudian español, matemáticas, historia y cultura de
México, geografía, y tecnología para la agricultura y para la
pesca.
d Las clases empiezan a las siete de la mañana.
e Las clases terminan a las doce y media.
f Hay treinta estudiantes en el instituto.

Valdemar
a Se llama el Colegio de San Idelfonso.
b No es un colegio normal. Un día cada año los alumnos
salen en la televisión y cantan los números de la lotería
nacional en la Navidad.
c Estudian matemáticas, inglés, historia, geografía y música.
d Las clases empiezan a las nueve.
e Las clases terminan a las cinco menos cuarto.
f Hay 300 estudiantes en el colegio.

AT3.4 | **4** Which school would you rather go to and why?
Explain in English using information from page 90.

Students give their own opinion on the two different
schools.

AT1.3 | **5** Escoge y copia cinco de los siguientes números.
Escucha y ver si ganas el gordo (a–c).

Students choose five numbers. They then have three
chances to 'win the lottery' as they hear three sets of
numbers in Spanish. You might like to explain here the
cultural significance of 'el gordo', the Spanish national
Christmas lottery draw with the biggest prize of the year.

CD 2, track 41   página 91, actividad 5

a 67 ... 87 ... 22 ... 15 ... 44
b 92 ... 7 ... 44 ... 53 ... 22
c 32 ... 15 ... 53 ... 87 ... 44

AT2.3   **6 Con tu compañero/a, alterna para decir estos números. Él / ella que se pare pierde.**

Students work in pairs and take it in turns to say the pairs of numbers in Spanish. The student who cannot say a number loses.

Answers: ocho, nueve; trece, quince; diecisiete, dieciocho; veinte, treinta; treinta y cuatro, treinta y cinco; cuarenta y uno, cincuenta y dos; sesenta y cinco, setenta y dos; noventa y nueve, cien

Repaso
           páginas 92–93

Resources
Students' Book, pages 92–93

Programme of Study reference
1c, 2a, 2c, 2f, 2h, 2i, 3b, 3c, 4a, 4c, 4d, 5d, 5e, 5g, 5h, 5i

AT3.1   **1 Copia y escribe el número correcto.**

Students copy and complete the table of the animals' life expectancies.

Answers: a ciento dos años; b ochenta años; c sesenta y ocho años; d cincuenta años; e treinta y seis años; f veintiocho años; g diez años.

AT 3.3/4   **2 Lee y decide qué clase es.**

Students read texts a–e and decide which school subject each one is describing.

Answers: a historia; b ciencias; c tecnología; d matemáticas; e educación física

AT1.4   **3 Escucha. Copia y rellena el cuadro para descubrir cuál es la asignatura más popular.**

Students listen and complete the table to find out which subject is the most popular.

Answers: English and music are the most popular.

 CD 2, track 42   página 92, actividad 2

– Pues, las matemáticas y la historia no me gustan mucho… creo que prefiero el inglés.
– ¡El inglés! Me parece que es aburrido. Prefiero la música.
– Sí, a mí también me gusta la música, es mi asignatura favorita.
– Pues la música a mí no me gusta. Me gustan las matemáticas.
– Odio la música, pero pienso que la historia es muy interesante.
– Prefiero el inglés. Me gusta el profesor y es muy útil aprender un idioma.

AT2.4   **4 Con tu compañero/a, pregunta y contesta.**

In pairs, students use the picture prompts to help them ask and answer the questions.

Vocabulario
           página 94

This page provides a theme-based Spanish–English summary of the key language of this unit. It can be used for reference throughout the unit or as an aid to learning vocabulary.

C95   Copymaster 95 contains a summary of the key language of the unit and can be given to the students at this point to help with revision.

W61   Page 61 of the *Uno/Dos* Workbooks also provides a summary of the key language of the unit.

Ya sé
           página 95

The *Ya sé* page provides an end-of-unit checklist of learning objectives. At the foot of the page are activities at three levels of difficulty to extend the work of the unit. Encourage students to select an activity at the most appropriate level.

C96   Copymaster 94 contains a checklist and activities to keep track of the students' progress.

W62   Page 62 of the *Uno/Dos* Workbooks gives an end-of-unit checklist in Spanish and English, together with activities to keep track of the students' progress.

Unidad 6 Uno página 106

Objectives

This reinforcement page is intended for those students who need further practice of core language of the unit. It can be used by students who finish other activities early or as alternative class or homework material.

Resources

Students' Book, page 106
CD 2, track 43

Programme of Study reference

1c, 2a, 2c, 2f, 3b, 3c, 3e, 4a, 5d, 5e, 5f, 5g, 5h, 5i

AT3.2 | **1 Pilla al intruso.**

Students find the odd one out in each of the three examples, using the glossary to check for meaning if necessary.

Answers: a la música; b odio; c comer

AT2.2 | **2 Juega al twister con los dedos.**

Students work in pairs to play finger twister. One student says a subject in Spanish and the other has to put their finger on the correct picture. They are only allowed to use one hand.

AT1.2 | **3 Escucha (1–5) y escribe las letras.**

Using the pictures in exercise 2, students listen and write down the letter of each subject mentioned.

Answers: 1 d; 2 e; 3 g; 4 a; 5 f

CD 2, track 43 página 106, actividad 3

1 – No me gusta el inglés. Es importante, pero es difícil.
2 – Me gusta la música. Mi parte favorita es tocar la trompeta.
3 – Me gusta la geografía. Es interesante.
4 – Me gusta el español. Es mi asignatura favorita.
5 – No me gusta la educación física. Odio el deporte.

AT1.3 | **4 Escucha otra vez y nota si la opinión es positiva o negativa.**

Students listen to the same track again and decide if the opinion about each subject is positive or negative.

AT4.3 | **5 Utiliza tus respuestas para escribir una frase sobre las cinco asignaturas.**

Students use their responses to exercise 4 to write a sentence like the example about each of the five subjects.

Unidad 6 Dos página 107

Objectives

This extension page is intended for more able students who are confident with the core language of the unit. It can be used by students who finish other activities quickly or as alternative class or homework material.

Resources

Students' Book, page 107
CD 2, track 44

Programme of Study reference

1c, 2a, 2c, 2d, 2e, 3b, 3c, 3e, 4a, 5d, 5g, 5i

AT1.3 | **1 Escucha a Inés y decide si cada asignatura le gusta, o no.**

Students listen to Inés and decide if she likes each of the subjects mentioned or not. They complete the box with a tick or a cross.

Answers: 2 ✗; 3 ✓; 4 ✗

CD 2, track 44 página 107, actividad 1

1 – ¿Qué piensas de la geografía?
  – Pienso que es importante y útil. Me gusta estudiar los mapas.
2 – ¿Te gusta la educación física?
  – Me gusta el deporte, pero en la educación física tengo que nadar, y no me gusta.
3 – ¿Y el inglés?
  – Mi madre dice que es importante, pero es difícil. Prefiero el italiano.
4 – ¿Te gusta la música?
  – Me gusta escuchar música, pero no puedo tocar instrumentos. Y no me gusta el profesor.

AT2.3 | **2 ¡A contrarreloj! Utiliza el cuadro para hacer frases sobre tus asignaturas. ¿Cuántas frases puedes hacer en dos minutos?**

Students work in pairs or small groups. They take it in turns to make up as many sentences as possible about school subjects in two minutes, using the information given in the box.

AT3.5 | **3 Lee y busca.**

Students read Danielle's note, and make notes under the five headings given.

Answers: Times 9.20, 11.00; Opinions – no me gusta, es muy aburrida; Questions – ¿Te gusta la geografía?, ¿A qué hora termina la clase?, ¿Por qué tengo que estudiar los ríos de Europa?; What she has to do – prestar atención; What she can't do – mirar por la ventana

AT4.5 | **4** Escribe una nota a un(a) amigo/a de otra clase. Utiliza el modelo de Danielle.

Students write a note in Spanish to a friend in another class using Danielle's as a model to help them.

Unidad 6 Lectura: uno
página 118

Objectives

This page is to encourage independent reading. Students should attempt it once they are confident with the core language of the unit. It can be used by students who finish other activities early or as alternative class or homework material.

Resources

Students' Book, page 118

Programme of Study reference

1e, 2a, 2c, 2d, 2i, 3b, 3c, 3e, 4a, 5a, 5e, 5f, 5g, 5i

AT3.2 | **1** Busca las palabras completas.

Students make complete words from the fragments given.

Answers: informática; español; música; matemáticas; inglés; dibujo; historia; geografía; ciencias

AT3.2 | **2** Mira los dibujos. Elige la opinión correcta.

Students look at the pictures and decide which is the correct opinion out of the two given.

Answers: a Me gusta el inglés; b La geografía es fácil; c La tecnología es aburrida; d Me encanta el dibujo; e La historia es divertida

AT3.3 | **3** Mira el horario. ¿Verdad o mentira?

Students look at the timetable and decide if statements a–h are true or false.

Answers: a M; b V; c V; d M; e V; f M; g M; h M

Unidad 6 Lectura: dos
página 119

Objectives

This page is to encourage independent reading. Students should attempt it once they are confident with the core language of the unit. It can be used by students who finish other activities early or as alternative class or homework material.

Resources

Students' Book, page 119
CD 2, track 45

Programme of Study reference

1c, 2a, 2d, 2i, 3b, 3c, 3e, 4a, 5a, 5e, 5f, 5g, 5i

AT1.4 | **1** Escucha y lee. ¿Cuántas cosas le gustan, cuántas no?

Students listen and read the text and count how many things the speaker likes, and how many things he dislikes.

Answers: Likes two things; does not like eight things

 CD 2, track 45 página 119, actividad 1

– Mamá: No quiero ir al instituto. No me gusta la geografía, no me gusta la música, no me gustan las matemáticas. El inglés es muy difícil, no entiendo las ciencias, y no puedo soportar la historia. No me gustan los profesores. Dicen que soy muy aburrido. No me gustan los estudiantes – son muy estresantes. Me gusta mirar por la ventana o pensar en las vacaciones. No quiero ir.

AT2.3 | **2** Lee en voz alta el chiste a tu compañero/a.

Students work in pairs and read the joke in exercise 1 to their partner.

AT3.4 | **3** Haz el cuestionario para buscar la asignatura que más te conviene.

Students complete the questionnaire to find out which subject suits them best, but the result may surprise them! They will probably need some help to read the upside-down comment, but allow them to work out as much as they can first.

Answer: You're very clever for having done a questionnaire in Spanish. It's a very difficult questionnaire and in Spanish. The perfect subject for you is therefore: Spanish.

AT4.4 | **4** Utiliza tus respuestas para escribir un párrafo sobre lo que te gusta hacer en el instituto.

Students use their replies to the questionnaire and any other relevant material to write a short paragraph about what they like to do at school.

Copymasters

Hoja 97 ¡A sus marcas!
This can be used after pages 82–83 in the Students' Book.

AT4.1   **1** Coloca las asignaturas que faltan.

Students complete the grid with the subjects from the list, following the instructions on the sheet.

Answers:

ciencias	matemáticas	inglés	**educación física**	geografía
educación física	inglés	geografía	ciencias	**matemáticas**
matemáticas	**geografía**	educación física	inglés	ciencias
geografía	educación física	ciencias	**matemáticas**	**inglés**
inglés	**ciencias**	matemáticas	geografía	educación física

AT3.2   **2** Decide cuál es la forma de transporte mejor.

Students choose the best form of transport for journeys 1–6 from the list on the right.

Answers: 1 en avión; 2 a pie; 3 en barco; 4 en tren; 5 en coche; 6 en bicicleta

AT1.1   **3** Juega a la lotería.

Students play bingo. Call out the numbers 10, 20, 30 etc. in Spanish, and the first student to cross off all five of their chosen numbers wins. This could also be a small group activity led by more confident students.

Hoja 98 Reto
This can be used after pages 82–83 in the Students' Book.

AT4.1   **1** Las palabras subrayadas se han escrito mal. Corrígelas en rojo.

Students correct the incorrectly spelt words in red.

Answers: a música; b religión; c educación física; d historia; e geografía; f tecnología

AT3.2   **2** Colorea las partes de la palabra que cambian.

Students colour in the parts of the words that change following the instructions given.

Answers:
Green: interesante/interesantes; aburrido/aburridas; clase/clases; divertido/divertidas; difícil/difíciles;
Red: hablo; pienso; juega; estudiamos
Blue: hablar; pensar; jugar; estudiar

AT3.3   **3** Haz corresponder las preguntas con las respuestas.

Students match questions 1–7 with answers a–g.

Answers: 1 g; 2 a; 3 f; 4 b; 5 e; 6 c; 7 d

Hoja 99 Escuchar: uno
This can be used after pages 82–83 in the Students' Book.

AT 1.2/3   **1** Escucha y escribe ☺ o ☹ para la asignatura correcta.

Students listen and complete the faces according to the opinions given.

Answers: Smiley: English; science; music; geography
Sad: maths; PE

 CD 3, track 48   Hoja 99, uno, actividad 1

a – No me gustan las matemáticas.
b – El inglés me gusta.
c – No me gusta la educación física.
d – Las ciencias me gustan.
e – Me gusta la música.
f – La geografía me gusta.

AT 1.2/3   **2** Escucha y subraya las palabras correctas.

Students listen and underline the word they hear in each sentence.

Answers: a la geografía; b divertida; c los volcanes; d las matemáticas; e aburridas; f el profesor

 CD 3, track 49   Hoja 99, uno, actividad 2

– Mi clase favorita es la geografía, porque es divertida. Puedo estudiar los volcanes.
No me gusta estudiar las matemáticas, porque son aburridas.
Pero me gusta el profesor.

Hoja 99 Escuchar: dos

AT1.3   **3** Escucha y completa el horario.

Students listen and fill in the timetable.

Answers: A ciencias; b. 10.00; c. 11.00; D historia; E español

 CD 3, track 50   Hoja 99, dos, actividad 3

– A las ocho y media tengo inglés. Luego tengo ciencias a las nueve y cuarto. Tengo música a las diez. Después del recreo, tengo educación física a las once. La clase de historia empieza a las doce menos cuarto. La última clase es de español a la una y media.

4 Escucha y rellena los espacios.

Students listen and fill in the missing words.

Answers: 1 estudio; 2 ciencias; 3 tengo; 4 dibujo; 5 miércoles; 6 clase

CD 3, track 51　　　　　Hoja 99, dos, actividad 4

– En el instituto el martes estudio inglés, matemáticas, español, ciencias, historia y geografía. No me gusta porque tengo español y es difícil. Prefiero el dibujo – es divertido. Creo que prefiero el miércoles porque tengo educación física y no tengo clase de español.

Hoja 100 Hablar: uno

This can be used after pages 82–83 in the Students' Book.

AT2.3

1 Da una opinión sobre esas asignaturas.

In pairs, students express an opinion about subjects as shown by the pictures. They should use all the opinion words at the bottom of the exercise, which their partner can tick as they listen. Alternatively, you could invite volunteers to the front for the class to check.

AT 2.3/4

2 Da tu propia opinión sobre esas asignaturas, y da una razón.

Students now express their own personal opinion about the subjects shown, and give a reason. They use the phrases on the right to help them.

Hoja 100 Hablar: dos

AT2.4

3 Contesta a esas preguntas.

Students answer the questions in Spanish. This could be done as a whole class survey activity.

Hoja 101 Leer y escribir: uno

This can be used after pages 82–83 in the Students' Book.

AT3.1

1 Rompe el código para descifrar esas palabras y el mensaje.

Students crack the code and write out the words correctly.

Answers: inglés; matemáticas; historia; ciencias; geografía; a las once en la cafetería

AT 3.3/4

2 Lee y completa el gráfico de barras.

Students read the text and complete the bar chart with Ramón's information.

Answers:

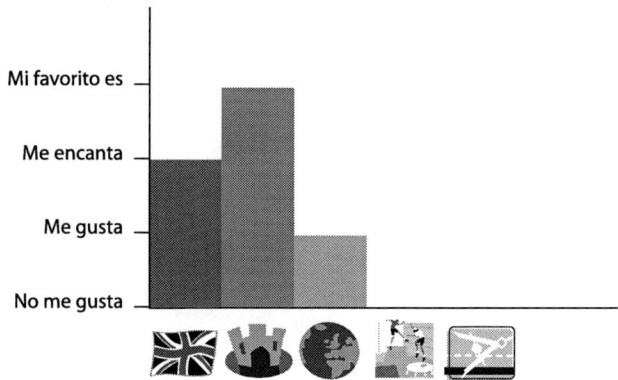

AT 4.3/4

3 Mira el gráfico de barras y escribe 5 frases.

Students use the information on the bar chart to write 5 sentences about subjects, giving opinions.

Answers:
... no me gusta el dibujo.
No me gusta la geografía.
Me gusta el español.
Mi asignatura favorita es la educación física.
Me encantan las matemáticas.

Hoja 102 Leer y escribir: dos

This can be used after pages 82–83 in the Students' Book.

AT3.4

1 Lee y rellena los espacios.

Students read the text and fill in the gaps with the words provided.

Answers: 1 autobús; 2 amigos; 3 español; 4 cuarto; 5 difícil; 6 matemáticas;7 dos

AT 3.4/5

2 Lee y haz corresponder la opinión con los alumnos.

Students read what the four students say, and complete the speech bubbles with the correct opinion phrase.

Answers: Lola: Son difíciles; Gregorio: Es útil; Enrique: Es divertida; Pili: Es aburrida

AT4.4

3 Contesta a esas preguntas en un párrafo.

Students write a full paragraph in Spanish in response to questions a–i.

Sample answer:
Voy al instituto a pie/en autobús/en coche/en tren. Las clases empiezan a las (...). El recreo es a las (...). Me gustan (... y ...) y mi asignatura preferida es/son (...) porque es/son (...). No me gusta/gustan (...) porque es/son (...). Las clases terminan a las (...).

Hoja 103 Gramática

This can be used after pages 82–83 in the Students' Book.

AT3.2

1 Look at the words in the box below. Underline the plural words in red.

Students identify the plural words from the selection given.

Answers: las matemáticas; las ciencias; los deportes

AT4.3

2 Use *me gusta / me gustan / no me gusta / no me gustan* to give your opinion of each subject from activity 1.

Students express their own opinion about the school subjects in activity 1, using the verb *gustar* correctly.

AT 3.3/4

3 This note has been smudged. Can you put in the correct form of *me gusta / me gustan*?

Students complete the note correctly.

Answer: Me gusta; me gustan; me gusta; me gustan

AT3.3

4 Read and summarise the opinion in two or three words. Pay attention to singular and plural.

Students decide what opinion is being expressed in statements a–f.

Answers: b No me gusta. c Me gustan. d No me gusta. e Es divertido. / Me encanta. f Me gustan.

Hoja 104 Técnica

This can be used after pages 84–85 in the Students' Book. It helps students to develop independence in consulting reference sources.

AT3.2

1 Underline the verb endings in this list that show 'I talk', 'you talk', 'he/she talks'. Complete the column in English.

Students underline the 1st, 2nd and 3rd person endings and translate the forms into English.

Answers: Hablo = I talk; Hablas = You talk; Habla + He/She talks

AT4.2

2 Use the verb endings in the table to change these verbs.

Students put the correct endings on the verbs.

Answers: a nado; b practica; c estudias

AT3.3

3 Underline the verb endings, then say what each sentence means.

Students identify the verb endings and write the sentence out in English.

Answers:
a hablamos: We talk in the Spanish lesson.
b bailas: Do you dance in PE?
c hablo: I talk to my friends.
d piensan: The teachers think that English is easy.

Hoja 105 Cultura

This can be used after pages 90–91 in the Students' Book.

AT3.3

1 Look at the information in the grid and answer these questions in English.

Students find out information about the Spanish education system.

Answers:
1 At 6 years old.
2 Culture, writing, speaking, maths, personal responsibility, English.
3 At primary school.
4 At 12 years old.
5 Up to 16 years old.
6 Science.
7 Humanities: geography, history and RE.
8 At age 16.
9 Arts and Literature, Science and Health, Humanities and Social Science, Technology.

AT3.4

2 Fill in the blanks with words or numbers from this page.

Students complete the paragraph about the Spanish education system.

Answers: 1 6/seis; 2 matemáticas; 3 inglés; 4 12/doce; 5 18/dieciocho; 6 10/diez; 7 16/dieciséis; 8 16/dieciséis

3 What are the differences and similarities between the English and Spanish systems? Which do you prefer?

Students express their opinions on the two systems in English. This could form the basis for a class discussion.

Hoja 106 Se pronuncia así

This can be used after pages 82–83 in the Students' Book.

AT1.1

1 Listen and tick the verbs you hear.

Students listen and identify the form they hear.

Answers: See transcript.

CD 3, track 52 Hoja 106, actividad 1

a hablar
b estudiar
c copia
d termina
e tocar
f practicar

AT2.1 **2** Practise saying these to a partner. Your partner will ring the one you say.

Students work in pairs to practise pronunciation.

AT2.2 **3** Practise saying these sentences. If the 'r' sound is hard, enjoy trying and don't give up! Then listen to check.

Students practise the pronunciation of both 'r' and 'rr' and then listen to see how accurate they are.

CD 3, track 53 Hoja 106, actividad 3

a – Bailar y cantar son realmente aburridos.
b – Ramón nada pero a Rafa no le gusta nadar.
c – ¿Por qué estudiar a los romanos en historia?
d – En la geografía prefiero mirar por la ventana.
e – Prefiero cantar pero mi perro prefiere bailar.

AT2.1 **4** Listen, and then practise saying the verb hablar with the stress in the right place.

Students do more pronunciation practice, this time working on stress, and then listen to check their accuracy.

CD 3, track 54 Hoja 106, actividad 4

hablo
hablas
habla
ha**bla**mos
ha**bláis**
hablan

Control Unidad 6

Resources

Copymasters 107–112
CD 3, tracks 55–57

Hoja 107 Escuchar: uno

AT1.1 **1** Pon las asignaturas en el orden (1–5) en que se mencionan.

Students put the correct number beside each picture in the order they hear them.

Answers: el español; la geografía; la educación física; el dibujo; ICT

Mark scheme:
1 mark for each correct answer = 5 marks

Assessment criteria: Students who order four or five words correctly show evidence of performance at AT 1.1.

CD 3, track 55 Hoja 107, actividad 1

1 – Me gusta el español.
2 – El martes tengo geografía a las nueve.
3 – No tengo educación física hoy.
4 – No me gusta el profesor de dibujo.
5 – La informática es muy importante.

AT1.3 **2** Escribe la asignatura que le gusta y que no le gusta a cada persona.

Students fill in the grid with the subjects each person likes and dislikes.

Answers:

	Andrés	Lidia	Marga	Malena	Paco
☺	inglés	dibujo	geografía	música	informática
☹	español	matemáticas	historia	educación física	ciencias

Mark scheme:
Students who attempt *uno* only: 2 marks for each correct answer = 20 marks. (1 mark for the correct word; 2 marks for the correct spelling)
Students who attempt *uno* and *dos*: 1 mark for each correct answer = 10 marks. (Half a mark for the correct word; half a mark for the correct spelling)

Assessment criteria: Students who identify eight or more of the subjects with the correct opinion show evidence of performance at AT 1.3.

CD 3, track 56 Hoja 107, actividad 2

Andrés
– Me gusta el inglés, pero no me gusta el español.
Lidia
– Prefiero el dibujo. Las matemáticas no me gustan.
Marga
– No me gusta la historia, pero la geografía es divertida.
Malena
– No me gusta la educación física. Mi asignatura favorita es la música.
Paco
– La informática es mi asignatura favorita. Odio las ciencias.

Hoja 107 Escuchar: dos

AT1.4 **3** Escucha. ¿Qué se describe? Escribe la letra a–e.

Students decide which item is being described and write a–e in the boxes in the order they hear them.

Answers: las tres y media – e; una bicicleta – a; un profesor – c; la educación física – b; la música – d

Mark scheme: 2 marks for each correct answer = 10 marks

Assessment criteria: Students who order four or five of the items correctly show evidence of performance at AT 1.4.

 CD 3, track 57   Hoja 107, actividad 3

a – Es muy práctico para ir al instituto si no tienes coche.
b – Es muy divertido si te gustan los deportes.
c – Dice que tengo que estudiar en silencio, "¡Silencio!"
d – Es una clase importante si quieres tocar un instrumento.
e – Es la hora a la que terminan las clases.

Hoja 108 Hablar: uno

AT2.3   **1a** Haz preguntas a tu compañero/a.

1b Responde a tu compañero/a.

Students work in pairs on the speaking test. They take it in turns to ask the questions given, and to respond to them using the word and picture prompts on the test cards.

Mark scheme: 5 marks for each correct question asked = 10 marks
5 marks for each coherent answer given = 10 marks
5 marks for communicative fluency and accent

Assessment criteria: Students who name two or more subjects and give an opinion show evidence of performance at AT 2.3. Where no opinion is given, performance is at AT 2.2.

Hoja 108 Hablar: dos

AT2.4   **2** Responde con más detalles.

Students working at a higher level fill out their answers using the words in the box.

Mark scheme: 5 marks for each correct question asked = 10 marks
5 marks for each coherent answer given = 10 marks
5 marks for communicative fluency and accent

Assessment criteria: Students who name two or more subjects and give an opinion show evidence of performance at AT 2.3. Where all the vocabulary from the box is used to give fuller answers, performance is at AT 2.4.

Hoja 109 Leer: uno

AT3.3   **1** Lee y haz corresponder la asignatura con el dibujo.

Students read the sentences and match the opinion about each subject with the pictures, putting the correct number (1–5) in the box.

Answers: a 5; b 1; c 3; d 2; e 4

Mark scheme:
1 mark for each correct answer = 5 marks

Assessment criteria: Students who match four or five opinions correctly show evidence of performance at AT 3.3.

AT3.3   **2** Lee y completa el horario en inglés.

Students read the paragraph and complete the timetable in English to show they have understood the information.

Answers: 9.00 English; 10.20 Spanish; 11.15 history; 11.55 PE; 12.35 science

Mark scheme:
2 marks for each correct answer = 10 marks

Assessment criteria: Students who complete four or five subjects correctly show evidence of performance at AT 3.3.

AT3.4   **3** Haz una lista de las asignaturas que le gustan a Chavo.

Students read the text, then write a list in Spanish of all the subjects Chavo likes.

Answers: historia; inglés; español; matemáticas; dibujo

Mark scheme: 2 marks for each correct answer = 10 marks

Assessment criteria: Students who list four or five subjects correctly show evidence of performance at AT 3.4.

Hoja 110 Leer: dos

AT3.3   **1** Lee e identifica cómo cada persona va al instituto.

Students read sentences 1–5 and match them with pictures a–e, putting the correct number in the box beside each picture.

Answers: a 1; b 2; c 3; d 4; e 5

Mark scheme: 1 mark for each correct answer = 5 marks

Assessment criteria: Students who match four or five sentences correctly show evidence of performance at AT 3.3.

AT3.3   **2** Lee y haz corresponder las opiniones con las razones.

Students match the sentence beginnings 1–4 with the endings a–d.

Answers: 1 d; 2 a; 3 b; 4 c

Mark scheme: 2 marks for each correct answer = 8 marks

Assessment criteria: Students who match three or four sentences correctly show evidence of performance at AT 3.3.

AT3.4 **3** Lee y contesta a las preguntas en inglés.

Students read the paragraph and answer the questions in English to show their understanding of what Antonio thinks of school.

Answers:
1 talk (1)
2 he likes them (1)
3 he likes the teacher, but he can't talk much, he thinks maths is important but hard (4)
4 he has to read and write a lot (2)
5 he can draw diagrams and maps (2)
6 English, it is very useful to speak another subject (2)

Mark scheme: See Answers.

Assessment criteria: Students who gain nine or more marks show evidence of performance at AT 3.4.

Hoja 111 Escribir: uno

AT 4.1/2 **1** Mira el horario y completa la lista.

Students look at the timetable and complete the list in Spanish.

Answers: español; inglés; geografía; educación física; dibujo

Mark scheme: 1 mark for each correct answer (half a mark for the correct word; half a mark for the correct spelling) = 5 marks

Assessment criteria: Students who identify four or five subjects show evidence of performance at AT 4.1. Students who in addition spell four or five subjects correctly show performance at AT 4.2.

AT4.2 **2** Completa esas frases, dando una opinión.

Students complete the beginning of each sentence saying if they like or dislike each subject, according to how each sentence ends, not personal opinion.

Answers: a Me gusta; b No me gustan; c Me gusta/Me encanta; d Me gusta/Me encantan; e No me gusta

Mark scheme: 2 marks for each correct answer (1 mark for appropriate opinion language; 1 mark for grammatical accuracy) = 10 marks

Assessment criteria: Students who give four or five appropriate opinions correctly show performance at AT 4.2.

AT4.3 **3** Contesta a esas preguntas con una frase.

Students answer questions A–E with a full sentence in Spanish.

Mark scheme:
2 marks for each correct answer (1 mark for communication; 1 mark for grammatical accuracy) = 10 marks

Assessment criteria: Students who score 5–7 marks show evidence of performance at AT 4.2. Students who communicate with good accuracy accurately, scoring 8 or more marks, show evidence of performance at AT 4.3.

Hoja 112 Escribir: dos

AT4.3 **1** Contesta a esas preguntas con una frase.

Students answer questions 1–5 with a full sentence in Spanish.

Mark scheme: 1 mark for each correct answer (half a mark for communication; half a mark for grammatical accuracy) = 5 marks

Assessment criteria: Students who score four or five marks show evidence of performance at AT 4.3.

AT4.3 **2** Escribe en español.

Students write out sentences 1–5 in Spanish.

Answers:
1 Las clases empiezan a las ocho.
2 El lunes tengo geografía primero.
3 Tengo matemáticas a las nueve y media.
4 Me encantan las matemáticas.
5 Las clases terminan a las dos.

Mark scheme: 1 mark for each correct answer (half a mark for communication; half a mark for grammatical accuracy) = 5 marks

Assessment criteria: Students who score 4 or 5 marks show evidence of performance at AT 4.3.

AT 4.3/4 **3** Escribe tres frases para cada asignatura.

Students write out three complete sentences in Spanish for each subject shown in the grid.

Sample Answers:
Me gusta el español porque es divertido. Me gusta porque puedo hablar con mis amigos. No me gusta porque tengo que leer y escribir mucho.
Me gusta la geografía porque es interesante. Me gusta porque puedo estudiar volcanes y ríos. No me gusta porque tengo que dibujar mapas.
No me gustan las matemáticas porque son aburridas. Me gusta porque puedo mirar por la ventana. No me gusta el profesor./No me gusta porque tengo que escuchar al profesor.

Mark scheme: 1 mark for communicating each sentence = 9 marks
6 marks for accuracy and variety
Total = 15 marks

Assessment criteria: Students who score 9 or more marks show evidence of performance at AT 4.3. Students who score 12 or more show evidence of performance at AT 4.4.

Control de fin de año

Resources
Copymasters 113–120
CD 3, tracks 58–63

Hoja 113 Escuchar: uno

 AT1.2 | **1** Escucha y pon el número correcto con cada imagen.

Students number pictures a–e in the order they hear them.

Answers: a 4; b 3; c 2; d 5; e 1

Mark scheme: 1 mark for each correct answer = 5 marks

Assessment criteria: Students who match four or five correctly show evidence of performance at AT 1.2.

 CD 3, track 58   Hoja 113, actividad 1

1 – Ese es mi perro David. Es muy grande.
2 – Mi hermana se llama Gabi. Lleva gafas.
3 – Mi casa es pequeña pero me gusta.
4 – Mi madre se llama Ernestina. Tiene treinta y dos años.
5 – Me llamo Luís y me gusta el esquí.

AT1.2 | **2** Escucha y señala si le gusta o si no le gusta.

Students listen and tick the correct box if the speaker likes or dislikes each item mentioned.

Answers:
☺ tennis; swimming; music; English
☹ rugby; geography; badminton

Mark scheme: 2 marks for each correct answer = 14 marks

Assessment criteria: Students who score 10 or more marks show evidence of performance at AT 1.2.

CD 3, track 59   Hoja 113, actividad 2

– Me gusta el tenis.
 Me encanta la natación.
 No me gusta el bádminton.
 Odio el rugby.
 La geografía es aburrida.
 La música es interesante.
 El inglés es divertido.

AT1.3 | **3** Escucha y señala lo que hay en Roda. Se mencionan 6 lugares.

Students listen and tick each place mentioned.

Answers: beach; restaurants; shops; supermarket; school; park

Mark scheme: 1 mark for each correct answer = 6 marks

Assessment criteria: Students who identify five or six of the places correctly show evidence of performance at AT 1.3.

 CD 3, track 60   Hoja 113, actividad 3

– Vivo en Roda: está en la costa y la playa es muy bonita. Es una ciudad tranquila: no hay tráfico, no hay fábricas. En el centro hay unos restaurantes y tiendas. El supermercado está en las afueras. Mi instituto está en el centro, y también hay un parque pequeño. Si quiero ir al cine, tengo que ir a Tarragona a unos ochenta kilómetros. No me gusta porque tengo que ir en autobús.

Hoja 114 Escuchar: dos

AT3.1 | **1** Escucha y completa la tabla para Rosa.

Students listen and complete the grid with the information about Rosa.

Answers: Ecuador; España; 13; 20/2; 2; No

Mark scheme: 1 mark for each correct answer = 6 marks

Assessment criteria: Students who complete five or six correctly show evidence of performance at AT 1.3.

 CD 3, track 61   Hoja 114, actividad 1

– ¿Cómo te llamas?
– Me llamo Tomás. ¿Y tú?
– Me llamo Rosa. ¿De dónde eres?
– Soy de España.
– Yo vivo en España, pero soy de Ecuador.
– Yo vivo en Castellón.
– Tengo trece años. ¿Cuántos años tienes?
– Tengo doce años y mi cumpleaños es el once de agosto.
– Mi cumpleaños es el veinte de febrero.
– ¿Tienes hermanos?
– Sí, tengo dos hermanos. No tengo hermana.
– Yo tengo un hermano y una hermana. ¿Tienes animales en casa? Yo tengo un hámster.
– ¿Un hámster? No, no tengo animales.

AT1.3 | **2** Escucha y rellena los espacios.

Students listen and fill in the gaps with the correct word in Spanish.

Answers: 1 historia; 2 profesor; 3 difícil; 4 encanta; 5 divertida; 6 bailar; 7 tenis

Mark scheme: 1 mark for each correct answer = 7 marks

Assessment criteria: Students who complete six or seven gaps correctly show evidence of performance at AT 1.3.

CD 3, track 62 Hoja 114, actividad 2

– Mi asignatura favorita es la historia, pero no me gusta el profesor. En geografía es más difícil porque hay mapas y diagramas. No me gusta, y no me gustan las matemáticas. Prefiero leer y escribir. Me encanta el inglés y me gusta ir a la biblioteca en el instituto. La educación física es divertida. Me gusta bailar y nadar. No me gusta el tenis.

AT1.4 **3 Escucha e indica si es Verdad (V) o Mentira (M).**

Students listen and note if statements 1–6 are true or false.

Answers: 1 M; 2 M; 3 V; 4 M; 5 M; 6 M

Mark scheme: 2 marks for each correct answer = 12 marks

Assessment criteria: Students who mark five or six sentences correctly show evidence of performance at AT 1.4.

 CD 3, track 63 Hoja 114, actividad 3

– Mi casa está en el campo, bastante lejos de la costa. Vivo cerca de la ciudad de Badajoz, en una granja. En mi dormitorio tengo un ordenador y mis libros. No tengo televisor en mi dormitorio. Hay un jardín donde puedo jugar al fútbol con mi hermano pero en mis ratos libres prefiero ir a la ciudad a ver a mis amigos. No hay autobús: tengo que ir en coche con mi padre.

Hoja 115 Hablar: uno

AT 2.2/3 **1 Contesta a esas preguntas.**

Two sets of questions are provided. You can ask individual students to prepare the questions in either A or B, or you can allow students to choose. Alternatively, students can carry out self-assessment in pairs while you monitor. Remind them that they can score higher marks by answering in full sentences.

Mark scheme: For each question, give 1 mark for a correct idea or for an idea expressed in a full sentence = 10 marks

Assessment criteria: Students who score 5–6 show evidence of performance at AT 2.2. Students who score 7 or more are performing at AT 2.3.

AT 2.3/4 **2 Utiliza esta información para describir la casa o el pueblo.**

Using either information card A or B, students describe the house or the town shown in the words and symbols. Depending on the level of the class, you could allow students to prepare this in advance or set it for students to give an unprepared response.

Mark scheme: 9 marks for communication; 6 marks for grammatical accuracy and variety = 15 marks

Assessment criteria: Students who score 8–10 show evidence of performance at AT 2.3. Students scoring 11 or more are performing at AT 2.4.

Hoja 116 Hablar: dos

AT 2.3/4 **1 Contesta a esas preguntas.**

Two sets of questions are provided. You can ask individual students to prepare the questions in either A or B, or you can allow students to choose. Alternatively, students can carry out self-assessment in pairs while you monitor. Remind them that they can score higher marks by answering in full sentences.

Mark scheme: For each question, give 1 mark for a correct idea or for an idea expressed in a full sentence = 10 marks

Assessment criteria: Students who score 5–6 show evidence of performance at AT 2.3. Students who score 7 or more are performing at AT 2.4.

AT 2.4/5 **2 Utiliza esta información para hablar de un instituto o los ratos libres.**

Using either information card A or B, students talk about their school or their free time, using the words and symbols to support them. Depending on the level of the class, you could allow students to prepare this in advance or set it for students to give an unprepared response.

Mark scheme: 9 marks for communication; 6 marks for grammatical accuracy and variety = 15 marks

Assessment criteria: Students who score 8–10 show evidence of performance at AT 2.4. Students scoring 11 or more are performing at AT 2.5.

Hoja 117 Leer: uno

AT3.1 **1 Lee y encuentra la persona que corresponde a 1–6. Escribe el nombre.**

Students write the correct name next to each sentence or according to the information shown in the picture. Some names are used more than once.

Answers: 2 Armando; 3 Armando; 4 Ramona; 5 Elena; 6 Ramona

Mark scheme: 2 marks for each correct answer = 12 marks

Assessment criteria: Students who answer five or six correctly show evidence of performance at AT 3.1.

AT 3.2/3 **2 Lee y contesta en inglés.**

Students read the text and answer the questions in English.

Answers: 1 in the east; 2 it's a flat and doesn't have a garden; 3 she walks the dog; 4 it's not a city for tourists but she likes it; 5 because there are shops and cinemas; 6 she prefers to go to the beach and play volleyball with her friends

Mark scheme: 2 marks for each correct answer, with 3 marks for question 6 = 13 marks

Assessment criteria: Students who score 10–12 show evidence of performance at AT 3.2. Students who score more than 13 are performing at AT 3.3.

Hoja 118 Leer: dos

AT3.2 **1** ¿Verdad (V) or Mentira (M)?

Students read about Javier's house and mark the sentences V or M.

Answers: 1 V; 2 V; 3 M; 4 M; 5 V; 6 M; 7 V; 8 M; 9 V

Mark scheme: 1 mark for each correct answer = 9 marks

Assessment criteria: Students who answer seven or more correctly show evidence of performance at AT 3.2.

AT3.4 **2** Lee y contesta en inglés.

Students read Anastasia's view of school and answer the questions in English.

Answers: 1 because she likes studying / because one day she's going to be a teacher; 2 any two from: she likes maths, it's very interesting, but it's difficult; 3 history; 4 she likes reading, thinking and writing; 5 she doesn't like speaking; 6 that she has to speak; 7 swimming; 8 basketball

Mark scheme: 2 marks for each correct answer = 16 marks

Assessment criteria: Students who answer six or more correctly show evidence of performance at AT 3.4.

Hoja 119 Escribir: uno

AT4.1 **1** Escribe las palabras en español.

Students label the pictures in Spanish.

Answers: 1 la playa; 2 la cocina; 3 la piscina; 4 el jardín; 5 mi perro

Mark scheme: 1 mark for each correct answer = 5 marks

Assessment criteria: Students who label four or five correctly show evidence of performance at AT 4.1.

AT 4.1/2 **2** Completa las frases con una palabra adecuada.

Students complete the text with appropriate words. Answers may vary but should make sense in the context. Sample **Answers:** 1 España; 2 años; 3 madre / hermana; 4 padre / hermano; 5 grande / pequeña etc. (feminine adjective); 6 moderna / antigua etc. (feminine adjective); 7 fútbol, tenis etc. (masculine sport or game); 8 la gimnasia, la equitación (activity used with *practicar*); 9 and 10 any school subject

Mark scheme: 1 mark for each correct answer: half for an appropriate word; half for the correct spelling = 10 marks

Assessment criteria: Students who score 5 –7 show evidence of performance at AT 4.1. Students scoring 8 or more are performing at AT 4.2.

AT4.3 **3** Escribe una frase para cada dibujo.

Students write a sentence for each picture. Answers may vary but should express appropriate ideas based on the pictures.

Sample Answers:

a Me gusta/encanta jugar al tenis pero no me gusta jugar al baloncesto.
b Hay mi padre, mi madre, mi hermana y mi hermano.
c La geografía es interesante. /Me gusta/encanta la geografía porque es interesante.
d Me gusta/encanta ir al cine.
e Me gusta ir a la piscina; nadar.

Mark scheme: 2 marks for each sentence: 1 mark for communication; 1 mark for grammatical accuracy = 10 marks

Assessment criteria: Students who score 7 or more show evidence of performance at AT 4.3.

Hoja 120 Escribir: dos

AT4.3 **1** Cambia esa descripción para que se refiera a ti.

Students write a paragraph following the model but changing the verbs and the information to write about themselves.

Sample answer: Me llamo (...). Tengo el pelo (...). Llevo / No llevo gafas. Soy de (...), y vivo en (...). Hablo español (...) y también inglés. En mis ratos libres prefiero jugar al (...) y (...).

Mark scheme: 6 marks for correct verb forms and 4 marks for other information given in Spanish = 10 marks

Assessment criteria: Students who score 7 or more show evidence of performance at AT 4.3.

AT4.4 **2** Escribe una descripción de tu pueblo. Utiliza 5 de las palabras de abajo.

Students write a short paragraph using five of the words in the box.

Mark scheme: 3 marks for communication; 2 marks for grammatical accuracy = 5 marks

Assessment criteria: Students who score 4 or 5 show evidence of performance at AT 4.4.

AT4.4 **3** Escribe un párrafo sobre lo que te gusta y no te gusta. Escoge <u>uno</u> de esos temas: Mi casa, Mi instituto, Mis ratos libres.

Students write a paragraph on one of the topics.

Mark scheme: 6 marks for communication; 4 marks for grammatical accuracy and variety = 10 marks

Assessment criteria: Students who score 8 or more show evidence of performance at AT 4.4.

Uno Workbook

Página 54 (6.1)

This page can be used with pages 82–83 of the Students' Book.

AT4.1

1 Escribe las asignaturas. Subráyalas.

Students label the pictures and use the different types of underlining shown on the page.

Answers: Reading across the rows:
Masculine singular: el dibujo
Feminine singular: la informática; la historia; la educación física; la religión
Masculine plural: los idiomas
Feminine plural: las matemáticas; las ciencias

AT3.2

2 Lee lo que dice Martín. ¿Verdad o mentira?

Students look at the pictures and mark the sentences true or false.

Answers: a V; b V; c M; 4 M; 5 M

AT3.3

3a Escoge los adjetivos correctos.

Students circle the correct form of the adjective in each sentence.

Answers: 1 difícil; 2 aburridas; 3 divertida; 4 útiles

AT4.2

3b Completa las frases para ti en la página 63.

Students use the verbs in exercise 3a to give their opinions about school subjects. They write their sentences on page 63, the spare page for writing at the end of the unit. When they have finished, remind them to check through their work, particularly for adjective agreement and the use of *me gusta/es* or *me gustan/son*.

Página 55 (6.2)

This page can be used with pages 84–85 of the Students' Book.

AT3.3

1a Lee lo que dice Pepe. ¿Cuál es Pepe: A, B o C? Pon una señal.

Students read Pepe's speech bubble and tick the correct picture.

Answers: Picture B

AT3.3

1b ¿Cuáles son las frases correctas? Indica a o b.

Students read Pepe's speech bubble again and tick sentence a or sentence b in each case.

Answers: 1 b; 2 b; 3 a; 4 b

AT3.1

2 ¿Estas palabras son positivas o negativas? Dibuja ☺ o ☹.

Students draw a happy or sad face according to whether the words are positive or negative in meaning.

Answers:
Positive: relajante; divertido; útil; fácil; interesante
Negative: aburrido; difícil; estresante

AT4.3

3 Escribe tu opinion sobre tres asignaturas en la página 63.

Using *puedo* and *tengo que*, students write more detailed opinions about three subjects on page 63. If time is short, they could simply fill out the sentences that they wrote for section 6.1. When they have finished, remind them to check through their work, particularly for adjective agreement and the use of *me gusta/es* or *me gustan/son*. Remind them too about the use of the infinitive after *puedo* and *tengo que*.

Página 56 (6.3)

This page can be used with pages 86–87 of the Students' Book.

AT3.2

1 ¿Qué hora es? Escoge a o b.

Students look at each clock, read the times and circle a or b.

Answers: 2 b; 3b; 4 a; 5 a; 6 b

AT3.3

2 Mira el horario de Marta. Lee las frases. ¿Verdad o mentira?

Students look at Marta's timetable and mark the sentences true or false.

Answers: a M; b V; c M; d V; e M; f M

AT4.3

3 Completa el texto sobre el día favorito de Javier.

Students look at the information and the pictures about Javier's favourite day and complete the text.

Answers: jueves; ciencias; nueve; diez; español; leer; educación física; fútbol

Página 57 (6.4)

This page can be used with pages 88–89 of the Students' Book.

AT4.1 **1 Identifica las formas de transporte.**

Students label the pictures with the phrases from the word box.

Answers: Reading across the rows: en barco; en avión; en tren; en bicicleta; en coche

AT3.3 **2 Lee el texto. Empareja las formas de transporte con las opiniones.**

Students read about transport in Peru. They then match the pictures with the words according to the information in the text. You might want to point out that some pictures match with two ideas.

Answers: by bus: practical, relaxing; on foot: not easy; by car: comfortable; by train: slow; by plane: fast, expensive

Página 58 (6.5)

This page can be used with pages 90–91 of the Students' Book.

AT3.3 **1 Lee el texto. Complétalo con las cifras de la casilla.**

Students complete the text with the numbers in the box. Ask them to try first without referring back to Valdemar's text on Students' Book page 90. (This is not a memory test. If they read the whole text first, most students should be able to follow the sense in order to do this as a comprehension exercise.)

Answers: 364; 1771; 9.00; 1.30; 4.45; 1; 300; 100

AT3.1 **2 Escribe los números.**

Students write the numbers in figures.

Answers: a 77; b 42; c 16; d 39; e 91; f 28

Página 59 Gramática

This page can be used with page 83 of the Students' Book. This page revises *gustar* and radical-changing verbs.

AT4.1 **1 Completa las frases con la forma correcta de gustar.**

Look at the first *Flashback* box with the class. Students then complete the sentences with the correct form of gustar.

Answers: a gustan; gusta; c gusta; d gustan, gusta

AT4.1 **2 Completa el cuadro con las formas de los verbos.**

Use the second *Flashback* box to remind the students about radical-changing verbs. Students then complete the verb table. Pay particular attention to the correct irregular first person forms *digo* and *tengo*.

Answers:
pienso **digo tengo**
piensas dices **tienes**
piensa **dice** tiene

AT3.3 **3 ¿Qué dicen?**

Students look at the pictures and complete the thought bubbles with the sentences in the box.

Answers:
¡Ay, no! Tengo que esperar.
Prefiero estar al aire libre.
En coche puedo ir a todos los sitios.
Pienso que es más rápido ir a pie.

Página 60 Reto

This page can be used with pages 92–93 of the Students' Book.

AT3.2 **1 Empareja las formas de transporte con los precios.**

Students match the forms of transport with the prices.

Answers: 1 e; 2 b; 3 d; 4 a; 5 c

AT4.2 **2 Mira la agenda de Raquel. ¿Verdad o mentira?**

Students look at Raquel's diary and mark the sentences true or false.

Answers: a M; b M; c V; d V; e M; f V

Dos Workbook

Página 54 (6.1)

This page can be used with pages 82–83 of the Students' Book.

AT4.1 **1 Escribe las asignaturas.**

Students label the pictures of the school subjects.

Answers: Reading across the rows:
las matemáticas; la informática
la historia; los idiomas; el dibujo
el deporte; la religión; las ciencias

AT4.2

2a ¿Qué asignaturas les gustan? ¿Qué asignaturas no les gustan? Escribe frases.

Students write four sentences giving the opinions shown in the pictures.

Answers:
1 No me gustan las matemáticas.
2 Me encanta la tecnología.
3 Odio el francés.
4 Me gustan las ciencias.

AT3.3

3a Completa las frases.

Students match 1–4 with a–d to make sentences.

Answers: 1 d; 2 a; 3 b; 4 c

AT4.3

3b Escribe dos frases para ti, como las del ejercicio 3a, en la página 63.

Students write two sentences giving their opinions of school subjects on page 63, the spare page for writing at the end of the unit. If there is time, you could ask them to write four sentences, using each of the verb forms in 3a. When they have finished, remind them to check through their work, particularly for adjective agreement and the use of *me gusta/es* or *me gustan/son*.

Página 55 (6.2)

This page can be used with pages 84–85 of the Students' Book.

AT3.3

1a Lee lo que dice Pepe. ¡Las líneas están desordenadas! Indica el orden correcto.

Students read Pepe's speech bubble and number the lines in the correct order.

Answers: 3; 5; 1; 6; 4; 2

AT3.3

1b Lee el texto de 1a. Escribe dos listas; a) los adjetivos positivos y b) los negativos.

Students make two lists, positive and negative, of the adjectives in 1a. (Students may want to include *perezoso* in the negative column.) They then add the adjectives from the box at the end of 1b.

Answers:

positive	negative
interesantes	aburridas
útiles	difícil
divertido	estresante
fácil	
relajante	

AT4.1

1c Añade las otras formas.

Students write out all the forms of the adjectives. (They don't need to work with *perezoso* here.)

Answers:
interesantes – interesante; útiles – útil;
divertido – divertida – divertidos – divertidas;
fácil – fáciles; difícil – difíciles;
estresante – estresantes; relajante – relajantes

AT4.3

2 Escribe tu opinión sobre las asignaturas en la página 63.

Using *puedo* and *tengo que*, students write more detailed opinions about school subjects on page 63. If time is short, they could simply fill out the sentences that they wrote for section 6.1. When they have finished, remind them to check through their work, particularly for adjective agreement and the use of *me gusta/es* or *me gustan/son*. Remind them too about the use of the infinitive after *puedo* and *tengo que*.

Página 56 (6.3)

This page can be used with pages 86–87 of the Students' Book.

AT3.2

1 Dibuja las horas.

Students draw the correct time on the clock faces.

Answers:
a 7.30, b 1.05, c 11.45, d 3.10, e 7.40, f 4.15

AT3.3

2 Mira el horario de Marta. Lee las frases. ¿Verdad o mentira?

Students look at Marta's timetable and mark the sentences true or false.

Answers: a M; b V; c M; d V; e M; f M; g M; h V; i M; j V

AT4.4

3 Describe el día favorito de Javier en la página 63.

Students use the picture prompts and the phrases in the box to write about Javier's favourite day on page 63. They use the first person, as if they were Javier. Answers will vary slightly as the students can choose different adjectives and reasons for why Javier likes/doesn't like certain subjects. When they have finished, remind them to check through their work, particularly for number and gender agreement of the adjectives and the use of *me gusta/es* or *me gustan/son*.

Página 57 (6.4)

This page can be used with pages 88–89 of the Students' Book.

AT4.1 **1 Identifica las formas de transporte.**

Students label the pictures with phrases. You may want to remind them about the meaning of *en* so that they understand that they are labelling the ways of travelling and not just the items in the pictures.

Answers: Reading across the rows: en barco; en avión; en tren; en bicicleta; en coche

AT3.4 **2 Lee el texto. Subraya las formas de transporte y las opiniones. Escribe ✓ para una opinión positiva y ✗ para una opinión negativa.**

Answers:
en autobús: práctico ✓ relajante ✓
trenes: lentos ✗
en coche: cómodo ✓
a pie: no es fácil ✗
en barco

AT4.4 **3 Describe el viaje.**

Students complete the account of the journey using the information given. You may want to ask them to write the times and numbers out in full for further practice.

Answers:
Salgo de casa a las 10.30/diez y media.
Voy al aeropuerto.
Tardo 70/setenta minutos.
El vuelo es a la 1.30/una y media. Tardo 3/tres horas 15/quince minutos.
Llego a Madrid a las 4.45/cinco menos cuarto.
Tengo que esperar 45/cuarenta y cinco minutos.
Tardo 20/veinte minutos.
Llego (al Hotel Espléndido) a las 5.50/seis menos diez.

Página 58 (6.5)

This page can be used with pages 90–91 of the Students' Book.

AT3.4 **1 Lee el texto. Escribe una lista en inglés de las diferencias entre este instituto y tu instituto.**

Students read the text and write a list in English of the differences between the school described and their own school. Students compare answers in pairs and then discuss them as a class.

AT4.4 **2 Escribe un email a Lety con información sobre tu instituto.**

Students write an email about their school using the notes given and Lety's text in 1 to help them. Answers will vary but as there is a fixed structure, this activity is suitable for peer correction.

Página 59 Gramática

This page can be used with pages 82–83 of the Students' Book.
This page revises *gustar* and radical-changing verbs.

AT4.1 **1 Completa las frases con la forma correcta de *gustar*.**

Look at the first *Flashback* box with the class. Students then complete the sentences with the correct form of *gustar*.

Answers: 1 gustan; 2 gusta; 3 gusta; 4 gustan, gusta; 5 gustan; 6 gusta, gustan

AT4.1 **2 Completa el cuadro con las formas de los verbos.**

Use the second *Flashback* box to remind the students about radical-changing verbs. Students then complete the verb table. Pay particular attention to the correct irregular first person forms *digo* and *tengo*.

Answers:

pienso	**digo**	**tengo**
piensas	dices	**tienes**
piensa	**dice**	tiene
pensamos	decimos	**tenemos**
pensáis	**decís**	tenéis
piensan	dicen	**tienen**

AT3.3 **3 Completa el texto con los verbos de la casilla.**

Students complete the text using the words in the word box.

Answers: dicen; pienso; tengo; puedo; dice; prefiero; piensas; tienen

Página 60 Reto

This page can be used with pages 92–93 of the Students' Book.

AT3.2 **1 Empareja las formas de transporte con los precios.**

Students match the forms of transport with the prices.

Answers: 1 e; 2 b; 3 d; 4 a; 5 c

AT4.3 | **2a** Escribe las opiniones de Jorge.

Students write what Jorge thinks about his school subjects.

Answers:
Me encanta el deporte.
Me gusta la informática.
No me gusta el dibujo.
Odio la geografía.

AT4.3 | **2b** Dibuja una línea para ti. Tu compañero/a tiene que apuntar tus opiniones.

Students draw their own opinion line about school subjects. In pairs, they each look at their partner's opinion line and write their partner's opinions.

AT4.4 | **3** Escribe sobre el día de Raquel en la página 63.

Students read Raquel's diary. They then write about her day, as if they were Raquel, on page 63. Remind the students to check their work carefully for adjective agreements and the correct use of *me gusta/me gustan*. Answers will vary, but you may want to prepare the sample answer, or your own, as an overhead or on the projector.

Sample answer:
Voy al instituto a las 8.30. Cuando llueve, voy en coche. Los martes, tengo matemáticas a las 9.00, pero no me gustan porque son aburridas. Tengo educación física a las diez, y me encanta. El recreo es a las 11.30 y puedo hablar con Elena. Tengo ciencias a las 12.10. El Señor Muñoz es mi profesor favorito. Es la hora de comer a la 1.10. Por la tarde tenemos tres clases. La música me encanta y me gusta también el inglés, pero odio la historia porque es aburrida. Voy a casa a las 5.30. Voy a pie.